The Native South

The Native
SOUTH

New Histories and Enduring Legacies

Edited by Tim Alan Garrison *and* Greg O'Brien

UNIVERSITY OF NEBRASKA PRESS | LINCOLN & LONDON

Some of the examples discussed by Mikaëla M. Adams in chapter 8, "Race, Kinship, and Belonging among the Florida Seminoles," were published in her book *Who Belongs? Race, Resources, and Tribal Citizenship in the Native South* (New York: Oxford University Press, 2016).

Library of Congress Cataloging-in-Publication Data
Names: Garrison, Tim Alan, 1961– editor. | O'Brien, Greg, 1966– editor.
Title: The native south: new histories and enduring legacies / edited by Tim Alan Garrison and Greg O'Brien.
Description: Lincoln: University of Nebraska Press, 2017. | Includes bibliographical references and index.
Identifiers: LCCN 2016041534
ISBN 9780803296909 (cloth: alk. paper)
ISBN 9781496216632 (paper: alk. paper)
ISBN 9781496204123 (epub)
ISBN 9781496201430 (mobi)
ISBN 9781496201447 (pdf)
Subjects: LCSH: Indians of North America—Southern States. | Indians of North America—Southern States—History.
Classification: LCC E78.S65 N386 2017 | DDC 975.004/97—dc23
LC record available at https://lccn.loc.gov/2016041534

Set in New Baskerville ITC Pro by John Klopping.

Contents

Acknowledgments

The editors wish to thank Theda and Mike for supporting the publication of this volume and for providing years of guidance. It is an honor to call them mentors and friends. The contributors to this volume are also friends, and we thank them for producing new essays and for exhibiting patience as we gathered the essays together and made them ready for publication.

Special thanks go to Kendon Levett (MA, UNC–Greensboro, 2013) for transcribing the interview with Mike and Theda and making useful suggestions about that chapter.

Tim Garrison thanks Cindy Garrison for thirty years of love, Sam Garrison for his growth and his commitment to excellence, and Talmadge and Jeannine Garrison and Jim and Dorothy Lamb for their steadfast support.

Greg O'Brien wishes to thank his former and current master's and doctoral graduate students at the University of North Carolina at Greensboro for contributing their own insights about the study of the Native South and early American history while this collection was under production. In alphabetical order: Hailey Ayers, Stephanie (Krysiak) Balaconis, Katie Bates, Sam Berton, Becky Byron, Sarah Cloutier, Matthew Esterline, Rebecca Fecher, Arlen Hanson, Jacquelyn Jones, Chris Jordan, Ellen Kennedy, Ellen Kuhn, Chris Kutas, Kendon Levett, James Marsh, Sarah McCartney, Jamie Mize, Ethan Moore, Kimberly Mozingo, Steven Peach, Kim Proctor, Melanie Staley, Jason Stroud, Monica Ward, Samantha Winer, and Ashley Wyatt.

We dedicate the book to the memory of Michael D. Green, who passed away while this volume was being assembled, and for whom we will always strive to, in his words, "know shit from apple butter."

Introduction

This collection of all original essays serves two main purposes. On one hand it provides a sampling of the latest work being done on the history of the Native South and Native peoples from the South. On the other hand, it honors two scholars who have done more to shape this field than anyone else: Michael D. Green and Theda Perdue.[1]

When Michael Green and Theda Perdue published their first monographs (Perdue: *Slavery and the Evolution of Cherokee Society, 1540–1866* in 1979 and Green: *The Politics of Indian Removal: Creek Government and Society in Crisis* in 1982), few historians focused on Indian people in the South.[2] Throughout most of the twentieth century anthropologists dominated understandings of Indian people in and from the South. James Mooney (1861–1921) lived for years among the Eastern Cherokees in North Carolina as an anthropologist working for the Smithsonian Institution's Bureau of American Ethnology in Washington DC. He learned the Cherokee language and conducted numerous interviews with Cherokees that led to important publications such as *Sacred Formulas of the Cherokees* (1891), *Myths of the Cherokee* (1900), and the posthumous *The Swimmer Manuscript: Cherokee Sacred Formulas and Medicinal Prescriptions* (1932). These works remain in print and have long served as a foundation for the scholarly understanding of Cherokee traditions.[3]

John Reed Swanton (1873–1958), who spent most of his career employed by the Bureau of American Ethnology, still influences the Native South field with his Boazian-derived structuralist interpretations. Swanton shaped the rise of ethnohistory as a methodology by utilizing a wide range of archival and printed documentary sources to gain insight into Indian culture that he could not attain through interviews and material remains. The sources he identified remain valuable to scholars, and his prolific publications remain in print.[4]

After Swanton's death the most important scholar working on the Native South was University of Georgia anthropologist Charles M. Hudson (1932–2013). Hudson focused his work on the Catawbas, the Cherokees, archaeology, the Mississippian chiefdoms encountered by Hernando de Soto, and he wrote the still-in-print magnum opus *The Southeastern Indians* (1976). Hudson trained numerous anthropologists who have focused on the Native South, and he also mentored history graduate students on occasion. His work provided an ethnohistorical bridge between anthropological and historical investigations of the Native South by tapping both archaeological sources and the documentary record in order to arrive at deeper understandings of the Indian past.[5]

In the 1970s, when Michael Green and Theda Perdue began their training, almost no historians studied the Indian people of the South. This situation shaped Green and Perdue's outlook and is shown in the roundabout way that each scholar came to this field. Green trained in western U.S. and frontier history while earning his PhD in history at the University of Iowa, while Perdue focused on southern U.S. history and race relations in her doctoral work at the University of Georgia. Both became adherents of the methodology of ethnohistory that was led at that time primarily by anthropologists studying Native America. Green discovered ethnohistory while searching for a more satisfactory way to understand American Indian history, while Perdue was introduced to ethnohistory by adding Charles Hudson to her doctoral committee at Georgia.[6]

Ethnohistory is a methodology that combines the anthropological focus on culture, comparative theory, ethnological study, and archaeology with the historical emphasis on documentary sources and appreciation of change over time. The perspectives and historical understandings of Native people provide a third leg to the ethnohistorical stool. We date the formation of the field of ethnohistory to the mid-1950s. In the aftermath of the U.S. Indian Claims Act of 1946, anthropologists and historians investigated Native histories to support the work of the Indian Claims Commission (ICC). The legislation sought to terminate the government-to-government relationship between the United States and Indian tribes through the ICC's proceedings, in which Indian groups were acknowledged as the previous owners of land and compensated for land taken from them. Anthropologists and historians involved in the ICC hearings formed the Ohio Valley Historic Indian Conference and an academic journal in 1953; both the organization and the journal were renamed Ethnohistory in 1966.[7]

Green sought out Perdue once he became aware of her book on Cherokees and slavery that was published in 1979. In the process of revising his dissertation on Creek Indian politics and the removal crisis, Green found a kindred intellectual spirit in Perdue. As two of the very few historians writing about Native southerners in the 1980s, Green and Perdue formed a working relationship that sought to legitimize their shared academic field and create a market for new studies of the Native South. Their ideas and promotion resulted in the start of the Indians of the Southeast book series with the University of Nebraska Press in the mid-1980s. This series has brought over twenty research monographs, document collections, and essay collections to print and effectively created the field of southeastern Indian history.[8] The professional relationship between Green and Perdue transformed into a loving relationship by 1992, and Green joined Perdue at the University of Kentucky.[9]

At Kentucky the couple started directing graduate students in southeastern Indian ethnohistory. In 1998 they moved to the University of North Carolina at Chapel Hill and directed dissertations there for over a decade, even after retiring from teaching (Green retired in 2009 and Perdue in 2011). In addition, they continued to publish books and essays, both individually and as joint authors.[10] Combined with editing the only book series that focused exclusively on the ethnohistory of Indian people in the South, and reaching out to colleagues and graduate students beyond their own department, they generated intense and rapidly expanding interest in their field of study.[11] Through the 1990s and into the 2000s, Green and Perdue had a hand in nearly every book-length ethnohistorical investigation on southern Indian history published in the United States, whether published in their series or not. Besides working with their own students, they served on doctoral dissertation committees of students at other universities. They worked the conference circuit tirelessly, participating in the Western History Association, Southern Historical Association, and Ethnohistory annual meetings every year and occasionally working in stops at the American Historical Association and the Organization of American Historians meetings as well. Additionally, they presented papers and commented on others at numerous regional and local conferences and gave invited talks at universities and organizations around the country.

Perdue has also served as president of the Southern Association for Women Historians (1985–86), the American Society for Ethnohistory (2001), and the Southern Historical Association (2010–11). She received the Lifetime Achievement Award from the Western History Association in 2008. Her book *Cherokee Women: Gender and Culture Change, 1700–1835* (2000) won both the James Mooney Prize (Best Book in the Anthropology of the South, Southern Anthropology Society) and the Julia Cherry Spruill Award (Best Book in Southern Women's History, Southern Association for Women Historians).[12]

At conferences, Green and Perdue made it a point to meet other scholars working in the larger field of American Indian studies and to promote work on the Native South. They sometimes criticized work they saw as deficient, but more often they offered support by providing contacts, offering to read drafts of articles and books, and building a network of like-minded scholars devoted to the ethnohistorical study of the Native South. Their outreach efforts developed the field of southeastern Indian history and opened it up at other universities besides their own. By the mid-1990s their example and success in exposing the rich, largely untapped historical study of the South's Indian people were encouraging a new generation of history PhD students throughout the country to pursue research in this quickly expanding field.

Over the last two decades the number of dissertations in southern Indian history has multiplied rapidly to the point that the field is largely self-supporting. The doctoral students trained by Green and Perdue teach at a variety of colleges and universities, and many of them now direct their own graduate students. Additional scholars and students of early American and southern history and anthropology have also migrated into the Native South discipline, fashioning a field that has reached the cutting edge of ethnohistorical sophistication and historiographical relevance. Along the way, the Indian role in all aspects and time periods of southern history is well on its way to being restored. Whereas only a couple of decades ago it was rare to find a course on southeastern Indian history being taught at any given southern college or university, today it has become expected nearly everywhere. Books and articles focusing on the Native South continue to grow in both quantity and quality, and the establishment of the journal *Native South* by the University of Nebraska Press in 2008 has added fuel to this scholarly fire.

Michael Green and Theda Perdue created intellectual legacies via their work, their actions on behalf of others, and their graduate students. While at the University of North Carolina, for example, they led efforts to create the American Indian and Indigenous Studies discipline within American Studies, to establish the American Indian student center, and to hire American Indian scholars in various disciplines. All the while, they mentored Native and non-Native graduate students in history. Green and Perdue promoted research on the Native South that placed Indian people at the center of their own history, and they encouraged their students to seek new narratives about what southern history means with Native people restored to a prominent place in that narrative. Working with a husband and wife team as doctoral advisers presented unique challenges to their students at times, but the circumstance also provided unique benefits. To have two experts in the same field providing constant feedback on your work and guiding you through the process of acquiring a job and publishing your research meant everything to us as new scholars. What all of Green and Perdue's doctoral students have come to realize over time is how much we also meant to them. As Christina Snyder remarked in 2015, "I know that I speak for many of Theda's students when I say that we are not just colleagues or friends; we are more like a family bound by ties of love and respect for one another and for the work we share."[13] Perdue is well-known among her graduate students for calling us her "intellectual children" or "academic children" and has even begun referring to the graduate students of her former students as her "academic grandchildren." Like the Native southerners they study and know, Green and Perdue have always insisted that such kinship ties are real and come with expectations and responsibilities.

When asked about their academic legacy, Green and Perdue have always emphasized their doctoral students first. "Legacy is something that other people talk about after you're gone," Perdue has stated, "but I can see mine. I know their names."[14] "Mike and I have had the great good fortune to see our legacy while we're still living. Our legacy is represented by the people who are contributing to this anthology as well as many others who are not. We have not only a body of work as a legacy but we also have had marvelous students."[15] Now that they are both retired, made doubly pertinent by the recent passing away of Michael Green, their graduate students in southeastern Indian history feel the time is appropriate to collectively show our appreciation of their efforts as mentors and academic leaders, as well as to provide a sample of where the Native South field stands at present. Green and Perdue refer to their former graduate students as their legacies, but their legacy is much deeper than us, however impactful our work might be. Their legacy created a new academic field that expanded and continues to enlarge our understanding of southern United States history.

This collection allows Mike and Theda to speak first through an interview that I conducted with them in the summer of 2012. They discuss their personal and academic backgrounds, their relationship with each other, their thoughts on ethnohistory as a discipline and organization, the reasons that the Native side of southern history needs to be emphasized, and their relationships with their graduate students.

The remaining essays in this volume follow a rough chronological organization. Each author was a doctoral student of Green and Perdue at either the University of Kentucky or the University of North Carolina at Chapel Hill. Each of us chose a topic that either builds upon our previously published work or stems from research that reflects our evolving interests into other areas of Native South history. Besides the academic kinship, these essays also share a commitment to exploring new lines of inquiry based on understanding Native southerners on their own terms, placing Indian people at the center of their history, and/or shedding new light on received notions about southern history and the people from the South. This collection is not meant to be a comprehensive overview of all the current research being conducted on the Native South—such an undertaking would now take several volumes. Taken as a whole, the collection allows readers to see where the field of Native South history has been, where it is now, and where it is going.

Notes

1. The editors have chosen the term "Native South" since it is the current designation for the field that studies the indigenous people originally from the North American Southeast. We are following the usage of the academic journal *Native South* published by the University of Nebraska Press.

2. Theda Perdue: *Slavery and the Evolution of Cherokee Society, 1540–1866* (Knoxville: University of Tennessee Press, 1979); Michael D. Green: *The Politics of Indian Removal: Creek Government and Society in Crisis* (Lincoln: University of Nebraska Press, 1982). Notable examples of books on the Native South published before 1980 include John Phillip Reid, *A Better Kind of Hatchet: Law, Trade, and Diplomacy in the Cherokee Nation during the Early Years of European Contact* (University Park: Pennsylvania State University Press, 1976); Arrell M. Gibson, *The Chickasaws* (Norman: University of Oklahoma Press, 1972); David H. Corkran, *The Creek Frontier, 1540–1783* (Norman: University of Oklahoma Press, 1967); David H. Corkran, *The Cherokee Frontier: Conflict and Survival, 1740–62* (Norman: University of Oklahoma Press, 1962); Angie Debo, *The Rise and Fall of the Choctaw Republic* (Norman: University of Oklahoma Press, 1961); Grant Foreman, *Indian Removal: The Emigration of the Five Civilized Tribes of Indians* (Norman: University of Oklahoma Press, 1953); Angie Debo, *The Road to Disappearance: A History of the Creek Indians* (Norman: University of Oklahoma Press, 1941); Angie Debo, *And Still the Waters Run: The Betrayal of the Five Civilized Tribes* (Princeton NJ: Princeton University Press, 1940); Grant Foreman, *Sequoyah* (Norman: University of Oklahoma Press, 1938); and Verner W. Crane, *The Southern Frontier, 1670–1732* (Ann Arbor: University of Michigan Press, 1929).

3. See a biography of Mooney in "James Mooney," *American Anthropologist*, n.s., 24, no. 2 (1922): 209–14. Mooney's major Cherokee publications include "Sacred

Formulas of the Cherokees," *Seventh Annual Report of the Bureau of American Ethnology*, 1892, 301–97; "Myths of the Cherokee," *Nineteenth Annual Report of the Bureau of American Ethnology*, 1902, 3–548; and *The Swimmer Manuscript: Cherokee Sacred Formulas and Medicinal Prescriptions*, Bureau of American Ethnology Bulletin, no. 99 (Washington DC: Government Printing Office, 1932).

4. Summaries of Swanton's career can be found in William N. Fenton, "John Reed Swanton: 1873–1958," *American Anthropologist* 61 (1959): 663–68; and Julian H. Steward, "John Reed Swanton, 1873–1958," *National Academy of Sciences Biographical Memoirs* 34 (1960): 329–49. Swanton's works on the Native South include *Indian Tribes of the Lower Mississippi Valley and Adjacent Coast of the Gulf of Mexico*, Bureau of American Ethnology Bulletin, no. 43 (Washington DC: Government Printing Office, 1911); "An Early Account of the Choctaw Indians," *American Anthropologist* 5, no. 2 (1918): 51–72; *Early History of the Creek Indians and Their Neighbors*, Bureau of American Ethnology Bulletin, no. 73 (Washington DC: Government Printing Office, 1922); "Religious Beliefs and Medical Practices of the Creek Indians," *Forty-Second Annual Report of the Bureau of American Ethnology*, 1927, 639–70; "Social Organization and the Social Usages of the Indians of the Creek Confederacy," *Forty-Second Annual Report of the Bureau of American Ethnology*, 1928, 279–325; "Chickasaw Society and Religion," *Forty-Second Annual Report of the Bureau of American Ethnology*, 1928; *Myths & Tales of the Southeastern Indians*, Bureau of American Ethnology Bulletin, no. 88 (Washington DC: Government Printing Office, 1929); "Modern Square Grounds of the Creek Indians," *Smithsonian Miscellaneous Collections* 85, no. 8 (1931): 1–46; *Source Material for the Social and Ceremonial Life of the Choctaw Indians*, Bureau of American Ethnology Bulletin, no. 103 (Washington DC: Government Printing Office, 1931); and *The Indians of the Southeastern United States*, Bureau of American Ethnology Bulletin, no. 137 (Washington DC: Government Printing Office, 1946).

5. Hudson's major publications include *The Catawba Nation* (Athens: University of Georgia Press, 1970); ed., *Red, White, and Black: Symposium on Indians in the Old South* (Athens: University of Georgia Press, 1971); *The Southeastern Indians* (Knoxville: University of Tennessee Press, 1976); *Black Drink: A Native American Tea* (Athens: University of Georgia Press, 1979); with Paul E. Hoffman, eds., *The Juan Pardo Expeditions: Exploration of the Carolinas and Tennessee, 1566–1568* (Washington DC: Smithsonian Institution Press, 1990); with Carmen Chaves Tesser, eds., *The Forgotten Centuries: Indians and Europeans in the American South, 1521–1704* (Athens: University of Georgia Press, 1994); *Knights of Spain, Warriors of the Sun: Hernando De Soto and the South's Ancient Chiefdoms* (Athens: University of Georgia Press, 1997); with Robbie Ethridge, eds., *The Transformation of the Southeastern Indians, 1540–1760* (Jackson: University Press of Mississippi, 2002); and *Conversations with the High Priest of Coosa* (Chapel Hill: University of North Carolina Press, 2003).

6. See interview with Green and Perdue, chapter 1 this volume.

7. For definitions and origins of ethnohistory see William C. Sturtevant, "Anthropology, History, and Ethnohistory," *Ethnohistory* 13, no. 1/2 (Winter/Spring 1966): 1–51; James Axtell, "Ethnohistory: An Historian's Viewpoint," *Ethnohistory* 26, no. 1 (Winter 1979): 1–13; and Michael E. Harkin, "Ethnohistory's Ethnohistory: Cre-

ating a Discipline from the Ground Up," *Social Science History* 34, no. 2 (Summer 2010): 113–28.

8. See the books in the Indians of the Southeast series at the University of Nebraska Press, http://www.nebraskapress.unl.edu/catalog/CategoryInfo.aspx ?cid=152 (accessed September 1, 2015).

9. See interview with Green and Perdue, chapter 1 this volume.

10. Green's and Perdue's joint publications include *North American Indians: A Very Short Introduction* (New York: Oxford University Press, 2010); *The Cherokee Nation and the Trail of Tears* (New York: Penguin, 2007); *The Columbia Guide to the American Indians of the Southeast* (New York: Columbia University Press, 2002); *The Cherokee Removal: A Brief History with Documents* (Boston MA: Bedford Books, 1995, 2nd ed. 2004); and "Native American History," in *A Companion to Nineteenth-Century America*, ed. William L. Barney (Malden MA: Blackwell Publishers, 2001).

11. Michael D. Green's other publications include the books *The Creeks* (New York: Chelsea House, 1990); *The Politics of Indian Removal: Creek Government and Society in Crisis* (Lincoln: University of Nebraska Press, 1982); and *The Creeks, A Critical Bibliography*, The Newberry Library Center for the History of the American Indian Bibliography Series (Bloomington: Indiana University Press, 1979).

Articles and book chapters: "William McIntosh and the Crisis of Creek National Identity," in *The Human Tradition in the American South*, ed. James Klotter (New York: Scholarly Resources, 2003); "Mary Musgrove: Creating a New World," in *Sifters: Native American Women's Lives*, ed. Theda Perdue (New York: Oxford University Press, 2001); "John C. Calhoun and the Crisis in Indian Affairs," *Proceedings of the South Carolina Historical Association* (Columbia SC, 2001); "Expansion of European Colonization to the Mississippi Valley, 1783–1880," in *Cambridge History of the Native Peoples of the Americas*, ed. Wilcomb Washburn and Bruce Trigger (New York: Cambridge University Press, 1996); "Grant Foreman," in *Historians of the American Frontier*, ed. John Wunder (New York: Greenwood, 1988); "'We Dance in Opposite Directions': Mesquakie (Fox) Separatism from the Sauk and Fox Tribe," *Ethnohistory* 30 (1983): 129–40; "The Creek Confederacy in the American Revolution," in *Anglo-Spanish Confrontation on the Gulf Coast during the American Revolution*, ed. William Coker and Robert Rae, Proceedings of the Gulf Coast History and Humanities Conference 9 (Pensacola: Perdido Press, 1982); "Alexander McGillivray," in *American Indian Leaders: Studies in Diversity*, ed. R. David Edmunds (Lincoln: University of Nebraska Press, 1980); "The Sac–Fox Annuity Crisis of 1840," *Arizona and the West* 16 (Summer 1974): 241–56; "Cumberland College in 1829," *Register of the Kentucky Historical Society* 66 (1968): 392–99.

12. Theda Perdue's publications include the single author books *Indians in the Segregated South, 1870–1970* (Chapel Hill: University of North Carolina Press, forthcoming); *Race and the Atlanta Cotton States Exposition of 1895* (Athens: University of Georgia Press, 2010); *"Mixed Blood" Indians: Racial Construction in the Early South* (Athens: University of Georgia Press, 2003; paperback ed., 2005); *Cherokee Women: Gender and Culture Change, 1700–1835* (Lincoln: University of Nebraska Press, 1998); *The Cherokees* (New York: Chelsea House, 1988); *Native Carolinians: The Indians of*

North Carolina (Raleigh: North Carolina Division of Archives and History, 1985; rev. ed. with Christopher Arris Oakley, 2010); and *Slavery and the Evolution of Cherokee Society, 1540–1866* (Knoxville: University of Tennessee Press, 1979).

Edited books: *Sifters: Native American Women's Lives* (New York: Oxford University Press, 2001); with Betty Brandon, Virginia Bernhard, Elizabeth Fox-Genovese, and Elizabeth Turner, eds., *Hidden Histories of Women in the New South* (Columbia: University of Missouri Press, 1994); with Betty Brandon, Virginia Bernhard, and Elizabeth Fox-Genovese, eds., *Southern Women: Histories and Identities* (Columbia: University of Missouri Press, 1992); *Cherokee Editor: The Writings of Elias Boudinot* (Knoxville: University of Tennessee Press, 1983, paperback ed., University of Georgia Press, 1996); and *Nations Remembered: An Oral History of the Five Civilized Tribes, 1865–1907* (Westport CT: Greenwood Press, 1980, paperback ed. with new introduction, University of Oklahoma Press, 1993).

Book chapters: "Southern Indians and Jim Crow," in *The Folly of Jim Crow: Rethinking the Segregated South*, ed. Stephanie Cole and Natalie Ring (College Station: Texas A&M University Press, 2012); "Native Americans, African Americans, and Jim Crow," in *IndiVisible: African-Native American Lives in the Americas*, ed. Gabrielle Tayac (Washington DC: Smithsonian Institution Press, 2009); "'A Sprightly Lover Is the Most Prevailing Missionary': Intermarriage between Europeans and Indians in the Eighteenth-Century South," in *Light on the Path: Essays in the Anthropology and History of the Southeastern Indians*, ed. Thomas Pluckhahn and Robbie Ethridge (Tuscaloosa: University of Alabama Press, 2006); "Matrilineal Kinship among the Cherokee Indians in the American Southeast," in *Major Problems in the History of American Families and Children*, ed. Anya Jabour (Boston MA: Houghton Mifflin, 2005); with John R. Finger, "History of the Old South Since Removal," in *Handbook of North American Indians, Vol. 14: Southeast*, ed. Raymond Fogelson (Washington DC: Smithsonian Institution, 2004); "George Washington and the 'Civilization' of Southern Indians," in *George Washington's South*, ed. Tamara Harvey and Greg O'Brien (Gainesville: University of Florida Press, 2003); "Indians Using a Strategy of Accommodation," in *Major Problems in American History, Volume 1: To 1877*, ed. Elizabeth Cobbs Hoffman and Jon Gjerde (Boston MA: Houghton Mifflin, 2002); "Catharine Brown: Cherokee Convert to Christianity," in *Sifters: Native American Women's Lives*; "Native Women in the Early Republic: Old World Perceptions, New World Realities," in *Native Americans in the Early Republic*, ed. Ronald Hoffman and Frederick Hoxie (Charlottesville: University of Virginia Press, 1999); "Writing the Ethnohistory of Native American Women," in *Rethinking American Indian History: Analysis, Methodology, and Historiography*, ed. Donald Fixico (Albuquerque: University of New Mexico Press, 1997); "Women, Men, and American Indian Policy: The Cherokee Response to 'Civilization,'" in *Negotiators of Change: Historical Perspectives on Native American Women*, ed. Nancy Shoemaker (New York: Routledge, 1995); "The Sequoyah Syllabary and Cultural Revitalization," in *Perspectives on the Southeast*, ed. Patricia B. Kwachka (Athens: University of Georgia Press, 1994); "Nancy Ward," in *Portraits of American Women*, ed. Catherine Clinton and Ben Barker-Benfield (New York: St. Martin's Press, 1991; repr., New York: Oxford University Press, 1998);

"Native American Revitalization Movements in the Early Nineteenth Century," in *New Worlds?: The Comparative History of New Zealand and the United States*, ed. Jock Phillips (Wellington NZ: Stout Research Center, 1989); "Indians in Southern History," in *Indians in American History*, ed. Frederick E. Hoxie (Arlington Heights IL: Harlan Davidson Inc., 1988); "The Trail of Tears: Removal of the Southern Indians," in *The American Indian Experience, A Profile: 1524 to the Present*, ed. Philip Weeks (Arlington Heights IL: Forum Press Inc., 1988, reprinted as "The Origins of Removal and the Fate of the Southeastern Indians," in *Major Problems in American Foreign Relations*, ed. Thomas G. Patterson and Dennis Merrill (Lexington MA: D. C. Heath, 1994); "Cherokee Relations with the Iroquois in the Eighteenth Century," in *Beyond the Covenant Chain: The Iroquois and Their Neighbors in Indian North America, 1600–1800*, ed. Daniel K. Richter and James H. Merrell (Syracuse NY: Syracuse University Press, 1987); "Southern Indians and the Cult of True Womanhood," in *The Web of Southern Social Relations: Essays on Family Life, Education, and Women*, ed. Walter J. Fraser Jr., R. Frank Saunders Jr., and Jon L. Wakelyn (Athens: University of Georgia Press, 1985) [and reprinted as "Domesticating the Natives: Southern Indians and the Cult of True Womanhood" in the following volumes: *Women, Families, and Communities: Readings in American History*, ed. Nancy A. Hewitt (Glenview IL: Scott Foresman and Company, 1990); *Half-Sisters of History: Southern Women and the American Past*, ed. Catherine Clinton (Durham NC: Duke University Press, 1994); *Major Problems in American Women's History: Documents and Essays*, ed. Mary Beth Norton and Ruth M. Alexander (Lexington MA: D. C. Heath, 1995); and *Myth America: A Historical Anthology*, vol. 1, ed. Patrick Gerster and Nicholas J. Cords (St. James NY: Brandywine Press, 1997)]; "Red and Black in Southern Appalachia," in *Blacks in Appalachia*, ed. William Turner and Edward Cabbell (Lexington: University of Kentucky Press, 1985), reprinted in *Southern Exposure* (November/December 1984): 17–24, reprinted in *Appalachia Inside Out*, ed. Robert J. Higgs, Ambrose N. Manning, and Jim Wayne Miller, 2 vols. (Knoxville: University of Tennessee Press, 1995); and "Cherokee Planters: The Development of Plantation Slavery before Removal," in *The Cherokee Indian Nation: A Troubled History*, ed. Duane King (Knoxville: University of Tennessee Press, 1979).

Journal articles: "The Legacy of Indian Removal," *Journal of Southern History* 78 (2012): 3–36; "American Indian Survival in South Carolina," *South Carolina Historical Magazine* 108 (2007): 215–34; "Race and Culture: Writing the Ethnohistory of the Early South, 1700–1840," *Ethnohistory* 51 (2004): 701–23; "Clan and Court: Another Look at the Early Cherokee Republic," *American Indian Quarterly* 24 (2000): 562–69; "Columbus Meets Pocahontas in the American South," *Southern Cultures* 3 (1997): 4–21 [reprinted in *Taking Off the White Gloves, Southern Women and Women Historians*, ed. Michele Gillespie and Catherine Clinton (Columbia: University of Missouri Press, 1998), and *Southern Cultures: The Fifteenth Anniversary Reader, 1993–2008* (Chapel Hill: University of North Carolina Press, 2008)]; "Pocahontas aikuisille: Mita paallikon tyttaren ja kapteeni John Smithin valilla todella tapahtui?" ("Pocahantas for Adults; Or, What Really Happened between Captain John Smith and the Chief's Daughter," translated by Tuija Modinos), *Kulturri Tutkimus* (Cultural Studies) 13 (1996): 21–28; "The Conflict Within: The Cherokee Power Structure and Removal," *Georgia Historical Quarterly* 73 (1989): 467–91, reprinted as "The Conflict Within: Cherokees and Removal," in *Cherokee Removal: Before and After*, ed. William Anderson (Athens: University of Georgia Press, 1991); "Cherokee Women and the Trail of Tears," *Journal of Women's History* 1 (1989): 14–30 [reprinted in the following volumes: *The American Indian: Past and Present*, ed. Roger L. Nichols (4th ed., New York: McGraw-Hill, 1992; 5th ed., New York: McGraw-Hill, 1999); *Unequal Sisters: A Multicultural Reader in U.S. Women's History*, ed. Vicki L. Ruiz and Ellen Carol DuBois (New York: Routledge, 1994); *Women and the American Legal Order*, ed. Karen J. Maschke (New York: Garland Publishing Inc., 1997); *American Encounters: Native and Newcomers from European Contact to Indian Removal, 1500–1850*, ed. Peter C. Mancall and James H. Merrell (New York: Routledge, 1999); and with a new introduction in *Native Women's History in Eastern North America before 1900: A Guide to Research and Writing*, ed. Rebecca Kugel and Lucy Murphy (Lincoln: University of Nebraska Press, 2007)]; "Cherokee Planters, Black Slaves, and African Colonization," *Chronicles of Oklahoma* 60 (1982): 322–31, reprinted in *Outstanding Articles on Slavery*, ed. Paul Finkelman (Hamden CT: Garland Publishing Inc., 1989/90); "Remembering Removal," *Journal of Cherokee Studies* 7 (1982): 69–72; "Traditionalism in the Cherokee Nation: Resistance to the Constitution of 1827," *Georgia Historical Quarterly* 66 (1982):159–70; "The Traditional Status of Cherokee Women," *Furman Studies* 26 (1980): 19–25; "Letters from Brainerd," *Journal of Cherokee Studies* 4 (1979): 4–9; "George Whitefield in Georgia: Philanthropy," *Atlanta Historical Journal* 22 (1978): 53–72; "George Whitefield in Georgia: Revivalism," *Atlanta Historical Journal* 22 (1978): 43–51; "Rising from the Ashes: The Cherokee Phoenix as an Ethnohistorical Source," *Ethnohistory* 24 (1977): 207–18; and "People Without a Place: Aboriginal Cherokee Bondage," *Indian Historian* 9 (1976): 31–37.

13. Deb Saine, "Theda Perdue: Academic Superhero," *Carolina Chronicle*, September 11, 2015, accessed September 15, 2015, carolinachronicle.unc.edu/2015/theda-perdue.

14. Kim Weaver Spurr, "Theda and Mike's Excellent Adventure," *Carolina Arts & Sciences* (Fall 2011): 15.

15. Interview with Green and Perdue, chapter 1 this volume.

The Native South

One

An Interview with Theda Perdue and Michael D. Green

GREG O'BRIEN

On July 11, 2012, Greg O'Brien conducted the following inter-view with Theda Perdue and Michael D. Green at their home in Chapel Hill, North Carolina.

Greg O'Brien (GO): First of all, tell us a little about your personal backgrounds, where you're from, where you grew up, what your parents did, and how you got interested in history as a profession.

Michael Green (MG): I was born and raised in Iowa. My dad was a Methodist minister. I've been interested in history since I can remember. When I was a kid in junior high and high school, I was a voracious reader and what I read was historical stuff. It was never a question what I was going to major in when I went to college. I went to Cornell College in Mount Vernon, Iowa, where I was a history and political science major because history and political science were joined together in the same department. When I went to graduate school to the University of Iowa I was a history major. I've always been, I've always had, the soul of a historian.

Theda Perdue (TP): I'm from McRae, Georgia, a town of 2,500 where my father was a farm equipment dealer. My mother had been a beautician during the late 1930s and through World War II, but by the time I was born she was a stay-at-home mom. I'm the only child, and my parents were middle-aged when I was born. I think I probably became a historian in part because my mother was an avid reader. She read constantly, and even in her late 80s, she could read a book a day. I remember going with her to the library where there was a series of biographies of famous women arranged alphabetically by their first name. I started with Abigail Adams, then Amelia Earhart, and I ended, I think, with Sarah Bernhardt the actress. So, I guess that hooked me. I began college at Emory University, then I transferred to Mercer University. By that time I wanted to be a lawyer. I entered law school early after my junior year in college, and I lasted one semester. I quit law school because I thought that the study of law was one of the most boring things I'd ever done in my life. It consisted largely of abstracting cases, but equally important, I was struck by what one of my professors said, which was that "there is no justice in the law." What he meant was that your client could be innocent and still not win, but it bothered me terribly, because this, after all, was 1971, at the height of the antiwar movement, and issues of social justice were still very much in the fore. I was appalled by the idea that you couldn't really be assured of justice in the American legal system. So I quit, I thought about what I wanted to do next, and I decided to go to graduate school in history. I ended up at the University of Georgia and became a historian.

GO: Okay. Mike, did you ever consider any other career other than being an academic historian?

MG: I briefly toyed with the idea of the State Department diplomatic corps, but when I graduated from college, I was faced with a real crisis, I guess. I graduated from college in 1963. I was married. I had a son who was two years old. I had not taken any education courses so I could not qualify to teach high school. I was a historian, and I had absolutely no idea what I was going to do, but I realized that I had to make up my mind immediately and graduate school was the only thing I could think of to do. That's how I ended up going to graduate school, and I discovered very quickly that I had blundered into the right decision. I was very happy as a graduate student, and I was very happy being a historian. So the question about whether or not I was going to become our ambassador to the Soviet Union slipped through my mind fairly quickly.

GO: Okay. Theda, other than possibly being a lawyer, did you ever consider any other careers by the time you were an undergraduate?

TP: No, I don't think so. I resisted education courses in the same way that I resisted typing courses in high school. (I still type with two fingers.) I don't know whether it was a kind of budding feminism or it was simply a reaction to my mother's situation. My mother was an extraordinarily bright woman who really never found an outlet for her intellect. I didn't want to get pigeonholed into a stereotypically female job as a schoolteacher or a secretary, so I shunned anything that smacked of that.

I never really thought about being a historian, it just sort of happened. I got a job, although, in the fall of 1974, there were not many jobs out there. I had not finished my dissertation or even taken qualifying exams when a job came open at Western Carolina University for a position in Cherokee history. Few people did Indian history in those days, and apparently I was one of two people in the country who applied. I managed to get the job. I was hired on December 30, and I started teaching the first half of world history on January 2. That was a humbling experience. But I took qualifying exams that spring, and by the next spring, I had a dissertation ready to defend. So, my career was something that just kind of happened. But once I got an academic position, I was absolutely certain that that's what I should do.

GO: Mike, I've heard you talk a lot before about academic legacies and your intellectual forebears, so I was wondering if you could spend a little time talking about that. Who have been your intellectual influences, either in your career or just in the way you approach history?

MG: Well, I suppose that the person most responsible for my becoming a student of American Indian history was Allan Bogue, who was my first professor at the University of Iowa. I went to Iowa with the intent of being a western historian. I took a seminar my first semester as a master's student with Bogue, and the first day, we went around the table talking about our projects for the seminar. I had no idea what a seminar was. I had no idea what my project was. I had no idea about anything. I wandered into graduate school as ignorant, as ill informed, as innocent of reality as anybody I could possibly imagine. And so when it came to me, I said that I wanted to do research on mountain men and the fur trade. Bogue gave me a sour look and didn't say anything. At the end of the hour as I was walking out the door, he said, "Come to my office." So I went to his office. He announced, "You can't do any work on the fur trade, there's nothing to be said about the fur trade"—this was 1963—"there's nothing new to be said about the fur trade, that's a waste a time, what other ideas do you have?" And I looked at him and said, "Er, uh, none." He got out a little 3x5 card-box and told me to start flipping through the cards, which had topics on them.

Bogue was a Canadian, and he'd been in the tank corps in the British Army during World War II. His tank had gotten blown up. The blast screwed up his back and he couldn't sit down, so his office was arranged for someone to stand up. The row of file cabinets had a sheet of plywood across the top, and he did all of his work—his writing, his typing, and everything—standing up, working off the top of his file cabinet. So I stood there next to him flipping through the card-box, and he said, "Hey, I know what you can do. I just got this collection of microfilm from the Oklahoma Historical Society. Go read that letter book and see what you can make out of it."

It was the letter books of an Indian agent for the Sac and Fox Indians named John Beach. I ended up writing this first seminar paper on John Beach and the administration of Indian policy among the Sac and Fox in the 1840s. That was the beginning of my focus on Native American history. So, I guess Allan Bogue was significant in heading me in that direction. I learned how to be a historian from Malcolm (Mac) Rohrbough, but basically I was a self-taught *Indian* historian. I learned how to be an ethnohistorian as a fellow at the Newberry Library in Chicago in the mid-1970s where director Francis (Fritz) Jennings and my colleagues inspired me, but I learned by floundering around, trying to figure things out and make as few mistakes as possible. I just really can't think of anybody that I would point to as being decisive in the development of my career as an Indian historian until Theda. I have learned so much from her, but that was of course after I had already gotten a start.

GO: Right. Okay. Theda, who do you see as intellectual forebears for you?

TP: The Charlies—Charles (Charlie) Crowe and Charles (Charlie) Hudson. I developed an interest in race when I was in high school. I will never forget shocking my high school history teacher by doing a book review on Martin Luther King's *Letter from a Birmingham Jail*. I was fascinated by the civil rights movement in part because it challenged the world I knew. I graduated in an all-white class in 1967. I think that I saw the injustice there, but my response was more intellectual than political or emotional. I was absolutely fascinated by how we became such a divided society and how we were going to change such an ingrained system.

When I went to Mercer, I enrolled in a course in African American history taught by a history professor from Fort Valley State College, a historically black institution. It was a life-changing experience. Everyone in the room except me was black. For the first time in my life, I was a racial minority and I was studying a history that was completely different from the histories I always had been taught. This was before African American history began to change the way that we teach American history or think about southern history. I found the experience to be disorienting on the one hand and thrilling on the other. All of a sudden I began to understand history not simply as the memorization of fact but as the understanding of human beings as actors and society as the creation of their decisions.

When I went to graduate school, I sought out the African American historian of the department, Charlie Crowe, who was white. (There were no black faculty members at the University of Georgia in the history department when I went there.) Charlie Crowe never saw a radical cause that he didn't like. Charlie had been fired from his first job at Old Dominion University because he got arrested for protesting the closing of the schools in Prince Edward County, Virginia. Charlie was a man who believed that resistance to injustice took precedence over everything else, and that included his academic job, which provided the income for his wife and his two small children. Charlie was a man driven—some would say a man possessed. I found his engagement with the present, one shaped by a profound understanding of the past, to be really exciting.

Charlie didn't know anything about Indians, but he knew who did, so he sent me to the other Charlie, Charles Hudson in the anthropology department. Charlie Hudson was a very different personality. Charlie thought that if you're going to write about the Indian past you have to put Indians at the center of it and you have to try to reconstruct their worldview. Charlie Hudson taught me how to do that. Charlie Crowe taught me how to write. Charlie never published very much, but what he did publish was beautifully written. The reason that I line edit my graduate students' work to this day is because that's what Charlie Crowe did for me. In the process of turning my rather awkward prose into something that was readable, he taught me the rules, and he convinced me that writing is mastering a skill set even more than it is innate talent. Many of the things that I have told my graduate students about good writing are the things that Charlie Crowe told me.

MG: Well, as you can see, her training is much more avant-garde than mine, which was very traditional, very old-fashioned.

GO: Let's talk a little bit more specifically about your own work. Mike, you first. How did you become interested in Creek Indian history and/or the removal era for southeastern Indians?

MG: After I got my master's degree on the removal of the Sacs and Foxes from Iowa Territory, I went to West Texas State University in Canyon in the Texas Panhandle for two years as an instructor. I taught five sections a semester of American survey for $54.50 a year. This was 1965–1967. By the time I got back to Iowa to do my PhD work, I really didn't have much of a notion of what I was going to do for a PhD. I didn't think that I wanted to continue with what I had started with Allan Bogue and the Sacs and Foxes. By this time, Mac's first book had come out and it was an administrative history of the General Land Office, and Mac thought of himself as an administrative historian. I got the bright idea that I would do a similar kind of study of the Bureau of Indian Affairs. Now I was going to be an administrative historian, study the Bureau of Indian Affairs, and do a dissertation that sort of replicated Malcolm's work on the General Land Office. I started doing research, and I just sort of floundered around.

I started reading microfilm with no guidance, no direction, no focus. I was just reading and taking notes. I spent a year doing that. I hadn't gotten very far and I got a little bit scared. I said to Mac, "You know, I don't really know how on earth I'm going to be able to fulfill our plan doing research for the next ten or fifteen years, because there's just so much stuff." He replied, "Well what have you got? Is there any way that you could proceed with something that you've got?" I said: "As a matter of fact, there is this hellacious controversy in Georgia in the 1820s between the state of Georgia and the federal government over the question of who's got authority over the administration of affairs with the Creeks. It's really interesting. I've done a lot of work. I think I know where I can find other stuff." And Mac said, "Well try that."

So that's what I did. I fell into the Creeks, I fell into Georgia in the 1820s, and I fell into the removal era. My career has been a succession of incredibly lucky accidents with essentially no plan, no preparation, no guidance. I don't know how on earth I ever made it to first base, but that's how it got started. I left Iowa in 1970 and went back to Canyon. I had taken a leave of absence with the idea that I was never going back, but by 1970 the jobs were all gone and they had to take me back. I taught at West Texas for another four years. I completed my dissertation and defended it in the spring of 1973. It took me three years to write it, and it was a very lackluster, ho-hum, uninteresting administrative history of this quite exciting controversy.

I was just about to finish it in the spring of 1973 when I went to Tahlequah, Oklahoma, to the first meeting of an Indian history, culture, and literature symposium sponsored by Northeastern Oklahoma University in Tahlequah. Francis Paul Prucha, Angie Debo, and two or three other major figures were on the program. That's when I met Angie—and talking about people who influenced me—Angie turned out to be a very good friend. I spent a fair bit of time with her, and we had marvelous conversations. I told her about my dissertation and my desire to turn it into a book. I asked her if she would read it, and she agreed to. She was pushing eighty by that time, long retired, and living in this little house in Marshall, Oklahoma. I didn't send it to her for a year or two, and by the time she got it, she had forgotten me, her promise, and our conversation—she told me later that she had no idea what was going on. But I had sent her a cover letter asking her to read it, and so she did. She had some good advice about what to do, but, she really wasn't, at that time, much of an ethnohistorian either, and so she didn't see where the real flaws in it lay. Fortunately, she thought what she saw was good, and she thought that what she saw in me was promise.

Then I got fired from West Texas State and became a gypsy for a year or two. I realized that there were no jobs, and the only way I was going to avoid becoming a car salesman or some such thing was to get a fellowship. About the only fellowship around was at the Center for the Study of the American Indian at the Newberry Library in Chicago. And I wrote an application and I asked Angie to write for me. D'Arcy McNickle was the director then, and my application said that I wanted to turn my dissertation inside out. This was a dissertation about the Creek Indians, but there were no Creeks in it. What I needed to do was to learn how to understand Creek culture and Creek society and put the Creeks in the center of the book. D'Arcy, I was told later, said, "That's not possible, he can't, there's no way he can do something like that." And somebody said, "Well, Angie Debo has written a letter for him." They read the letter, and D'Arcy conceded, "Angie says if anybody can do this, he can." So that's how I got the fellowship. And that's how, totally by accident, I became a student of Creek history and American Indian history.

GO: Now of course you're not giving yourself enough credit, you know, saying that you bumbled into this by accident. Obviously you had a nimble mind and you came to realize, with some influence of others, what needed to be done to turn that manuscript into a proper book.

MG: Well, I did figure it out. And, I figured it out pretty much by myself. The Newberry was a wonderful place, because it provided the setting and a certain degree of institutional support, but mostly, what it provided was a stipend. There were six fellows there: three postdocs, three predocs, and the director, Francis (Fritz) Jennings. Fritz became a very dear friend, but Fritz didn't know shit from apple butter most of the time, especially not about the Creeks and especially not about ethnohistory. And he didn't think that studying culture really was significant. I had time and I had support, but I had to figure it out for myself.

TP: I was lucky. I had a lot of help. I came up with my dissertation topic because at some point while I was in graduate school, I was driving around in north Georgia and happened on the James Vann house, which was built in the early nineteenth century by a Cherokee slaveholder. Cherokee slavery seemed to me to be a reasonable topic for a dissertation. Comparative studies of slavery were very popular, in particular comparing slavery in North America and various parts of the Caribbean and South America. When I raised this topic with Charlie Crowe, he thought it was a great idea. It played to his strength and his interest in African American history. So, that's how I ended up writing on Cherokees. By the time I had finished my dissertation, Charlie Hudson had arranged a session at the American Society for Ethnohistory meeting in Chicago. At the meeting, he introduced me to Ray Fogelson of the University of Chicago. Between Ray and Charlie I had an awful lot of help in teaching me how to think like an ethnohistorian. Charlie Crowe taught to be a historian, but it was Ray and Charlie Hudson who taught me to be an ethnohistorian. And so it's really out of that context that my own work emerges. I, too, went through the Newberry Library in 1978. Most of the major scholars of American Indians of our generation had fellowships at the Newberry at some point, and I am enormously grateful for that opportunity because it did a number of things for me. The fellowship gave me time to finish my book on Cherokee slavery, and it put me in contact with other people who were doing American Indian history. Until then, I was the only historian I knew who was writing about American Indians. I knew anthropologists, but I didn't know anybody doing Indian history. And so it was a really important point in my career. The fellowship made it clear to me that, even after the slavery book was done, I would write other books. I actually started doing research on the Cherokee women book while I was at the Newberry.

GO: Let's transition into ethnohistory a little bit and think about ethnohistory as a field and the American Society for Ethnohistory as an organization. First of all, just in your careers, what are some significant ways that ethnohistory—either the organization or ethnohistory as an approach to history—has changed since you first encountered it?

TP: I think that when we first encountered ethnohistory, it was dominated by anthropologists. It's not surprising, I think, that the people who introduced me to ethnohistory were anthropologists, not historians. In the era in which I was in graduate school, people were much more disciplinarily focused, that is, you just didn't read very much outside your own discipline. Things changed very quickly. As historians began to publish books that put Indians at the center of the story, other historians began to be inspired. I will never forget the first Western History Association meeting I attended, and I didn't know anybody much there. I knew John Finger from the University of Tennessee and that was probably about it. My book had just come out, so this would have been 1979 or 1980, and I was either delivering a paper or commenting on a session. The room was absolutely packed although the topic was something on southern Indians and didn't have anything really to do with the West. After the session was over, I asked, "Why would all these people come to this session?" And someone said: "They came to hear you. They've read your book." I didn't normally go to the Western History meeting, I'm a southern historian, and people began to engage me in conversations about how you write about the South and how you put Indians at the center of what is essentially a southern story. They were grappling with how you put Indians at the center of western history in ways other than the Indian wars. I think it was the first time I realized that somehow I had stumbled onto something that was really new. I was using the methods of historians—in particular, archival research—but I was thinking like an anthropologist. That is how I first realized that writing the history of Native people was in the process of changing.

MG: It always seemed to me as though it changed very slowly. Ethnohistory meetings continued to be very heavily influenced, if not dominated, by anthropologists, and you can't hardly blame them because if they didn't do history they'd have to do anthropology, and who wants to do that. Back in the old days, when I first started going to the ethnohistory meetings in the early and mid-1970s, it was just awful because everybody was an anthropologist, they were asking dumb questions and offering dumb answers, and it was just really frustrating.

GO: Can you think of any examples?

MG: Well, the only example that I can think of that's concrete was the session at the Ethnohistory meeting, which I think was in Albany, that was focused on Rutgers historian Calvin Martin. His book, *Keepers of the Game: Indian–Animal Relationships and the Fur Trade*, had just come out, and there was this session about it. I think virtually all the panelists were anthropologists, and they just shredded Calvin. Calvin's book was wrong, and Calvin was so arrogant that he could not possibly engage in conversation about it. I was sitting right behind him in the audience, and he started bouncing up and down in his chair as they came one right after another. These anthropologists were telling him he was wrong about this, he was wrong about that. And you nearly could see the smoke pouring out of Calvin's ears. He had read the stuff ahead of time, so he had prepared comments, but they were incoherent. I think that part of the reason for ganging up on Calvin was that Calvin had presented an idea that rested on no factual evidence that anybody could discover and therefore it needed to be shot down. But I think that the enthusiasm that these people brought to their task was largely based upon a kind of disciplinary chauvinism.

TP: In those days anthropologists thought no more of us than we thought of them. I mean Ethnohistory was really in many ways a very tense meeting because it was almost as though the historians and the anthropologists were speaking different languages.

MG: And we dug in our heels and we, we resisted mightily. And. . . .

TP: There was the footnote controversy!

MG: Oh yes, absolutely. The great footnote controversy over whether or not you cited your articles in the *Ethnohistory* magazine parenthetically the way the anthros do or numbered with footnotes or endnotes. Oh my God. We had a business meeting in which that was virtually the only topic of conversation. All of the historians who had tried to publish in *Ethnohistory* had been confronted with this because the editor of the journal, whose name I've forgotten, was absolutely stubborn in his refusal to compromise. But the person who ended up winning that fight was James (Jim) Axtell. And Axtell did a marvelous job of characterizing the narrow-minded disciplinary chauvinism of the anthropologists who edited the journal. That, plus the fact that the editor was incompetent, brought change. At that time, the journal was about four years behind schedule. Historian John Wunder actually took it over and rammed through two years and two volumes in an effort to try and catch it up.

TP: I think looking at the divide between the historians and the anthropologists is kind of hard for someone of younger generations to imagine, but anthropologists were very suspicious of historians because we didn't do fieldwork. They were very suspicious of whether you could write an Indian-centered history out of the archives, out of the documents, since documents were generally not—or they believed that documents were not—generated by Indians. I think the historians were very suspicious of anthropologists because they had this idea that anthropologists just went out on a kind of lark in Indian Country, came back, and wrote something up. There presumably was no documentary evidence to support it, and they had not done scholarship in the way that historians understood it. There was real methodological divide. The footnote war was really over a lot more than footnotes. It resulted in a deep and searching consideration of what ethnohistory was and what we should be doing.

MG: The problem with ethnohistory was that anthropologists and historians had not been trained in ethnohistorical methodology. I mean we all came to this from the outside. One of the things I think is that in the 1970s, the whole idea of the ethnographic present was for the first time really being questioned. Cultural anthropologists found themselves in a situation where the old verities were being challenged, and it wasn't real clear what the new verities were going to be. What they found particularly disconcerting was the idea that change over time could be documented or inferred on the basis of evidence. That, of course, was what historians were doing. And therefore what historians were engaged in was not only doing scholarship that didn't seem to make a lot of sense to cultural anthropologists, they were also doing the scholarship that seemed to verify the sort of intellectual changes in cultural anthropology that were taking place and disrupting things.

TP: At the same time historians were abandoning white man's history. The impetus for that came out of African American history, but it affected everything, not just Indian history, but labor history, women's history, immigration history, et cetera. All this comes out of this attempt to curtail the writing of elitist Whiggish history and focus instead on the diversity of the past and the role that people who were not in positions of power played. Both disciplines were really in a period of enormous changes.

By the mid- to late 1970s many American Indian peoples were taking control of their own pasts. They were increasingly regulating access to their reservations and to their intellectual resources, or those over which they had control. The kind of participant observation that anthropologists had been able to do a generation earlier was becoming less and less possible as Indians began to say, "Wait a minute. We don't want to be the mere subjects of your academic research. We don't want to be the fuel that fires your academic career. We want control over what goes on in our communities." Tribal self-determination meant that both historians and anthropologists had to do things differently.

MG: One result was that whole generations of graduate students of cultural anthropology were driven into the library and were forced to write dissertations out of the archives because they were prevented from going into Native communities.

TP: And at the same time historians were forced to take Indian viewpoints into account. This shift away from white man's history was partly driven by Indian people's insistence that their voices had to be incorporated in this history. It was a *really* exciting period.

MG: Yeah, it sure was.

TP: These debates between historians and anthropologists that took place in journals and scholarly meetings were really the things that made us the historians that we became.

MG: The 1970s and 1980s annual meetings of various organizations—the Western and Ethnohistory, in particular, were the two that I went to—were always exciting. There was the "gang of four" in the Western History Association—Richard White, Bill Cronon, Patty Limerick, and Donald Worster. We would go to the annual meetings, into the sessions, into the business meetings, and there would be fundamental debates.

TP: It happened in national meeting, too. I will never forget the AHA meeting where Fritz Jennings stood up and denounced the description of Indians as a "race." It was a really exciting time to be a young scholar.

MG: And we were aware of it. I mean, this is not looking back on the good old days that were more fun than they are now. We were aware of it then. We knew what was going on.

GO: Before we go any further, in the great footnote controversy, the solution was to use both citation styles in *Ethnohistory* depending on whether it was a history article or an anthropology article.

MG: The thing that finally settled it was the argument that Jim Axtell and I as well as several others made that parenthetic footnotes for lengthy citations of unpublished manuscript material from complicated collections simply could not be incorporated without doing violence to the flow of the text. We demonstrated why parenthetical notes did not work for most historians. And so the final result was that we didn't force our system on them, but we got them to promise not to force their system on us.

GO: You mentioned the broader trends within American history during the 1970s and 1980s. In recent years, there has even been a debate in some quarters about the relevance of ethnohistory, and I was wondering if you could talk a little about that. Is ethnohistory still relevant as a distinct field or is it merely one expression, say, of social history? What do you think about the future of ethnohistory?

MG: I think that ethnohistory is a methodology. And I think because it's a methodology it can be applied in a wide range of scholarship. But it still irritates me when I get the *Ethnohistory* journal, and every article in it is about Madagascar or some such place. I do think that what really excites anthropologists who are ethnohistorians is the methodology. It is a means to an end; and for that reason, I think that it is an invaluable tool for doing the history of people without a written record. But whether or not it's necessary to have an organization is another question. I think the national organization is bankrupt. I have thought it has been bankrupt for years and years and years. Every year I swear up and down I'm never going back, but I always do because there are friends there that I want to see, but I don't think that intellectually it makes sense at all.

TP: Mike probably doesn't want to admit this, but his main meeting has become the Southern Historical Association.

MG: Yeah, I go with Theda, but I have sort of become acculturated.

TP: I think one of the reasons you find the Southern intellectually satisfying is because good southern historians are also ethnohistorians [MG: Yeah], and I don't think that they came to this perspective through the American Society for Ethnohistory. I don't think they came to this through the writing of Indian history. But I think that ultimately the methods of ethnohistory have become so universal in good history that the term itself is almost meaningless now. I have always thought that one of the great classics of ethnohistory is Charles Joyner's *Down by the Riverside*. Ethnohistory—as something that is distinct—just really doesn't exist anymore. It's simply just good history.

MG: I think that a lot of historians, and perhaps ethnohistorians too, are more comfortable thinking of what they do as the new social history, but the American Society for Ethnohistory has an important history. When it was founded in the late 1940s and 1950s in the midst of the research for the Indian Claims Commission, it was enormously important as a way to bring together for the first time people who were engaged in a scholarly, historical, culturally informed, and culturally sensitive Native American history. But now, if the ASE decided to pack up its tent, I don't think very much would be lost except the social dimension. I increasingly believe that the primary purpose of national meetings is to provide the opportunity for people to make new professional friends and to rekindle old friendships. You know, there was a while when I knew everybody in the profession and I knew 'em because I saw 'em every year. That was good. I learned a lot and maybe I taught a lot.

TP: The professional networks are important. When you work in Indian history, you are likely to be the only person in your department who does that. And that makes, in my mind, the American Society for Ethnohistory important because it gives you an opportunity to have discussions with people who are in your discipline and working in your field within that discipline. That is really important. Whether NAISA [Native American and Indigenous Studies Association] is going to replace ASE, I'm not really sure. It may. Certainly there is more intellectual energy at NAISA than there is at Ethnohistory meetings. But I think that if the American Society of Ethnohistory exists for no other purpose than to enable scholars to create those networks that transcend their own institutions, then it's worthwhile.

There is another shift that currently is taking place that is at least as significant as the one that went on in the late 1970s and 1980s. We seem to be moving away from tribal studies. And I think that this is both good and bad. I think that it's unfortunate because there are a lot of tribal stories that need to be told. Every tribe has its own distinct culture and history, and it is important for there to be an intellectual recognition of this uniqueness of each tribe.

It is also important for political reasons because if we are going to have an intellectual basis for tribal sovereignty it has to be rooted in tribal studies. This is one of the things that concerns me about the move toward indigenous studies. Although indigenous peoples who have been victims of colonization globally have many things in common and exploring those commonalities is important, we need to remember that tribal sovereignty in the United States rests on a unique government-to-government relationship and that Indian tribes currently are able to exercise their sovereign rights because of unique treaty relationships. If there is no ongoing investigation of specific examples of the exercise of tribal sovereignty historically, it seems to me to endanger the whole concept of tribal sovereignty.

While I am not arguing against indigenous studies, I am arguing for a continuation of tribally specific studies. Nevertheless, scholars are paying attention increasingly to problems that cut across tribes rather than the way a specific tribe works those difficulties out. We recently have had two graduate students, Christina Snyder and Mikaëla Adams, who have done wonderful dissertations that cut across tribal boundaries. They make major contributions to this new move toward investigations that explore a problem across a number of tribes rather than in a specific tribe. This approach may change the way we think about the ethnohistory.

MG: I agree, but I think that there's a danger of putting the cart before the horse, in a sense. It's going to be hard to do the kind of broad-gauged, multitribal studies that some may pose without doing the basic legwork with tribal histories themselves. But there's room for both, and they both are very important exercises. I agree absolutely with Theda though that indigenous studies could perhaps deflect our attention away from what is uniquely significant about American Indian history. And I think about that both in terms of efforts to do comparative studies across international boundaries but also the growing interest in incorporating Native Hawaiians into a Native American perspective. I think that tribalism, the treaties, the assumptions of sovereignty, all of which define American Indian experience and history, really need to be kept at the forefront of our interest for political, cultural, and historical reasons.

TP: Mike and I both are increasingly concerned about preserving tribal sovereignty. We have, since the mid-1970s, seen a kind of renaissance in Indian Country—not everywhere, but in many places—in which Indian peoples have seized control of their own futures. They have figured out ways to define their problems and to come up with solutions to those problems. It is really scary to imagine what might happen if they lost the foundation on which this rests, that is, tribal sovereignty, the right to govern yourself.

MG: Just imagine what would happen if a significant tribal sovereignty case came to this Supreme Court.

TP: We have seen what happened with the Violence Against Women Act and all of the concerns raised by the Republicans about expanding tribal judicial authority over crimes against Indians on Indian reservations. How could you possibly be opposed to letting tribes punish people who commit sexual violence on their reservations?

MG: But we can't do that because they might not be Indian [sarcasm].

TP: Increasingly our own work intellectually is geared towards shoring up tribal sovereignty. I think as historians, as academics whose careers rest on writing the history of Native people, we have an obligation to take our reputations and our skills and put them to use to defend the rights of Indian people to govern themselves.

GO: Let's go in a slightly different historiographical direction. I wonder if you see any connections between changes in ethnohistory with the kind of broader trends within early American history, especially with the rise of Atlantic history, which, from my perspective, tends to subsume understanding of Native peoples and particularly the distinctiveness of various Native groups into a kind of broader colonial interaction between Europeans and Indians? And I wonder if you see a danger with the rise of Atlantic history, at least in terms of how it impacts Indian history in early America? Similarly, do you view the "new Indian history" as something distinct from ethnohistory or is it just another label for the same thing?

MG: I think one of the interesting things about what's happened in the last twenty or thirty years is the way in which Indian history has transformed colonial history. It is no longer possible to be a colonial historian and ignore Indians. That is not true in any other period in American history. Whenever I think of Atlantic history, I think of Bernard Bailyn's book of twenty years ago *The Peopling of British North America* in which he has this long half-page footnote about how he has deliberately chosen to ignore

Indians because there's no legitimate and acceptable literature on Indians that would have helped him incorporate them into this story. Fred Hoxie had a nice article (*The Social Science Journal* 25) taking on Bailyn's assertion. I don't have any particular feelings about Atlantic history one way or the other. I think that it is perfectly all right for people to do what interests them. I don't have any interest in Atlantic history myself, but I don't think of it as a movement that is likely to threaten the existence of Indian history in the colonial period in any particular way. I don't think I know what the "new Indian history" is.

GO: That's actually what I was trying to get at since it's a label that's bandied about a lot.

MG: Oh.

TP: I think the Atlantic World history is another way to put Europeans at the center of the history and to put Africans and Indians on the periphery because Europeans were the people to whom the Atlantic was important as a connector and as a source of power. The Atlantic did not empower Africans, it helped enslaved them. The Atlantic did not empower Indians, it led to their dispossession. So I think there are real problems with Atlantic World history. I think people should do whatever kind of history they want to do, but we need to look beyond catchy titles and think critically about the intellectual assumptions that are driving the inquiry. So that's my take on Atlantic history. When you use the term "new Indian history," I assume you are referring to people like James Merrell and Daniel Richter.

GO: Maybe Richard White to some degree—

TP: I think that's a different kind of history from the kind of ethnohistory that Mike and I normally do, or that we did earlier in our careers. It does put Indians and Europeans on a kind of level playing field in a sense. The kind of history I write puts Indians at the center of the narrative. I think there are other ways to include Indians as players, as rational people making rational decisions, other than the kind of history I write. And so I see the "new Indian history" as making Indians believable actors in the past but not the center of the story. Centering the interaction between the Indians and Europeans is extraordinarily useful and may represent a step forward. I'm not dismissive of it in the way I am of Atlantic World history. I think that the new Indian history is extraordinarily useful because it draws in lots of readers who might never read Indian history in another context. If Indians are major actors in any book, it helps people develop a fuller understanding of early America.

MG: You may remember the opening days of my graduate reading seminar when I talked about Robert Berkhofer and Axtell and the two primary approaches to Native American history, where one was focused internally on Indians and one was sort of new frontier history. When I think about what you call "new Indian history," I think of it as a new frontier history. Most of the new frontier history I read is by scholars whose previous work focused on Indians. Richter started out with one of the most brilliant ethnohistorical studies I ever read on the Iroquois. Merrell, as far as that goes, did the same with his Catawba book. I haven't read any of Richter's new stuff, but I have read Merrell's, and I think that what they're doing is what I would call the new frontier history. What it does is that it writes culture out of the story, which I think is very interesting.

We have a very good friend who is a significant cultural anthropologist and a colleague in the anthropology department here. She takes great pleasure in announcing that "we cultural anthropologists reject the idea of culture, we don't talk about culture anymore, culture is no longer thought of as a focus or a body of interest." The first time I heard her say this in a public forum, my jaw bounced off the floor like yours just did. I asked her to explain herself. She tried but not terribly successfully. I think that what these guys are doing is a reflection of this, a frontier scholarship that puts, as Theda said, Indians and non-Indians onto a level playing field. The problem with this is that the unspoken cultural baseline is the non-Indian cultural baseline. That's the world out of which the scholars are operating, and that's the world out of which the documentary evidence comes. In one sense I think that this scholarship is a step backwards because it is removing uniqueness based upon culture.

I disagree with my good friend and colleague in anthropology that culture is no longer a valid concept to think about. But I'm not 100 percent certain that I'm right because I also really like the new frontier scholarship that I've read. There's an awful lot of it that I haven't read, but what I have read I'm very impressed by and I think that it's doing great things. But I'm a little bit nervous about the absence of culture as an analytical construct. I've heard these guys swear up and down that they are absolutely not ethnohistorians, almost to the point that if you call me an ethnohistorian them's fightin' words. I don't quite understand that level of bitterness and assertion. But, it certainly seems to be their perspective.

GO: That's something I've picked up on as well, and I think others of my generation have too. There is a certain divide and I'm not exactly sure what the roots of it are. There is Indian history that is very ethnohistorically informed and Indian history that is much less culturally and ethnohistorically informed yet it is still quality history. There does seem to be kind of a fundamental difference between the two, and I'm sure it has something to do with whom the people trained with in graduate school and their approach to doing either early American or Indian history.

MG: With Merrell and Richter it's a kind of a rejection of their first entry into the field. But I think it's significant that everybody that we can think of who takes this position are colonialists. It's a reflection of what's happened to colonial American history: Indians have become so totally and completely integrated into the story that it's no longer novel.

TP: Ten years or so ago when we were hiring colonialists, the top twenty candidates all did some Indian history. They weren't solely Indian historians, but Indians played a role in their work. I think it is a really good indication of how colonial history has changed, and I absolutely applaud it. Let me go back to what Mike said about our colleague in anthropology and the notion of culture. I think that her reaction to the word "culture" is very much grounded in an old-fashioned anthropological use of the word "culture," which is static practices and beliefs apparently frozen in time. As historians we see culture as the ways people essentially organize their world and that is constantly changing. I think in part that's a disciplinary difference.

GO: Let's move to the South specifically. You and your students, as well as those outside your immediate circle on whom you've had some impact, have produced a plethora of works on the Native South over the past few decades. I want you to talk a little bit about how our understanding of southern history changed as a result of this outpouring of scholarship on southeastern Native people.

TP: I'm not sure it has.

MG: It's about to though.

TP: I've been holding my breath for the last twenty years waiting for it to change. I think we may just about be there. Having been in the profession at the very time when African American history was transforming the way we wrote about the South, I am optimistic that Indian history is going to have some impact on the way we write about the South. I haven't seen it yet, but I'm looking forward to it. An editor I know told me at a meeting this summer that a very prominent southern historian told him that the conferences he had been to in the last year or so had convinced him that including Indians really changes the story and that it's something that southern historians need to take into account. I consider this to be a huge triumph, and so I'm hopeful that southern history is going to change. But if it doesn't, I think that the fact remains that the scholarship is there and that if southern historians choose to ignore it, they do so at their own peril.

MG: I think you're right. We, and particularly our students, have changed the narrative. And when the changes that Theda talks about come, if they do, it's going to be in part their work, as well as the book that Theda's working on, that bring them about. But I don't think we set out to rewrite southern history. We came together because I did Creek history and she did Cherokee history and they were neighbors.

TP: But we met at the Southern Historical Association.

MG: We met at the Southern Historical Association, but my first conversation with her was over the phone after I had read and reviewed her slavery book. I was finishing up my Creek book, and I wanted to know if she thought an argument that she developed might be applicable for understanding Creeks. She said she didn't know because she didn't know anything about Creek history. [**GO:** (laughs)] But it was a great conversation nevertheless. That was the beginning of our acquaintance and our friendship. When we started directing graduate students together at the University of Kentucky we made a conscious decision to limit ourselves to southern Indian history because that was what we knew. We believed very, very firmly, and I think absolutely correctly, that you cannot adequately train graduate students until you know the source material yourself and the field. Then you can help your students figure out from the very beginning how to make those first tentative steps. I didn't have that, and I wasted a lot of time. I didn't want to see that happen to my students.

TP: I think there's another important part of this: we've also made southern Indian history a part of Indian history [**GO:** Yes]. The fact that Malinda Maynor Lowery's book, *Lumbee Indians in the Jim Crow South: Race, Identity, and the Making of a Nation* (2010), just won the NAISA's prize for the best first book is a really good indication of how southern Indians are no longer on the margins of scholarship on American Indians. I can remember the days when people writing the history of the Sioux or Navajos or other western tribes laughed when you said you worked in Cherokee history because the assumption was that Cherokees weren't real Indians. I don't think anyone can make that argument anymore. Certainly southern Indians have a different history. But it is a history that has a great deal to offer the field of American Indian history more generally. Our students and the people who have published in our series at the University of Nebraska Press, in particular, have made that case. I am enormously greatly to Nebraska for having hosted the series all these years. Publishing a series on southern Indians with a press well-known for its American Indian list more broadly was a really important thing to do.

GO: So where's the field of southeastern Indian history going? What topics need to be investigated?

TP: Well I'm really happy to see interest in Indian Territory. I think that lots needs to be written about Indian Territory. Rose Stremlau's recent book, *Sustaining the Cherokee Family: Kinship and the Allotment of an Indigenous Nation* (2011), has revealed the wealth of material that is available in allotment records. I think there is an enormous amount that we don't know about how tribes operated in the period between removal and Oklahoma statehood. We know even less about the period after Oklahoma statehood, when people in eastern Oklahoma managed to retain a sense of tribal identity in the virtual absence of a tribe. I think issues of race will continue to produce very good work. Mike tends to be somewhat more suspicious of that line of inquiry than I am, and I think there are a number of dangers associated with that topic. African American history opens up possibilities for Indian historians, but I would never want Indian history to be subsumed by African American history in the same way that I would never want American Indian history to be subsumed by indigenous history. I think that there's integrity in Indian history that I would like to see preserved, but at the same time, for southern Indians, in particular, race has to be a major concern.

I see lots of really good work on the horizon that deals with issues of race. Katherine Osburn's *Choctaw Resurgence in Mississippi: Race, Class, and Nation Building in the Jim Crow South, 1830–1977* (2014) is one of these. Mississippi Choctaws exploited white southern notions of race, segregation, and white power in order to achieve their own goals. I think that is a very useful line of inquiry, and I would like to see more done. Warren Milteer, a graduate student at UNC–Chapel Hill, has a fascinating dissertation on how people with Indian, African, and European ancestry end up with a particular racial classification. More work is needed on how people see themselves, how they envision their own past, and what happens when their own view of the past and the documentary record do not coincide. These are really interesting issues to me.

MG: I would agree with much of what Theda said. Whenever I say, "there's nothing more to be done," I think of Allan Bogue telling me in 1963 that there was nothing more to be done in fur trade history. So who knows? I really applaud the growing interest in Indian Territory. I think that the number of questions that have not been addressed is huge, particularly in the era of allotment. I'm not real comfortable with the racialization of Indian history. I'm not real comfortable with using black history as a kind of methodological guide or an interpretive guide to the study of Indians. So I'm perhaps somewhat less welcoming than Theda is of this direction, but I basically think that if it's good, any new stuff is worth doing and we can all learn more.

GO: Okay, that's fair enough. How would you answer a new graduate student who asked, "I'm interested in doing southeastern Indian history, so what are the one or two main things I need to know right off the bat, in terms of doing this sort of history?"

MG: Jesus.

GO: [Laughs] What I had in mind was the emphasis that you have always placed on the role of kinship, for example, among Native people and that understanding the importance of kinship is fundamental in determining a whole host of actions by Native people. I think that is expressed in a lot of your students' work as well.

MG: Learn the rules of kinship and understand how they apply. Of course, you know the rules of kinship are more or less significant depending on your question [GO: Right]. But understanding and appreciating kinship, I think, would entail learning as much as you can about the culture of the tribe that you're interested in and the time period that you're interested in. Become confident in your ability to use that understanding to interpret the documentary record.

TP: I would say that if you were going to write about southern Indians, you better understand about race, particularly if you're going to write about southern Indians from the late eighteenth century onward because in the twentieth century race increasingly trumps kinship. I think this brings us to perhaps an even more important thing, and that is the need to get into the archives. You don't go into archives blind, but historians work from the documentary record. They don't go into the archives looking for things to support a preconceived conclusion. Instead, they go to the archives to see what they can find. I know from working southern archives that there are lots of topics out there that I could write on, but I didn't know that before I went into those archives. You get a general topic, but then you go into the archives and you start looking to see what you can find. It's almost like a mystical experience, I think, for most historians. It's hard to describe to someone who has never experienced it. You begin reading the documents, and slowly your topic begins to emerge from the records themselves. I have always had difficulty with anthropology graduate students who come to research seminars and have a thesis that they want to prove, or they have a theoretical method that they want to apply to a particular tribe or to a particular period. They go to the archives looking for evidence to support that model. That is absolutely the opposite of the way that historians work. It's not that we are oblivious to theory, quite the contrary, but ultimately our work emerges from the archives themselves.

GO: And asking questions.

TP: I think you discover the questions in your research. Now having said that, I was not this good at directing dissertations when you were a graduate student [GO: (laughs)] but I think I got good at knowing what was workable and what was not as a topic. I have had students show up with topics they wanted to work on, and I would say, "Absolutely not, that's not doable. You can't do it. Why don't you see what you can find about this." With Mikaëla Adams, I said: "Why don't you go see what you can find out about creating tribal rolls?" And with Christina Snyder, I said, "Why don't you see what you can find out about captivity?" Ultimately, though, you can help students settle on a topic, but they themselves have to figure out where to take that topic.

MG: So I think that instead of saying they have to know about kinship, or they have to know about this or that . . .

TP: They have to know about Indians.

MG: They have to know how to do research. They have to *do* research. They have to have an open mind. They have to use imagination.

TP: They have to know how to read a document. They have to know not to take a document at face value. You have to know the context in which it was written, the purpose for which it was written. You have to be able to distinguish the information and the interpretation in the document itself.

MG: It takes at least five years to get a PhD because there are lots of things that you have to know.

GO: From what I'm hearing, you're saying, "Get into the documents, start doing the research." At what point do you make sure they have a thorough working knowledge of the relevant historiography?

TP: Before they go to the archives. That's why we have comprehensive exams. You need to know *something* before you go the archives otherwise it's a waste of time.

MG: That's why we have reading seminars.

TP: I think the dissertation prospectus is useful in pointing you in a particular direction, but having done a prospectus and defended it, it's okay then to leave it behind because what you find in the archives may lead you in a very different direction.

GO: I certainly remember that in my own work. This is a good segue into talking about working with graduate students. From talking with friends I have across the country in a variety of fields, I know that working with you guys was somewhat unique, first of all because you're a husband and wife team and essentially you're co-mentors, even if one of you might be officially the mentor. I'll never forget receiving draft chapters back from each of you with different comments and different advice about what to do and then calling you up and saying, "Okay now, whose advice do I abide by here?" And then you discussed that further between yourselves and decided what to do. It worked very well. Getting direct and immediate feedback from two scholars from the same field was invaluable. Since many of your students are now also mentors, at least of undergraduates if not also of graduate students, what would you recommend to them as mentors? What's your guide to mentoring?

MG: Don't let your students make mistakes if you can help it.

TP: I think you can either learn from your mistakes or you can learn how to avoid mistakes. And I always thought it was a lot simpler to help your students learn how to avoid mistakes. But let me back up a minute. I think you must be careful about who you take as a student. I think you only accept as a graduate student someone who is interested in what you yourself know. Mike touched on this earlier: there's only one graduate student that we ever directed in Indian history outside the South, and that was a unique situation. She wrote a publishable dissertation, but she had a lot of help from other people who were actually in her field. Everyone else we've directed in Indian history has worked on the South, which we know, and so we were actually able to direct.

The second thing is that you don't take more graduate students than you can give undivided attention to. We have tried very hard to accept only a student a year so that when it gets to the dissertation, particularly that final year, we can focus on that student, we can make sure that the dissertation is polished and not far from being a book, and that the graduate student does not have to compete against our other graduate students on the job market. I think that is extraordinarily important.

In accepting students I always try to talk to students or have them visit before I've accepted them because not everybody can work with me. I'm very opinionated, I'm very direct, and I expect graduate students to do what I tell them to do. There are lots of really smart people who can't deal with someone like me, and that's all right. It's just that life is too short and my time's too valuable to invest a lot of energy in someone who is not going to do what I say. I think I'm autocratic, I'll admit that, but I also think that there is a level of trust that you develop with your students. When you tell them something, they believe you, and they trust that you're right about it. I'm not always right, but I think I'm more likely to be right than my graduate students left to their own devices. So I've been very careful about trying to admit students that I was fairly certain that I could work with. They have to be able to trust me, and I have to able to trust the fact that they will do what they're supposed to do, that they'll work hard, that they'll be conscientious. I have just been enormously fortunate in having really wonderful graduate students. I don't just mean intellectually, I mean in, in terms of wonderful human beings.

Other things that I think go into being a successful mentor is that I've never permitted students to dawdle. I see some graduate students who take eight, nine, ten years to finish a degree in U.S. history, and I just can't deal with that. I would get bored with a topic by then. But I think it's extraordinarily important for graduate students to be fairly single-minded for the five years it takes them to go from an undergraduate degree to a PhD. And getting it done means that you don't do much else. I have had graduate students with families, and I greatly admire the sacrifices that they were willing to make to get the degree. But I think that's important because it shapes a work ethic. It sets you up for the rest of your career if you're able to work consistently at that level. My advice to mentors is to make sure that your graduate student understands that being a graduate is a full-time job and it takes constant attention. There are no vacations, no weekends off. You just get it done.

Graduate students need to be integrated into the broader profession. Mike and I have always insisted that our graduate students go to professional meetings, deliver papers, apply for funding for their research, publish book reviews, and have an article published before you finish your degree. These things integrate you into the profession and also make you marketable.

MG: Because what we're trying to do is basically two things: one is to teach you how to be a scholar and a historian; two is how to become a professor with a real job. I think that over the period of our career together, we've done more things right than wrong. We did not sit down and draw up a plan. Our style of working together sort of evolved. I know that we have a reputation for having been important mentors to our students. I know that we have a reputation for expecting a lot from our students. I know that we have been enormously successful, and I think basically the secret to our success has been our partnership. Neither one of us could have done it alone. We wouldn't have had the time. We wouldn't have had the stamina. We wouldn't have had the interest. We wouldn't have had any of the things that really made it work. What really made it work was our partnership.

TP: Mike is absolutely right about that. Our different training and different perspectives explain your experience of us writing radically different comments. You know, I suspect that was an important learning experience for you in the end.

MG: Yeah, you loved that, didn't you? [laughs]

GO: [laughs]

TP: In the end, though, you did what you thought was right.

GO: Well, what I did was call Mike, and Mike said, "You better go by what Theda told you to do."

MG, TP, & GO: [laugh]

TP: Mike's a very wise man. But I do think that our constant disagreements over chapters and haggling over students' dissertations also meant that you got a second perspective on your writing that ultimately forced you to understand that there are perhaps several equally valid ways of seeing the past. And I can't help but think that that's very useful.

GO: Oh yeah, absolutely.

TP: Mike and I also bring very different strengths to dissertations, I think. Mike has a much better command of the secondary literature than I do. I don't have a very good mind for details or factual information. I rarely can remember both the author and the title of a book. Mike can remember the author, the title, and usually the year it was published.

MG: Now, I'm not David Nichols.

TP: You're not David Nichols, that's right. You can't usually remember the journal and page number of articles. My really strong suit in the dissertation is that I can help students figure out an organization that works. So normally, Mike gets students to the point that they go to the archives, and then I take over and shepherd them through the note taking, the outline, and the organization of the dissertation. When it gets to actually writing it, we begin to pass it back and forth.

MG: We pass dissertation chapters back and forth in the same way that when we write a book together, we pass our own chapters back and forth.

TP: I think it has worked extraordinary well. So, I think Mike's right: our success is because there are two of us. Of course, I also have directed southern history dissertations. There is that whole segment of my mentorship that's not reflected in this anthology, but I am enormously proud of those southern history dissertations, the books written from them, and the professors their authors have become. But working with Mike has been easier, I must say, because Mike's strengths are my weaknesses and vice versa.

I will never forget when I told John Wunder that Mike and I were getting married. He said, "Getting married! You can't even agree on a manuscript!" And he was essentially right, but our arguing about manuscripts and our arguing about dissertations I think has made our marriage an ongoing seminar.

MG: Yep.

TP: And you guys have been the subjects of the seminar.

GO: But the beneficiaries too, yes. Do you have any last comments, points, lessons, legacies you would like to get across?

TP: Shall I give him my legacy line?

MG: Yeah, give him your legacy line . . .

TP: When people talk about legacies, they're usually talking about what you leave behind when you die. And Mike and I have had the great good fortune to see our legacy while we're still living. Our legacy is represented by the people who are contributing to this anthology as well as many others who are not. We have not only a body of work as a legacy but we also have had marvelous students. There are few people who, at the end of their professional careers, can see their legacy quite as vividly as we can. And we can not only see it, we know its name: it's named Greg O'Brien, and Tim Garrison, and Jamey Carson, and David

Nichols; it's named Christina Snyder, and Malinda Lowery, and Mikaëla Adams, and Julie Reed, and Rose Stremlau and Meg O'Sullivan; it's named Karl Davis, and Joe Anoatubby, and John Hall, and Lorri Glover, and Rowena McClinton, and Izumi Ishii, and Cary Miller, and Andrea (Ramage) Watkins, and Randolph Hollingsworth; it's named Matt Schoenbachler, and Craig Friend, and George Ellenberg.

MG: All I can say is that I agree.

Two

The Enterprise of War

The Military Economy of the Chickasaw Indians, 1715–1815

DAVID A. NICHOLS

After interacting for several centuries with the Indians of eastern North America, many Europeans and Euro-Americans had concluded that Native Americans were innately violent, possessed of what Henry Knox called a "passion for war." Modern ethnohistorians believe that Indians had no more innate inclination to violence than their European contemporaries, but they do acknowledge that, like Europeans, Native North Americans had inherited a long military tradition, predating European contact by many centuries. The evidence for this lies in archaeological sites bearing traces of ancient warfare, in art objects bearing images of military weapons (like the engraved copper plates found at the Etowah site), and in the derogatory names that some Indians gave their neighbors—like "Sioux," an Anishinaabe word meaning "snakes" or "enemies." Scholars also note that warfare served vital social and cultural functions for Indians, allowing young men to acquire sacred power and demonstrate their masculinity, allowing families to replace fallen kinsmen with captives, and letting communities avenge interethnic attacks and correct the cosmic imbalances such transgressions caused. What early modern Europeans attributed to nature or race actually grew out of indigenous religious beliefs, social needs, and North America's long precontact history.[1]

Some Indian nations enjoyed a greater reputation for martial enthusiasm than others. The Chickasaws, a southeastern nation from present-day Mississippi, belonged to this select group. The Chickasaws' military history began before they became a unified nation. One of their predecessor peoples, the Summerville culture of present-day Alabama, left persuasive archaeological evidence of internecine warfare—the remains of a palisade and of a man with a projectile in his chest. The nation's other principal precursor, the Chicaza chiefdom of eastern Mississippi, gave Hernando de Soto an equally persuasive demonstration of their acumen in 1541, when the would-be conquistador demanded his hosts provide him with two hundred porters. Instead of submitting, the Chicazas attacked Soto's camp, killing twelve Spaniards and forcing the expeditionaries to flee. The Chickasaws, into whom the Summerville Indians and Chicazas coalesced by the seventeenth century, gave up some of their ancestors' customs but retained their study of war. One of their English allies, Thomas Nairne of South Carolina, described them in 1708 as "the most military power in the region." "We are not acquainted," added veteran trader James Adair, who lived with the Chickasaws for much of the eighteenth century, "with any savages of so warlike a disposition as the Catawba and Chickasaw."[2]

The Chickasaw Nation began constructing its outsized martial reputation during the era of the Indian slave trade (ca. 1670–1715), when Native American raiders captured and sold twenty or thirty thousand southeastern Indians to English traders, wreaking havoc on the entire region. Chickasaw warriors played an important role in this grim story, ensnaring about two thousand slaves in the Mississippi Valley and along the Gulf Coast. The Indian slave trade collapsed during the Yamasee War, but Chickasaw men and women knew little peace in its aftermath: like their English allies, the Chickasaws found themselves at war one year out of every two between 1715 and 1815. They fought a desultory war with the Choctaws and French in the early 1720s, and a longer and deadlier conflict with those nations between 1731 and 1758, during which two French armies attempted to conquer the Chickasaws' homeland. Farther from home, the Chickasaws continued a war they had begun in the seventeenth century with the Illinois confederation; a map drawn in the 1730s by Mingo Ouma (Red King), the nation's principal military leader, included an active *chemin de guerre* (war road) between Chickasaw and Illini country. Chickasaw warriors raided Creek and Yamasee towns on behalf of British Carolina in the 1720s, and during La Guerra del Asiento, or the War of Jenkins's Ear (1739–48), Chickasaws from an emigrant settlement in Georgia accompanied James Oglethorpe's raids into Florida. One Chickasaw leader, probably Paya Mataha, accompanied Oglethorpe himself to Scotland and campaigned with him against the Jacobites. In the late 1750s Chickasaws destroyed a settlement of French-allied Shawnees on the Tennessee River, and served the British Army as auxiliaries in the Anglo-Cherokee War of 1759 to 1761.[3]

During the decade after the Seven Years' War, Chickasaw men generally stayed home or tended to their hunting, but in 1772 they formed an alliance with their old adversaries, the Quapaws, and joined that nation's war with the Osages. Chickasaws would periodically participate in this conflict for the next thirty years. In the American War of Independence, Chickasaw warriors patrolled the Mississippi River for Britain and small parties helped British troops defend Pensacola and Mobile from Spanish attack, while a larger force attacked Fort Jefferson, a Virginia outpost on Chickasaw territory, and compelled its defenders to withdraw. Late in that war, Chickasaw raiders plundered Spanish shipping in the Mississippi River and attacked the Spanish garrison at Arkansas Post. Following the American Revolution, a faction led by Piomingo (Mountain Leader) and the biracial sons of trader James Colbert became allies of the United States, and some scouted for the U.S. Army during the Northwest Indian War of the 1790s, while those back home in Mississippi fought an intense war with the Creeks. Finally, in 1814 Chickasaw rangers served with American forces in the Creek War, and Chickasaw gunmen destroyed one of the Red Stick Creeks' refuges. Just a few years before this last conflict began, when traveler Rush Nutt asked Chickasaws to comment on the "fortifications" he encountered in their homeland, they told him that "as far back as they can learn by their ancestors . . . there was nothing but war . . . with all nations." This was only a modest exaggeration.[4]

While one of their French foes commented on the Chickasaws' "turbulent and restless spirit," more lay behind their century of conflict than bloody-mindedness. Warfare provided the Chickasaws, as it did the Iroquois and the Comanches, with tangible economic benefits and with even more important social and political compensation. The economic proceeds included captives, whom Chickasaws could ransom or adopt, and plunder, which Chickasaws could sell or use themselves. Less tangibly, but more importantly, endemic warfare built the nation's strong military reputation, which allowed the Chickasaws to retain their independence in an era when other Indian nations faced enslavement or involuntary incorporation into other Native polities. The Chickasaws' reputation also brought economic gains: it made them valuable allies for Europeans and other Indians, and thus the recipients of gifts, territorial concessions, and other benefits from diplomatic suitors. As Sechin Jagchid observed about the Mongol nomads of central Asia, war could serve for indigenous peoples as an effective means of production. Like many other modern means of production, however, warfare's costs proved difficult, in the long term, to sustain.[5]

In the shorter term, warfare generated the direct material benefit of plunder, a product of the Chickasaws' raids on river shipping and, more infrequently, of attacks on other Indians' towns or of battlefield salvage. In the 1730s and 1740s, for instance, Chickasaw warriors captured French bateaux on the Mississippi and Ohio Rivers and took abandoned guns and provisions from the field after a failed French attack on the town of Chokkalissa' (1736). During the American War of Independence, James Colbert and his sons led a campaign of piracy against the Spanish that yielded liquor, clothing, firearms, and money destined for Spain's garrisons or its Indian allies. Many of the goods that Chickasaws purloined were European wares they could not make themselves and upon which they had come to rely while trading with the British (for example, firearms or woolen and cotton cloth). Harvesting these goods from the field of battle helped decrease the nation's dependence on British traders and on their tenuous overland trading link to South Carolina.[6]

More valuable than European trade goods were horses, which the Chickasaws captured from their Indian adversaries' towns. Carolina and Caddo traders had introduced the Chickasaws to these animals in the early eighteenth century, and within a few decades they had become a regular feature of Chickasaw life, honored in one of the nation's dances, the *issoba-hihla*. They constituted a military and economic asset, with which raiders and hunters could increase their range by hundreds of miles. While Chickasaw men bred and raised their own equines by midcentury, taking horses from their adversaries diminished their foes' military strength and provided surplus animals for trade or gift-giving.[7]

At the apex of the Chickasaws' small mountain of trophies stood human prisoners, whom the Chickasaws, like Indians elsewhere in North America, either adopted as new kinsmen or redeemed for ransom. During the Franco–Chickasaw wars, French officials paid Chickasaw leaders gifts and deerskins when they returned captives. Spanish officials followed suit after Spain took over the western half of Louisiana. In December 1789, for example, the commandant of Arkansas Post gave the leaders of a war party a substantial quantity of clothing, ammunition, mirrors, knives, rum, and tobacco, along with 335 person-days of rations, in exchange for four Illini prisoners the Chickasaws had taken on the Ouachita River. The redemption of captives resembled the Indian slave trade, whereby many Chickasaws had once made their fortunes, except that it was a safer practice, less likely than enslavement to lead to retaliatory violence.[8]

Why did the Chickasaws, who suffered from severe population losses in the eighteenth century, not adopt more of their captives, as the Iroquois and other nations did? Part of the explanation lies in the other mechanisms the Chickasaws could use to augment their numbers, like polygynous marriages and the office of the *fanimingo* (squirrel chief), who could ceremonially adopt families from other nations and incorporate them into the Chickasaw polity. Moreover, the material benefits of the Indian slave trade and of the plundering campaigns that followed it altered the balance of power in Chickasaw communities, increasing the prestige of warriors at the expense of chiefs and of the clan matrons who regulated adoption. Warriors probably tended to perceive their captives as "prestige goods" rather than potential kinsmen, and they therefore tended to sell or ransom rather than adopt them.[9]

The most valuable of all the proceeds of warfare, arguably, was the reputation for boldness and military acumen that the Chickasaws garnered. This reputation acted as a kind of capital, which leaders could combine with warriors' military labor to persuade other nations that the Chickasaws' friendship was worth a good price. Chickasaw men built this reputation both individually and collectively, through acts of war and through their oral and symbolic communication of these acts to others. They staged public war dances for their kinsmen and visitors, during which warriors took turns reciting their martial exploits. They adorned their bodies with tattoos, produced by incising the body with gars' teeth and rubbing soot into the wound; the images denoted past acts of heroism and "registered them among the brave." War-party captains tattooed themselves with the totemic animal of their community, so that survivors of their raids could tell others the attackers' identity. The female canoeists encountered by Robert La Salle in 1682 probably used such symbols, emblazoned on the attackers' bodies or carved into their war clubs, to identify the destroyers of an Acolapissa town as "Auma, Auma, Chiquilosa," the latter referring to the Chickasaws' town of Chokkalissa'. Even when at peace with a particular nation, Chickasaw men preserved their martial image by behaving in a "fierce, cruel, insolent, and haughty manner" toward former enemies, like the Quapaw diplomats whom a Chickasaw warrior insulted and sprayed with rum in 1771.[10]

The Chickasaws' warlike reputation made them attractive allies to European empires seeking to strengthen their position in the Southeast's borderlands. Chickasaw leaders knew that many colonial governments wanted to employ their nation as a piece (an important one, if the Chickasaws had any say) in imperial games. Spanish officials in Florida, for instance, hoped to entice the Chickasaws to resettle in that depopulated province, and in 1747, hearing that the Chickasaws resented the aid that Britain had given Red Shoes's faction of Choctaws, Florida's governor tried to exploit their disaffection by offering gifts to Chickasaw leaders. Officials in South Carolina countered with more lavish presents of uniform coats and lace-trimmed hats. The British colony continued to arm the Chickasaws into the 1750s, needing them as proxies against the French in the Mississippi Valley.[11]

While the French terminated their North American empire in 1763, Britain subsequently exercised only nominal sovereignty in the continent's interior, a point that the Great Lakes Indians made abundantly clear in Pontiac's War (1763–65). After that conflict General Thomas Gage and Southern Indian Superintendent John Stuart believed Britain still needed the Chickasaws' services: to escort an army regiment to Illinois, to help police the Illinois country, and to help defend the new British colony of West Florida. The need grew with the outbreak of the American War of Independence, and with the rebels' seizure of the old French Illinois settlements on the Mississippi River. Stuart and other agents sent regular supplies to Chickasaw country and made sure that warriors had new muskets and "new fine ruffled shirts" to remind them of Britain's friendship.[12]

When the Revolutionary War ground to a halt in 1782, Chickasaw leaders divided on which of the victors should enjoy their nation's good offices: Spain or the United States. (The Chickasaws' need for trade goods precluded their selecting "none of the above".) One faction, based in Chokkalissa' and headed by Paya Mataha and Ugulaycabe (Wolf's Friend), signed a commercial treaty with Spain in 1784. Spanish officials, who hoped to turn the southeastern Indians into a barrier to American expansion, subsequently gave their allies medals, regular gifts, and a chiefly salary or two. The other faction, based in Chokka' Falaa' and headed by Mountain Leader and the Colbert clan, sought an alliance with the United States, with whom they signed a treaty in 1786 and whose army employed them as scouts and skirmishers in the Northwest Indian War (1790–94). While the Americans initially found it difficult to give their partisans more than unfulfilled promises, the more stable and solvent federal government created by the U.S. Constitution proved more capable of rewarding its Native American allies. The War Department sent the Chickasaws weapons and ammunition—enough in one 1793 shipment to arm every adult male in the nation—and during the Creek–Chickasaw war American settlers in Nashville provided Chickasaw communities with supplies and light artillery. Even after 1795, when Spain scaled back its support for the southeastern Indians, the U.S. government remained sufficiently worried about its influence to continue courting the Chickasaws. Congress voted the small nation a $3,000 annuity in 1795, and a few years later the War Department opened a trading factory for them at Chickasaw Bluffs (present-day Memphis), where hunters could sell their skins and buy inexpensive merchandise from a federally employed factor.[13]

The Chickasaws' military prestige drew Native American allies as well. Despite a reputation for arrogance, the Chickasaws periodically allied with other Indian nations in wartime or in anticipation of war. Indeed, after the French destroyed the Natchez Indians, Chickasaw leaders tried to create a regional anti-French alliance, an effort that helped precipitate the Franco–Chickasaw war of 1731 to 1758. During the latter years of that conflict, some Chickasaw women formed marital alliances with men from their nation's sometime enemies, the Cherokees and Shawnees. Their husbands provided the Chickasaws with additional manpower, and helped correct (in a limited way) the gender imbalance created by earlier Chickasaw war losses. Occasionally, too, inter-Indian alliances brought not merely additional warriors but economic returns. In the 1770s the Quapaws offered Chickasaw hunters access to the rich hunting ranges of the Arkansas Valley in return for assistance against the Osages. Chickasaw chiefs accepted the alliance, and the lands west of the Mississippi River later provided the Chickasaws with abundant furs and pelts, including most of the 300,000 pounds of deerskins they sold to the factory at Chickasaw Bluffs.[14]

Warfare carried substantial costs, of course, a lesson the Chickasaws had learned during their slaving campaigns in the early eighteenth century, when smallpox and enemy muskets reduced their population by 65 percent. Their subsequent wars were less deadly but still costly. Enemy war parties attacked Chickasaw towns and took captives and horses, as the Choctaws did in the 1740s and 1750s, and as Spanish-allied Kickapoos did in 1782. They destroyed Chickasaw crops and inhibited hunting, depriving families of food and the means to buy trade goods. These stresses continued to deplete the Chickasaws' population, which fell from 2,800 in 1715 to 1,900 (a 30 percent decline) by 1760. The losses produced a significant change in Chickasaw culture, as the matrons and uncles who arranged marriages for young women encouraged polygyny as a way to replenish the nation's population. Merely "fashion"[able] in the early eighteenth century, polygamy had, according to one trader, become nearly universal by the 1750s. War could also prove psychologically taxing; one French captive reported that Chickasaw men had to sleep with their guns near their heads for fear of Choctaw raiders, and during a visit to Georgia the Chickasaw captain Postube declared that "we now have so many enemies round about us that I think of nothing but death."[15]

Given these costs, it seems likely that Chickasaw men went to war less to obtain plunder or captives (though these remained important considerations) than to build their nation's reputation, which served the Chickasaws both as an economic asset and a defensive shield. Chickasaw leaders recognized that eighteenth-century North America was a dangerous place for small nations. In the era of the Indian slave trade, Denise Bossy has noted, southeastern Indians could become either "slave raiders" or "targets," and the Chickasaws had chosen the former. Even after that trade collapsed, the Chickasaws still lived among Europeans who believed that fostering internecine warfare would protect their own fragile colonies; as one councillor advised Governor Bienville in 1723, better "to give the Choctaws . . . this bone [the Chickasaws] to gnaw" than have them attack French settlements. In this fractious environment, the Chickasaws had a choice. They could hunker down, gradually lose land and population to their enemies, and wind up like the Chakchiumas, who by the 1730s had just a few hundred people, and whom a French official then ordered to abandon their pretense of autonomy and merge with the Choctaws. Or, they could retain their independence and seek Indian and European allies, which meant they had to be willing to fight and have a reputation for fighting well. The latter option, at least, gave individual warriors the opportunity to win laurels and influence, and gave the nation as a whole access to resources they would not otherwise have enjoyed.[16]

When warfare eventually declined as an important part of the Chickasaw economy, it did so because decreased competition among European empires made the Chickasaws' military labor and reputation less valuable to them. As long as the British needed a proxy in the Deep South, the Spanish wanted a barrier against American expansion, or the Americans worried about their control of the Mississippi River, they found the Chickasaws useful as warriors, and warfare gave the Nation reliable returns. By the second decade of the nineteenth century, however, the contest between rival imperial powers had resolved itself in favor of the United States, which wanted the Chickasaws' lands rather than their military services.[17]

The Chickasaw Nation's economic survival now lay in its ability to subsist on a reduced land base, for which purpose many needed to adopt commercial agriculture and home manufacture. Some Chickasaw families had begun making the transition to the new economy in the 1770s, and by 1790 visiting army officer John Doughty could report that Chickasaw men "verg[ed] fast toward the state of farmers." Rush Nutt, a decade and a half later, claimed (only slightly prematurely) that "the men have laid down their gun & tomahawk and taken up the implements of husbandry." Chickasaw survival also lay in the ability of men such as George and Levi Colbert to communicate effectively with American commissioners, obtain adequate compensation for road easements and land cessions, and resist pressure to cede the entirety of the Chickasaw homeland. Cultivating these skills required substantial changes in the training and mindset of Chickasaw men, who had defined themselves as hunters and warriors, not farmers and negotiators. Change, however, had become the one constant in Indian Country by the nineteenth century, and the Chickasaws would embrace the new order as willingly as they had once devised a military economy.[18]

Acknowledgments

The author presented an earlier version of this essay at the Fourteenth Biennial Maple Leaf and Eagle Conference in Helsinki, Finland, May 11, 2012. He thanks James Gustafson, John Craig Hammond, Jacob Lee, Chris Olsen, Shawn Phillips, and Barbara Skinner for helpful comments on subsequent drafts.

Notes

1. Bernard Sheehan, *Seeds of Extinction: Jeffersonian Philanthropy and the American Indian* (Chapel Hill: University of North Carolina Press, 1973), 185–212; Henry Knox

to William Blount, January 31, 1792, in Clarence Carter et al., eds., *Territorial Papers of the United States*, 26 vols. (Washington DC: Government Printing Office, 1934–73), 4:115–16 (quote); Colin Calloway, *New Worlds for All: Indians, Europeans, and the Remaking of Early America* (Baltimore MD: Johns Hopkins University Press, 1997), 92–114; Matthew Jennings, *New Worlds of Violence: Cultures and Conquests in the Early American Southeast* (Knoxville: University of Tennessee Press, 2011), 3–26; James Loewen, "Arizona Navajo Reservation: Calling Native Americans Bad Names," posted to H-AmIndian, December 11, 1998, accessed September 19, 2013, http://h-net .msu.edu/cgi-bin/logbrowse.pl?trx=vx&list=h-amindian&month=9812&week=b&msg =dRmdybLlslyulh0uyaajqq&user=&pw=; Daniel Richter, "War and Culture: The Iroquois Experience," *William and Mary Quarterly*, 3rd ser., 40 (October 1983): 528–59; Gregory Evans Dowd, *A Spirited Resistance: The North American Indian Struggle for Unity, 1745–1815* (Baltimore MD: Johns Hopkins University Press, 1992), 9–16; James Adair, *The History of the American Indians* (London, 1775; http://olivercowdery.com /texts/1775adr1.htm#title, accessed February 15, 2016), 148–51.

2. Ned Jenkins and Richard Krause, *The Tombigbee Watershed in Southeastern Prehistory* (Tuscaloosa: University of Alabama Press, 1986), 95–97; Charles Hudson, *Knights of Spain, Warriors of the Sun: Hernando de Soto and the South's Ancient Chiefdoms* (Athens: University of Georgia Press, 1997), 259–60, 267–71; Robbie Ethridge, *From Chicaza to Chickasaw: The European Invasion and the Transformation of the Mississippian World* (Chapel Hill: University of North Carolina Press, 2010), 65–76; Alexander Moore, ed., *Nairne's Muskhogean Journals: The 1708 Expedition to the Mississippi River* (Jackson: University Press of Mississippi, 1988), 38 (first quote); Adair, *History of the American Indians*, 224 (second quote).

3. Allan Gallay, *The Indian Slave Trade: The Rise of the English Empire in the American South, 1670–1717* (New Haven CT: Yale University Press, 2002), 294–99; Ethridge, *From Chicaza to Chickasaw*, 167, 189, 198, 227, 235, 238, 244; Christina Snyder, *Slavery in Indian Country: The Changing Face of Captivity in Early America* (Cambridge MA: Harvard University Press, 2010), 58–63; Claiborne Skinner, *The Upper Country: French Enterprise in the Colonial Great Lakes* (Baltimore MD: Johns Hopkins University Press, 2008), 115, 123–34, 159; Jacob Lee, "'At War with All Nations': Chickasaw Indians and the Greater Illinois Country in the Eighteenth Century" (paper presented at the Annual Meeting of the Southern Historical Association, November 3, 2012); Edward Cashin, *Guardians of the Valley* (Columbia: University of South Carolina Press, 2009), 6, 45–49, 57, 84–85, 111–12, 119–22. On Mingo Ouma (or Houma) see James Atkinson, *Splendid Land, Splendid People: The Chickasaw Indians to Removal* (Tuscaloosa: University of Alabama Press, 2004), 27, 95.

4. Kathleen DuVal, *Native Ground: Indians and Colonists in the Heart of the Continent* (Philadelphia: University of Pennsylvania Press, 2006), 140, 151–55, 173, 185, 208–9; Colin Calloway, *The American Revolution in Indian Country* (Cambridge MA: Cambridge University Press, 1995), 221–30; Jim Piecuch, *Three Peoples, One King: Loyalists, Indians, and Slaves in the Revolutionary South* (Columbia: University of South Carolina Press, 2008), 118–19; John Campbell to Lord Germain, August 6, 1780, in K. G. Davies, ed., *Documents of the American Revolution, 1770–1783*, 21 vols. (hereafter

cited as DAR; Shannon: Irish University Press, 1972–81), 16:377; Kenneth Carstens, "George Rogers Clark's Fort Jefferson, 1780–1781," *Filson Club History Quarterly* 71 (July 1997): 259–84; D. C. Corbitt, "James Colbert and the Spanish Claims to the East Bank of the Mississippi," *Mississippi Valley Historical Review* 24 (March 1938): 457–72, esp. 457–62, 466–71; Wendy St. Jean, "How the Chickasaws Saved the Cumberland Settlement in the 1790s," *Tennessee Historical Quarterly* 68 (Spring 2009): 6–8, 14; David Nichols, *Red Gentlemen & White Savages: Indians, Federalists, and the Search for Order on the American Frontier* (Charlottesville: University of Virginia Press, 2008), 140, 198; Statement of Chickasaws Employed as Rangers in the Service of the United States against the Hostile Creeks, October 1, 1813, to May 31, 1814, Letters Received by the Secretary of War Relating to Indian Affairs, 1800–1823 (U.S. National Archives Microfilm m-271), reel 1:969. The "fortifications" Nutt saw were probably burial mounds and ceremonial earthworks. See Jesse Jennings, ed., "Rush Nutt's Trip to the Chickasaw Country," *Journal of Mississippi History* 9 (January 1947): 34–61, esp. 51–52 (quote 52). My thanks to Jacob Lee for this reference.

5. Jean-Baptiste Le Moyne Bienville to Jean-Frédéric Phélypeaux, Comte De Maurepas, April 23, 1734, in Patricia Galloway et al., eds., *Mississippi Provincial Archives: French Dominion*, 5 vols. (Jackson and Baton Rouge: Mississippi Department of Archives and History and Louisiana State University Press, 1927–34 and 1984; hereafter cited as MPAFD), 1:228; Pekka Hämäläinen, *The Comanche Empire* (New Haven CT: Yale University Press, 2008), 18–106; Jagchid quoted in Jack Wetherford, *Genghis Khan and the Making of the Modern World* (New York: Crown Publishers, 2004), 108. See also Michael Khodarovsky, *Russia's Steppe Frontier: The Making of a Colonial Empire, 1500–1800* (Bloomington: Indiana University Press, 2002), 19, 22–24, 66–67, 83, 136–37. I am grateful to Barbara Skinner for the Khodarovsky reference.

6. Skinner, *Upper Country*, 115, 127, 131–34; Bienville to Maurepas, September 5, 1736, MPAFD, 1:326–29; Account of the March and Defeat of D'Artaguette, in Caroline Dunn and Eleanor Dunn, eds., *Indiana's First War*, Indiana Historical Society Publications 8 (Indianapolis: William Burford, 1924), 131; Deposition of Anicanora Ramos, May 30, 1782, in Louis Houck, ed., *The Spanish Regime in Missouri*, 2 vols. (Chicago IL: R. R. Donnelly & Sons, 1909), 1:227–28; Calloway, *New Worlds for All*, 46–47; James Axtell, *The Indians' New South: Cultural Change in the Colonial Southeast* (Baton Rouge: Louisiana State University Press, 1997), 62–64.

7. Cashin, *Guardians of the Valley*, 101, 117–18; Moore, *Nairne's Muskhogean Journals*, 47; Daniel Usner Jr., *Indians, Settlers, and Slaves in a Frontier Exchange Economy* (Chapel Hill: University of North Carolina Press, 1992), 177–78; H. B. Cushman, *History of the Choctaw, Chickasaw, and Natchez Indians* (Greenville TX: Headlight Printing House, 1899), 499.

8. Cashin, *Guardians of the Valley*, 70; DuVal, *Native Ground*, 99; R. G. McWilliams, ed. and trans., *Iberville's Gulf Journals* (Tuscaloosa: University of Alabama Press, 1981), 173; Louis Billouart de Kerlérec to Antoine Louis Rouillé, August 20, 1753, MPAFD, 5:131; Joseph Vallières to Esteban Miró, January 12, 1790, in Lawrence Kinnaird, ed., *Spain in the Mississippi Valley, 1765–1794*, 3 vols. (Washington DC: Government Printing Office, 1949), 2:293.

9. Ethridge, *From Chicaza to Chickasaw*, 179, 227–29; Snyder, *Slavery in Indian Country*, 65–67; Moore, *Nairne's Muskhogean Journals*, 40; Patricia Galloway, "'The Chief Who Is Your Father': Choctaw and French Views of the Diplomatic Relation," in *Powhatan's Mantle: Indians in the Colonial Southeast*, ed. Peter Wood, Gregory Waselkov, and Thomas Hatley (rev. and expanded edition; Lincoln: University of Nebraska Press, 2006), 345–70, esp. 362–64. On slavery and "prestige goods," see Claude Meillassoux, *The Anthropology of Slavery*, trans. Alide Dasnois (Chicago IL: University of Chicago Press, 1991), 36–40, 110; Patricia Galloway, "Choctaws at the Border of the Shatter Zone: Spheres of Exchange and Spheres of Social Value," in *Mapping the Mississippian Shatter Zone*, ed. Robbie Ethridge and Sheri Shuck-Hall (Lincoln: University of Nebraska Press, 2009), 333–64, esp. 341–45, 356–57.

10. Moore, *Nairne's Muskhogean Journals*, 41; Adair, *History of the American Indians*, 389 (first quote); Jean-François-Benjamin Dumont de Montigny, *The Memoir of Lieutenant Dumont, 1715–1747: A Sojourner in the French Atlantic*, ed. Gordon Sayre and Carla Zecher (Chapel Hill: University of North Carolina Press, 2012), 356; Patricia Galloway, "The Minet Relation: Journey by River," in *La Salle, the Mississippi, and the Gulf: Three Primary Documents*, ed. Robert Weddie (College Station: Texas A&M University Press, 1987), 57 and 57 n. 65; Bernard Romans, *Concise Natural History of East and West Florida*, ed. Kathryn Braund (Tuscaloosa: University of Alabama Press, 1999), 121–23 (third quote). I define capital as both the product of "accumulated labor"—in this case, military labor—and as "a social relation of production," an accumulation of "social magnitudes" that the holder could transform into means of subsistence or production without depleting the original principal. See Karl Marx, *Wage Labor and Capital*, trans. Harriet Lothrop (New York: New York Labor News Company, 1902), 35–37.

11. Cashin, *Guardians of the Valley*, 75, 81; Journal of John Buckles, April 12, 1754, in *Colonial Records of South Carolina: Documents Relating to Indian Affairs*, ed. William McDowell, 2 vols. (Columbia: South Carolina Archives Department, 1958), 1:511.

12. Colin Calloway, *The Scratch of a Pen: 1763 and the Transformation of North America* (New York: Oxford University Press, 2006), 67–91; Clarence Alvord and Clarence Carter, *The New Regime, 1765–67* (Springfield: Collections of the Illinois State Historical Library, 1916), 130; John Thomas to the Earl of Hillsborough, December 1, 1770, DAR, 1:216; Thomas Gage to Hillsborough, October 1, 1771, DAR, 1:409; John Thomas to John Stuart, January 27, 1772, DAR, 4:104; Stuart to Lt. Col. McGillivray, March 28, 1778, DAR, 13:269; Alexander Cameron to Lord George Germain, November 30, 1780, DAR, 16:449; Robert George to John Montgomery, September 2, 1780, reprinted in Carstens, "George Rogers Clark's Fort Jefferson," 279 (quote).

13. Nichols, *Red Gentlemen & White Savages*, 8; David Weber, *The Spanish Frontier in North America* (New Haven CT: Yale University Press, 1992), 282–85; Charles Weeks, ed., "Of Rattlesnakes, Wolves, and Tigers: A Harangue at the Chickasaw Bluffs," *William and Mary Quarterly*, 3rd ser., 67 (July 2010): 499; Henry Dearborn to James Robertson, September 14, 1802, Records of the Office of the Secretary of War, Letters Sent, Indian Affairs (U.S. National Archives Microfilm M-15, Washington DC), 1:278; Henry Knox to William Blount, May 14, 1793, in Walter Lowrie and

Walter Franklin, eds., *American State Papers, "Indian Affairs"*, 2 vols. (Washington DC: Gales and Seaton, 1834), 1:430; Statement of the Annuities . . . Payable Each Year under Indian Treaties to the Year 1819, in Lowrie and Franklin, *American State Papers*, 2:215–16; St. Jean, "How the Chickasaws Saved the Cumberland Settlement," 10–11, 14; David Nichols, *Engines of Diplomacy: Indian Trading Factories and the Negotiation of American Empire* (Chapel Hill: University of North Carolina Press, 2016), 50–52. On the spelling of Chickasaw place names see John Dyson, *The Early Chickasaw Homeland: Origins, Boundaries, and Society* (Ada OK: Chickasaw Press, 2014), esp. 98, 137.

14. Louis Billouart de Kerlérec to Jean-Baptiste de Machault d'Annouville, September 15 and December 18, 1754, MPAFD, 5:143–46, 158; Kathleen DuVal, "Interconnectedness and Diversity in 'French Louisiana,'" in *Powhatan's Mantle: Indians in the Colonial Southeast*, ed. Gregory Waselkov, Peter Wood, and Thomas Hatley (rev. and exp. edition; Lincoln: University of Nebraska Press, 2006), 148; DuVal, *Native Ground*, 128, 134–35, 140; John Treat to Henry Dearborn, November 15, 1805, in Carter et al., *Territorial Papers of the United States*, 13:277, 280. For shipments from the Chickasaw Bluffs Factory, see Nichols, *Engines of Diplomacy*, 50, 96, 134–35.

15. Paul Kelton, "Shattered and Infected: Epidemics and the Origins of the Yamasee War," in *Mapping the Mississippian Shatter Zone*, 312–32; Bienville to Maurepas," 28 May 28, 1740, February 18, 1742, and February 4, 1743, MPAFD, 3:733–34, 3:758–59, and 3:773–74, respectively; Kerlerec to De Machault d'Annouville, February 18, 1754, MPAFD, 5:158; DuVal, *Native Ground*, 153–54; Report of Sieur Drouet de Richardville, June 10, 1739, in Dunn and Dunn, *Indiana's First War*, 139, 141; Petition of the Chickasaw Head Men, August 23, 1753, in McDowell, *Colonial Records of South Carolina*, 1:458; Cashin, *Guardians of the Valley*, 30 (first quote); Moore, *Nairne's Muskhogean Journals*, 46 (second quote); John Buckles to Governor Glen, June 26, 1754, in McDowell, *Colonial Records of South Carolina*, 1:510, 514.

16. Denise Bossy, "Indian Slavery in Southeastern Indian and British Societies," in *Indian Slavery in Colonial America*, ed. Alan Gallay (Lincoln: University of Nebraska Press, 2009), 207–50, esp. 215 (first two quotes); Minutes of the Superior Council of Louisiana, July 23, 1723, MPAFD, 3:357 (third quote); Perier to Maurepas, January 25, 1733, MPAFD, 1:167; Gregory Dowd, *War Under Heaven: Pontiac, the Indian Nations, & the British Empire* (Baltimore MD: Johns Hopkins University Press, 2002), 262–64.

17. Daniel Walker Howe, *What Hath God Wrought: The Transformation of America, 1815–1848* (Oxford UK: Oxford University Press, 2007), 74–75, 96–97, 107–9.

18. Romans, *Concise Natural History*, 128; John Doughty to Henry Knox, April 17, 1790, Josiah Harmar Papers (William Clements Library, Ann Arbor, Michigan), 12:85 (first quote); Jennings, "Rush Nutt's Trip to the Chickasaw Country," 43, 49 (second quote); Atkinson, *Splendid Land, Splendid People*, 183–85, 189–97, 205–12. On adaptation and change as constants in Indian societies, see Patricia Nelson Limerick, *The Legacy of Conquest: The Unbroken Past of the American West* (New York: Norton, 1987), 189.

Three

Quieting the Ghosts

How the Choctaws and Chickasaws Stopped Fighting

GREG O'BRIEN

One of the hallmarks of newer scholarship on southeastern Indian peoples over the past couple of decades has been the use of ethnohistorical methodology to ascertain Indian motivations and to place Indian people at the center of their own history. There are still many events in southern Native history that need to be reconsidered with this basic assumption in mind, one of which is when, why, and how the Choctaws and Chickasaws ended decades of internecine fighting in the eighteenth century. The usual explanation of the Choctaw–Chickasaw peace is that France's defeat in the Seven Years' War forced the Choctaws to open relations with Britain and arrange peace with the British-allied Chickasaws after 1763. However, the Choctaws and Chickasaws, along with the lesser-known Chakchiumas, forged the peace on their own terms and for their own reasons, rather than at the behest of shifting European powers.[1]

For nearly seventy years before the Seven Years' War in the 1750s, Chickasaws had raided Choctaw villages and hunting parties, and Choctaws retaliated in a seemingly endless cycle of revenge killings. Though closely related through culture, language, and occasional intermarriage, Chickasaw and Choctaw relations fell apart with the establishment of the Chickasaw–British alliance after the founding of Charles Town (Charleston) in 1670. Chickasaws supplied the British demand for Indian slaves by using their British guns to attack their neighbors to the south and sell thousands of Choctaw captives into the Charles Town–Caribbean slave market.[2] French intrusion in the lower Mississippi Valley, starting at the beginning of the eighteenth century, enabled the Choctaws to acquire their own guns and to counter Chickasaw raids with equally deadly ones of their own. On behalf of France, and sometimes with French forces at their side, Choctaws mounted major unsuccessful campaigns against the Chickasaws in the early 1720s and late 1730s, and both groups assaulted each other nearly continuously through the 1750s.[3]

Though war was naturally violent and resulted in deaths and injuries, it was also a significant aspect of normal life and culture among all southeastern Indians. Choctaw and Chickasaw males attacked each other in order to become men or to develop into men with greater status and authority. Southeastern Indian boys, no matter their actual age, remained children until they participated in a successful raid on an enemy. Only then did they acquire a title bestowed by accomplished war leaders and elders that designated them men. Men who killed an enemy with their own hands, especially an enemy warrior rather than a woman or child, gained higher status and new titles. Ever higher status and authority could be gained for those men who then successfully led warriors into battle, success being judged by the killing of an enemy and minimal loss of one's own forces. Veteran war leaders sometimes became diplomats entrusted with forging peace with other peoples because they had proven that they could negotiate the hazards presented by the outside world. What successful war making proved was that a man could tap into spiritual forces to defend his people and conquer his enemies. Moreover, war was rarely a large-scale event characterized by annihilation of the enemy. Rather, southeastern Indian warfare, like that between the Choctaws and Chickasaws, usually involved small-scale attacks on hunting parties or unguarded individuals tending to crops or venturing out to travel and trade with other villages. Such warfare still invoked terror because of the unpredictability of attacks, but the numbers of people killed generally remained relatively low.[4]

Besides male status, though often conflated with it, motivations for war also stemmed from the need to avenge the death of one's kinsman or kinswoman. When someone was murdered, only revenge and the death of the murderer or the murderer's relative could restore the balance between two peoples. Women, as the leaders of their matrilineal kinship groups, played a key role in demanding revenge for their deceased relatives and in singing "the enlivening war song in the time of an attack" in order to "inflame the men's spirits" to fight. Choctaw people, according to an anonymous French source from the early eighteenth century, talked about relatives killed in war as "ghosts" who "have not been given certain effects on dying of which they had need in the other world." Ghosts needed to be quieted by vengeance and proper ceremony. Chickasaw people believed similarly that the soul (or ghost) of a relative slain in war "would haunt the eaves of the house until equal blood had been shed for him." These cultural imperatives to wage war provided fuel to the engine of continuous warfare.[5]

When Choctaw and Chickasaw men attacked each other at the insistence of the French or British, they often did so because they could use such actions to enhance their status or gain greater access to European-made merchandise. Only when European demands for attacks meshed with Indian motivations did such attacks occur, but the competing European powers did, nonetheless, provide further incentive to engage in war against other Native peoples. Despite the strong Choctaw–French alliance in existence since the early eighteenth century, chiefs and other ranked men of the Western Division (one of three major Choctaw ethnic and political divisions referred to as the Western, Eastern, and Six Towns) had persistently contacted British traders and officials throughout the eighteenth century. One of them, the famous war leader Red Shoes, who apparently counted a Chickasaw woman among his multiple wives and ironically rose to a position of prominence through leading a successful war party against the Chickasaws in the early 1730s, led a delegation of Choctaws to the Chickasaw villages in 1738 to make peace and gain access to British traders. However, most Choctaw chiefs refuscd to rccognize the agreement, and warring between Choctaws and Chickasaws resumed within months.[6] In 1744, during King George's War between France and Britain, the Choctaws and Chickasaws again temporarily ceased hostilities as the Choctaws sought access to British trade via the Chickasaw villages. Foreshadowing events in the mid-1750s, France was unable to supply the Choctaws with trade goods because of the disruptions of the war, forcing the Choctaws to find British goods even if that meant crafting a temporary truce with the Chickasaws.[7]

Red Shoes led another Choctaw peace delegation to the Chickasaw towns in 1746 after a Frenchman reportedly raped one of his wives. Red Shoes then instigated the Choctaw Civil War by killing three Frenchmen later that year, forcing French officials to encourage the Eastern and Six Towns Divisions to attack Red Shoes and his Western Division kinsmen. Choctaw and Chickasaw relations with the French and British, thus, helped to cause the destructive Choctaw Civil War that lasted from 1746 to 1750.[8] That conflict arose, in part, over disagreement about which European country—France or Britain—could better supply their trade needs. Western Division fighters maintained access to British trade through the Chickasaw villages during the civil war. In 1750, after hundreds of deaths among the Choctaws, the Choctaw division allied most strongly with France, the Eastern Division, won the civil war. The alliance between France and the Choctaws seemed secure, putting the Choctaws and Chickasaws again at war.[9] Thus, by the early 1750s, the Choctaws and Chickasaws had fought a nearly constant seventy-year conflict spurred on by Britain and France, as well as by Choctaw and Chickasaw cultural pressures to enhance male status and seek clan vengeance to "quiet the ghosts." With the opening of the Seven Years' War, there was little reason to think this scenario would alter significantly, much less permanently.

After the start of fighting between France and Britain in the Ohio Country in 1754 and 1755, southern Indians heard of the growing conflict. As in previous wars between their European neighbors, southern Indians played the sides off each other where possible and jockeyed for the best possible trade position. The outbreak of war between France and Britain provided Native southerners an opportunity to negotiate from a position of strength as both European powers sought their allegiance. Although the outcome of the Seven Years' War resulted in the defeat of France and the eventual evacuation of French forces from the South (France occupied New Orleans until 1766, however), the Choctaws, Chickasaws, and other southern Indians began to establish the groundwork for fundamental geopolitical changes as soon as the Seven Years' War commenced and not simply as the result of the European outcome of the war.

The war brought about new opportunities and incentives to further harmony. Since 1752 the Lower Creeks, especially the chief Malatchi of Coweta, had begun constructing peace with their longtime enemies the Cherokees. Upper Creek leaders made the Creek–Cherokee peace a reality. The "Gun Merchant" of the town of Okchai led a peace delegation to Cherokee country from August 1754 to April 1755. Along with other men, women, and children, he spent the winter of 1754–55 in the Cherokee towns of Tellico and Chote at the invitation of the "King of Chote." While there they hunted together, discussed trade exchange rates offered by British fur traders, and cemented a peace between these specific Creek and Cherokee villages.[10]

Meanwhile, French goals at the start of the war with Britain enabled southern Indians to negotiate with one another without fear of attack from other Indians. As early as the spring of 1755, French Louisiana governor Louis Billouart de Kerlérec encouraged Indian delegations from throughout the South to visit him at Fort Toulouse. Fort Toulouse, or "the Alabama Fort" as the British called it, was located at the southwestern edge of Upper Creek territory among the Alabama Indian villages near where the Alabama River originates at the confluence of the Coosa and Tallapoosa Rivers just north of present-day Montgomery. Positioned at the crossroads of competing European empires and Indian nations, Fort Toulouse and the Alabama Indian villages played a key role in diplomatic strategies during the French and Indian War. The potential for European trade and the chance to meet with French officials provided part of the incentive for southern Indians to journey to the Alabama villages in the 1750s, but the Alabamas themselves seem to have held a unique status as economic and diplomatic brokers that dated back decades. As early as 1715 Alabama leaders coordinated a trade agreement between the French and all of the primary Creek provinces, the Abikas, Tallapoosas, and Cowetas. Alabama leaders invited French officials in Mobile to establish a fort and trading post in their midst, resulting in the construction of Fort Toulouse in

1717. Alabamas exploited the geographic significance of their position at the crossroads of competing European and Indian nations and where two rivers joined to form one, a site rife with latent sacred and historical significance.[11]

Fort Toulouse and the Alabama villages attracted Indian and European diplomats throughout the French and Indian War. Kerlérec mediated a peace there between the Alabamas and visiting Choctaw emissaries in early 1755. The two Indian groups had long attacked one another in a series of revenge killings. Since both the Alabamas and the Choctaws counted the French as a trading partner, Kerlérec did not gain a new ally for France with this negotiation, but Indian motivations coincided with his desire to keep France's Native allies at peace with one another and united for possible action against British subjects in the South. In fact, since southeastern Indian diplomacy to end conflicts required that a third party act as a mediator, the Choctaws and Alabamas used Kerlérec's offer to meet as a welcome means to end their ongoing quarrel.[12]

Following up on the peace efforts between the Okchai Creeks and the Tellico and Chote Cherokees, Creek leaders also accepted Kerlérec's offer to meet. A delegation of both Upper and Lower Creek Indians visited with Kerlérec at Fort Toulouse in the spring of 1755 after refusing a request of South Carolina governor James Glen to visit Charles Town. The French governor hosted the Creek delegation, doled out gifts, and promised future trade. More importantly, he furthered southern Indian goals of peace and cooperation by hosting a small Choctaw delegation at the same time and mediating an agreement between them and the visiting Creeks. Both Upper and Lower Creek chiefs participated in this meeting with their longtime enemies, along with about two hundred to three hundred other Creek residents. The Creeks and Choctaws had also sporadically warred against each other for decades. This initial agreement at Fort Toulouse enabled the Creeks and Choctaws to begin more serious and larger-scale meetings in the coming months and years. Besides having French officials host and mediate the peace meeting, the former enemies also required leading chiefs, or "headmen," to visit the villages of the other group to assure their people that war had ended and peace reigned. Creek chiefs punctually traveled to the Choctaw villages in 1756 after this peace agreement was established.[13]

Kerlérec had encouraged an end to the warring between the Choctaws and Creeks and the Choctaws and Alabamas a few months earlier when he met with thousands of Choctaws from all three ethnic and political divisions for their annual gift-giving congress at Mobile in October to November 1754. These follow-up meetings in the spring of 1755 at Fort Toulouse provided the needed physical and cultural environment for that diplomacy to take place. Apparently, the Eastern Division Choctaws, who counted kinfolk among the Alabamas and the Upper Creeks, represented all three Choctaw divisions in these early meetings at Fort Toulouse. The Choctaws who had met with Kerlérec at Mobile a few months earlier bestowed a title upon him, *Youlakty Mataha Tchito, anké achoukema*, that Kerlérec translated as "King of the Choctaws and greatest of the race of the Youlakta [or *Inhulahta*] which is the finest and the oldest."[14] The Inhulahta ethnic identity dominated the Eastern Division Choctaws who had supported the French interest and prevailed in the Choctaw Civil War that culminated just four years prior to this meeting in Mobile. It is consistent that they in turn led the negotiations with their neighbors and relatives among the Alabamas and Creeks with Kerlérec's support.[15]

Finally, Cherokees from the Tellico village visited Fort Toulouse in 1756 to discuss trade possibilities with the French. The Cherokee diplomatic mission found shelter and protection in Gun Merchant's village of Okchai, perhaps visiting new kin established during the Creek visit to their village. During their visit to Fort Toulouse, the Cherokee delegation also met with a visiting party of Choctaws who told the Cherokees "that notwithstanding they had for a long time been at war with them and kill'd great numbers of their people[,] they were extremely proud to see them and had forgot all past injuries."[16] The Choctaws then attempted, according to a British source, to convince the Cherokees to join them in alliance with France. Rather than seeking an alliance with the Cherokees on behalf of the French, however, the Choctaws who met with the Cherokee chiefs at Fort Toulouse more likely wanted peace with the Cherokees for their own reasons involving access to British trade and safer travel through-out the Southeast. For their part, the Cherokees already enjoyed greater quantities of trade goods from the British at lower prices than the French could ever supply, so they did not necessarily need French trade goods. Despite British fears and rumors, the Cherokee mission to the Creek and Alabama villages appears to have had more to do with strengthening peace ties to the Creeks and establishing new relationships with the Alabamas and Choctaws than with serious consideration of joining a French alliance. As a sign of this diplomatic priority, the Choctaws promised to visit the Cherokee Tellico village the following spring to verify the new peace.[17]

These French-sponsored peace negotiations between the Alabamas, Choctaws, Creeks, and Cherokees in 1755 and 1756 resonated throughout the South. The two leading chiefs of the Upper Creek village of Okchai, the brothers-in-law Gun Merchant and the Mortar, worked diligently in 1757 to continue the momentum for intertribal peace. Mortar met with Cherokee delegates at his home in May while the Gun Merchant met nearly simultaneously with a Choctaw delegation he had invited in order to discuss ending the Choctaw conflict with the Chickasaws. Meanwhile, French officials at Fort Toulouse also sent three messages to the Chickasaws in 1757 to encourage them to abandon their decades-long war against France and the French-allied Choctaws and join an anti-British alliance. The Chickasaws refused all calls for diplomacy across the Southeast at first, pledging to continue their decades-long war against France and the Choctaws while remaining firmly in the British alliance and trade network. Reports from British fur traders confirmed that the Chickasaws and Choctaws continued to harass and kill one another in 1757. Nevertheless, the French-sponsored meetings during the first couple of years of the Seven Years' War encouraged dramatic new understandings, as various southern Indian delegations continued to visit one another all over the region.[18]

While the French seemed to benefit from these initial diplomatic efforts in 1755–57, and Fort Toulouse would remain an important international meeting site, southern Indians enacted their own agendas. Conferences held over the next few years at

Fort Toulouse, the Alabama villages, Creek towns, and at other Indian sites if anything benefited Britain more than France as all of the southern Indians sought British trade goods. Even so, Indians controlled the agenda and set the parameters about what such trade relationships meant, and Indians clearly acted out of their own interests and not on behalf of some overarching French or British alliance. They refused to engage in combat on behalf of either France or Britain throughout the entire French and Indian War, for example. Peace among the southern Indian nations had its own benefits in lessened violence and an easing of tensions, but for the Indian groups who counted France as a trading partner, such as the Choctaws, lack of French trade goods had caused an economic and political crisis. Louisiana lagged behind the British colonies on the Atlantic coast in both quantity and quality of supplies for the Indian deerskin trade, and the outbreak of war in the mid-1750s further exacerbated this discrepancy. From the declaration of war between France and Britain until 1758 not one French ship arrived in New Orleans loaded with Indian supplies.[19]

In early 1757 Choctaw "deputies" visited the French governor in New Orleans to give him a chance to produce the trade goods and annual presents they expected of their European neighbors and as had been custom in their relationship with France. After three years of no manufactured goods from the French, the Choctaws told the governor "that the nation could no longer do without receiving the English among them."[20] Kerlérec appealed to his superiors in France later that year that the "King's warehouses are stripped," and "we are daily annoyed by the Choctaws, who are in want of everything. They threaten us more than ever to resort to the English and to introduce their traders into their country."[21]

Choctaw leaders decided to reach beyond Governor Kerlérec to British trade and successfully take advantage of the enhanced British and French demand for their attention in the wake of the French and Indian War.[22] In the spring of 1757, various Choctaw groups used the newly formed peace alliance with the Alabamas and Creeks that Louisiana governor Kerlérec had helped make possible to journey east to visit their new Native partners with the hope of finding British trade goods. Building upon the peace and fictive kinship established at the Alabama villages two years earlier, Choctaws now sought trade with the Alabamas and Upper Creeks. British traders had also invited Choctaw and Chickasaw chiefs to a meeting at the Creek village of Okchai (home of Gun Merchant and the Mortar) that spring to discuss an end to the fighting between them. However, only two Chickasaw chiefs from the "Breed Camp" (a group of a couple of hundred Chickasaws who lived a few miles north of Okchai) attended, and they could not speak for the main Chickasaw villages. The twenty-five Choctaws who journeyed to the Alabama villages in the spring of 1757 told South Carolina governor William Henry Lyttelton's agent Daniel Pepper that they would report back to their nation and encourage a larger delegation with more authority to return later in the year, as well as perhaps send a small delegation to Charles Town to meet directly with British government officials. Pepper, hoping to secure the Choctaws in a pro-British and anti-French alliance, subsequently sent a letter to the Chickasaws urging them not to attack any Choctaws in anticipation of a future peace between the two nations. What the Choctaws wanted, though, was trade, and they rebuffed efforts to commit to a military alliance.[23]

During a December 1757 visit to the Alabama towns, Choctaws exchanged their deerskins with the Alabama Indians, rather than with British traders, for Alabama-owned "old Cloaths [sic]" and "their Blanketts [sic], Flaps, Shirts &c." In turn, the Alabamas, perhaps trying to enrich themselves as middlemen or possibly at French insistence, since Fort Toulouse was nearby, traded the Choctaw deerskins for new goods with the British traders, rather than allowing direct contact between the Choctaws and British. As a sign of just how literally the Alabama towns were located at a crossroad of empire, British traders and officials noted that the French troops at Fort Toulouse often provisioned themselves with British goods via trade with the Alabamas since supplies from France or other French posts remained in perpetual short supply. Choctaw eagerness to trade with Britain soon circumvented any Alabama or French interference. As promised during the spring 1757 visit to the Alabama villages, an unnamed Choctaw chief accompanied a Creek delegation to Charles Town in early 1758, and Governor Lyttelton sent him home with a letter of greeting to the Choctaws.[24]

One major obstacle to the opening of direct Choctaw–British trade remained. Before trade between the Choctaws and Britain could commence, the Choctaws and Chickasaws also had to establish peace. Britain refused to trade with the Choctaws "as long as matters were indeterminate between that nation & the Chickasaws."[25] The decades-long war between the two nations raged on, however, as the Choctaws simultaneously tried to reach British traders to their east among the Alabama and Creek Indians and engaged in revenge killings against the Chickasaws.

The Chickasaws told fur trader Jerome Courtonne that in early 1756 they fought "the largest Army of Chactaws that they had ever seen" to a draw. A group of about thirty Chickasaw warriors subsequently killed and scalped three Choctaws and brought one Choctaw captive back to their villages to be burned to death. The Choctaws killed one Chickasaw hunter in October 1756, another Chickasaw man died similarly in November, and three more perished in December. In retaliation, a Chickasaw war party of 130 men left their villages from December 25 to January 4, 1757, to attack the Choctaws, returning with ten Choctaw scalps. Throughout the spring of 1757, "gangs" of Choctaws and Chickasaws attacked each other at remote hunting camps. Some prisoners were tortured to death, women fell to enemy scalping knives, and the Chickasaws were unable to effectively hunt for deerskins in order to trade with the British, while running out of ammunition and gunpowder for their guns. A force estimated at two hundred Choctaws abandoned their attack on the Chickasaw villages in April 1757, and instead split up and harassed Chickasaw hunting camps, killing three Chickasaws at one camp and stealing their horses, deerskins, and supplies.[26]

In the summer of 1757 Choctaws burned a Chickasaw house, wounded a child and killed a man as they slept in a corn house scaffold, and picked off lone Chickasaw travelers who strayed too far from their villages. In September the Choctaws killed three Chickasaws out hunting, and at least five more Chickasaws were slain in October while hunting. Five "gangs" of Chickasaws set out against the Choctaw villages in September and October, one of them returning with a Choctaw scalp. In December the Chickasaws succeeded in redeeming a woman and children and killing five Choctaw warriors who had kidnapped them and killed the father. In early 1758 the attacks continued, with two Chickasaw women murdered by Choctaws within sight of their villages, and another large group of Choctaws estimated to number two hundred forced to retreat after stealing ten Chickasaw horses. As usual since the outbreak of the Seven Years' War, Quapaws from west of the Mississippi River and "northern Indians" also assaulted the Chickasaws. Despite a relatively small population and losses from the ongoing war against the Choctaws and others, Chickasaw chiefs remained defiant but beseeched Governor Lyttelton in May 1758 to send them ammunition, a call that the British answered with a new shipment of goods. In June the Chickasaws again took the fight to the Choctaws, returning home with four scalps and two captives who they "would have Burnt directly" had not British fur trader John Buckles intervened to save their lives. Buckles saved the two Choctaw men "finding that they were two belonging to the Towns that was formerly in our Interest [the Western Division]." Rather than dying a tortuous death, the two Choctaw men went home with blankets, shirts, paint, and other items supplied by Buckles in order to put them in a good frame of mind toward the British.[27]

Choctaw attitudes toward the British had begun to change long before, but it was the intervention of another, more obscure group of Indians who began to turn the tide of the Choctaw–Chickasaw conflict. In late July 1758 Chickasaw warriors captured a man who they thought at first to be a Choctaw but who turned out to be a Chakchiuma Indian. Culturally and linguistically related to both the Choctaws and Chickasaws, the Chakchiumas supposedly disappeared as an identifiable group after Chickasaw and Choctaw attacks decimated them in the 1730s.[28] Courtonne described the Chakchiumas in 1758 as a "formerly distinct people and a Nation of themselves, but they were reduced by the Chickasaws some Time ago and since [then] the best Part of them have resided in the Chickasaws."[29] In fact, some Chakchiumas joined and intermarried with the Choctaws, many of the rest did so with the Chickasaws, while still more Chakchiumas lived among the Quapaws west of the Mississippi River. Both French and English records describe the movement of multitudes of Chakchiumas away from their own independent villages to live among the Western Division Choctaws in the mid-1730s, including a contingent of several dozen Chakchiumas who joined the famous Red Shoes's village. English trader James Adair described the freedom of movement enjoyed by these Chakchiumas to travel between the Choctaw and Chickasaw towns and serve as the gateway for English contact with the Western Division Choctaws before the Choctaw Civil War. The Chakchiumas aided the Choctaw Western Division in the Choctaw Civil War, but with the defeat of their side some of them joined their relatives among the Chickasaws.[30]

Although the Chakchiumas had amalgamated with various politically distinct Indian groups, they maintained powerful connections across the Choctaw–Chickasaw border. The Chakchiuma man captured by the Chickasaws in July 1758 appealed to his relatives among the Chickasaws and was soon released and then queried about circumstances in the Choctaw Nation. He reported the extreme want of European merchandise among the Choctaws and the readiness of the Choctaws to make peace with the Chickasaws. Meanwhile, war continued as two Choctaws died at Chickasaw hands in August, and four Chickasaws and five Choctaws died in a pitched battle in November. Then on December 12, 1758, another Chakchiuma "fellow" arrived in the Chickasaw towns on a peace mission from the Choctaws.[31]

The unnamed Chakchiuma diplomat lived among the Choctaws but counted numerous Chakchiuma relatives living among the Chickasaws, enabling him to communicate and travel safely between the nations. This circumstance made him an ideal mediator between the two old enemies. He informed the Chickasaws that the Choctaws had prepared to send several war parties against the Chickasaws but "had resolved on making a Peace with the English & Chickasaws" instead. The Chakchiuma man explained the seriousness of the Choctaw proposal for five days and then the Chickasaws had a "general meeting" to consider the offer. The Chickasaws agreed to the peace if the Choctaws proved their commitment to ending the conflict. They sent the Chakchiuma diplomat back to the Choctaws "with all the usual Tokens of Peace as are Customary in such Cases amongst Indians, such as a White Flag, a string of White Beads, Tobacco & Pipes & so forth."[32] White was the universally recognized color of peaceful intentions, and smoking from a shared pipe similarly expressed open intentions and the desire for honesty. Southeastern Indians always insisted on a neutral third party to host talks and act as the conduit of communication in order to establish a lasting peace between warring nations, a role played in this case by surviving Chakchiumas. The Chakchiumas were perhaps the only population in the region who could move between the Choctaws and Chickasaws with impunity. The Chickasaws had clearly grown weary of the constant attacks, and, just as clearly, the Choctaws too suffered from the violence and lack of access to European trade.

The Western Division Choctaws maintained close relations and cultural ties with the Chickasaw Indians to their north, and they accordingly led the effort to end the long-standing war against the Chickasaws, just as the Eastern Division Choctaws led the similar peace process with their relatives among the Alabamas and Creeks.[33] Since the Chakchiumas lived exclusively among the Western Division Choctaws, it is also probable that many of the Western Division Choctaw and Chickasaw intermarriages of the eighteenth century (such as Red Shoes's "Chickasaw" wife) actually derived from the dispersed Chakchiuma population, furthering the Chakchiuma role as Choctaw–Chickasaw intermediaries. Chakchiuma identity persisted among the Choctaws and Chickasaws, even if European and American officials did not always notice it or think it important. For example, in the mid-eighteenth century and around the time that Chakchiuma diplomats helped to secure the peace between the Choctaws and Chickasaws, British fur trader James Adair collected an origin story that explained that the Choctaws, Chickasaws, and Chakchiumas migrated to central and northern Mississippi at the same time and were related to one another, thus tying the fates of those three groups together for eternity. The early nineteenth-century

Choctaw chief of the Western Division, Apuckshunnubbee, and his successor and maternal nephew Robert Cole both claimed Chakchiuma ancestry through their mothers, as apparently did the famed late eighteenth-century Chickasaw leader Piomingo. Robert Cole's mother (and apparently Apuckshunnubbee's sister) was a Chakchiuma woman named Shumaka who reportedly lived to be over one hundred years old, having been raised among the Choctaws since a girl. Apuckshunnubbee's maternal uncle (and therefore presumably Shumaka's uncle), Payehuma, was also apparently a Chakchiuma Indian and served as the principal war leader for Franchimastabe, one of the most important Western Division chiefs of the late eighteenth century. In the mid-nineteenth century, Choctaw leader Peter Pitchlynn related the oral tradition of how the Choctaws incorporated some of the Chakchiumas into their society by making them dress like other Choctaws and speak the Choctaw dialect of the western Muskogean language, thus remembering the long-standing ties between the Choctaws and Chakchiumas that subsequent generations have largely forgotten.[34]

The presence and continued resilience of the Chakchiumas made the Choctaw–Chickasaw peace efforts possible and undoubtedly helped ensure their permanent success. By May 8, 1759, word reached Governor Lyttelton that "the Chactaws and Chickesaws have made a Peace."[35] But the real affirmation of the new agreement came on May 28, 1759, when a Choctaw delegation of eighty-six people arrived in the Chickasaw villages bearing a white flag, tobacco to facilitate negotiations, and a "Peace Talk" from various Western Division villages and some Six Towns Division towns. An Eastern Division delegation of forty-six individuals reached the Chickasaws a few days later with another white flag, and they were "received with all the Serimoney [sic] usuall [sic] on such occasions." The Choctaw delegates emphasized their need for a consistent trade in order to hunt and trade deerskins, and they promised to live at peace with the Chickasaws, leaving six warriors among them as a symbol of their good intentions. Visitations by high-ranking former enemies were a mainstay of postwar diplomacy among southeastern Indians, as they provided tangible proof that a new era of peaceful coexistence and cooperation existed. Although the British reported that a few Choctaw chiefs and villages remained allied with France, chiefs from all three Choctaw divisions played major roles in the peace with the Chickasaws and in approaching negotiations with British officials, demonstrating that the various Choctaw divisions were cooperating in a time of crisis and beginning to form greater cohesion in the aftermath of their civil war.[36] Their Chakchiuma relatives played a significant role in creating intertribal and interdivisional cooperation. Another immediate impact of the peace between the Choctaws and Chickasaws was that the Chickasaws—perhaps the Chakchiuma population among them— repopulated villages on the southern Chickasaw boundary that had been abandoned due to the constant warfare between the Choctaws and Chickasaws.[37]

Once the Choctaws and Chickasaws affirmed their new peace in 1759, a new series of diplomatic maneuvers burst out among all of the Indian nations of the South. The Choctaw–Chickasaw peace removed the final major stumbling block to region-wide intertribal and international cooperation. Chiefs among the Choctaws, Chickasaws, Creeks, and Cherokees began an elaborate new series of diplomatic meetings that summer in an attempt to formally incorporate them all into a British trading alliance. On July 18, 1759, the Choctaws and Britain signed a formal treaty. Delegates representing all three Choctaw divisions agreed to maintain peace with the Creeks and Chickasaws and to protect British traders visiting their towns. The Choctaws made demands that reflected their attempts to preserve divisional cooperation. For example, the two divisions most responsible for constructing peaceful relations with the Creeks and Chickasaws, the Eastern and Western, picked one village each to be the sites where British traders should conduct trading. In addition, three villages, Yazoo in the Western Division, Coonsa in the Eastern Division, and "Shinnyahsah" in the Six Towns Division, were chosen as the places where a British flag should fly to let everyone know that the Choctaws and Britain lived in peace. This divisional unity was further expressed by the chiefs who signed the treaty: a chief named "Ocahpuckano-mingo" signed as "Chief or Ruler of the Town of Coonsa and Speaker for the Eastern Division." A man named "Oquatchitoby" signed as "Chief and Speaker for the Western and 6 Towns Divisions."[38]

Sixty-two Choctaw towns, and all three divisions, participated in the treaty and expected to reap the forthcoming benefits. The Choctaw and British leaders concluded the meeting by exchanging gifts and agreeing to an exchange rate of deerskins for thirty-six separate trade goods, with guns as the most expensive item at sixteen deerskins each. British Indian superintendent Edmond Atkin loaded his new Choctaw friends with gifts for their return journey, and British fur traders William Hewitt and a Mr. Thompson soon arrived in the Choctaw towns with goods accompanied by a Choctaw escort.[39]

Although British gifts and traders had made their way to Choctaw country by mid-August 1759, Choctaws sought still more presents and traders. A group of thirty-six Choctaws, carrying a letter from trader William Hewitt, found Atkin at the Creek village of Tuckabatchee on September 17 and told him that a high-level delegation was on the way to demand more trade of him. Choctaws felt emboldened to demand British acquiescence to their requests because French Louisiana had finally received and distributed gifts to the Choctaws at Mobile in early May 1759, coincidentally at the same moment that the Choctaws concluded their peace with the Chickasaws.[40] Atkin deeply resented this attempt of the Choctaws to "play-off" Britain and France, but in October he faced another seventy-three Choctaw chiefs and warriors and three women at the Upper Creek village of Okfuskee who had escorted British traders back from their villages, and who now demanded a new affirmation of the British alliance.

These Choctaw emissaries insisted, and Atkin accepted their portrayal, that their visit was a necessary ratification of the peace treaty conducted in July. It is in this October 1759 conference that the Choctaws most clearly acknowledged that Britain constituted the trading partner of the future, even though France had just recently distributed trade goods and still controlled Mobile, New Orleans, Baton Rouge, and Natchez close to the Choctaw homeland. Nevertheless, as a result of having successfully established peace with Britain and her Native allies, the Choctaws then initiated a new trade strategy at this follow-up meeting with Atkin that recognized forthcoming changes in the geopolitical makeup of the region while simultaneously constructing as much Choctaw control over the new trade relationship as possible. At several points in their talks with Atkin the Choctaw speakers applauded the fact that "we have got the English fast" and did not intend to let them go. Closely related to that declaration was Choctaw and Chickasaw commitment to never again go to war against each other. Moreover, Atkin and the Choctaw chiefs shared laughs more than once over the imminent removal of the French and inevitable relocation of British territory to points nearer the Choctaws. Even so, Choctaws did not wait for the end of the war to seek out yet more British trade, as they sent a trade delegation to Savannah, Georgia, in October 1760 and from there to Charles Town, South Carolina.[41]

Choctaw–Chickasaw relations were forever altered by the events of 1758 to 1759, as they never again fought a war against each other and became forever linked in their origin stories and subsequent history. Their reasons for establishing peace and making paths between the nations "white and clean" derived in part from economic issues related to the deerskin trade and the circumstances of the Seven Years' War, while their techniques for making peace relied upon kin relationships via the Chakchiumas. Rather than acting at the instigation of Europeans, as French and British officials hoped and feared, the Choctaws, Chickasaws, and Chakchiumas pursued their own goals that forged peace out of war. We should honor their accomplishments during this era and remember that Native southerners made peace as skillfully as they made war.[42]

Notes

1. Two recent works on the Chickasaws cite the Paris Peace Treaty in 1763 and the end of French rule as the timing and reason for Choctaw–Chickasaw cooperation and peace while failing to cite or notice the diplomatic efforts by both groups during the war: James R. Atkinson, *Splendid Land, Splendid People: The Chickasaw Indians to Removal* (Tuscaloosa: University of Alabama Press, 2004), 88–89; Wendy St. Jean, "Trading Paths: Chickasaw Diplomacy in the Greater Southeast, 1690s–1790s" (PhD diss., University of Connecticut, 2004), 127, 150.

2. Alan Gallay, *The Indian Slave Trade: The Rise of the English Empire in the American South, 1670–1717* (New Haven CT: Yale University Press, 2002), 296–99.

3. My interpretation of decades of war between the Choctaws and Chickasaws runs counter to Wendy St. Jean's argument that the Chickasaws continually tried to establish peace with the Choctaws but that French interference prevented success. Wendy St. Jean, "Trading Paths," *The American Indian Quarterly* 27, no. 3 (2003): 758–80.

4. Greg O'Brien, *Choctaws in a Revolutionary Age, 1750–1830* (Lincoln: University of Nebraska Press, 2002), 27–49.

5. John R. Swanton, "An Early Account of the Choctaw Indians," *American Anthropological Association Memoirs* 5, no. 2 (1918): 69; John R. Swanton, *Chickasaw Society and Religion* (Lincoln: University of Nebraska Press, 2006), 84; James Adair, *The History of the American Indians*, ed. Kathryn E. Holland Braund (first published 1775; Tuscaloosa: University of Alabama Press, 2005), 326.

6. Dunbar Rowland, A. G. Sanders, and Patricia Kay Galloway, eds., *Mississippi Provincial Archives: French Dominion*, 5 vols. (Jackson MS, 1927–1932 and Baton Rouge LA, 1984; hereafter cited as MPA:FD), 3:709–13, 718–19, 4:162–64; Patricia Galloway, "Choctaw Factionalism and Civil War, 1746–1750," *Journal of Mississippi History* 44 (1982): 289–327, also in Greg O'Brien, ed., *Pre-removal Choctaw History: Exploring New Paths* (Norman: University of Oklahoma Press, 2008), 80. On the origins of the Choctaw Confederacy, see Patricia Galloway, *Choctaw Genesis, 1500–1700* (Lincoln: University of Nebraska Press, 1995). For the Choctaw terms for their divisions, see John R. Swanton, *Source Material for the Social and Ceremonial Life of the Choctaw Indians*, Bureau of American Ethnology Bulletin 103 (Washington DC: Smithsonian Institution, 1931), 55–57.

7. *MPA:FD*, 4:225–26.

8. The best analysis of the Choctaw Civil War is Galloway, "Choctaw Factionalism and Civil War." For the actions of Red Shoes, see also Adair, *History of the American Indians*, 322–26.

9. *MPA:FD*, 5:216–19. On Red Shoes see also Richard White, "Red Shoes: Warrior and Diplomat," in *Struggle and Survival in Colonial America*, ed. David G. Sweet and Gary B. Nash (Berkeley: University of California Press, 1981), 49–68. On Chickasaw–Choctaw relations in the 1730s–1750s, see also Atkinson, *Splendid Land, Splendid People*, 65–87.

10. "Journal of an Indian Trader, January–May 1755," William L. McDowell Jr., ed., *Colonial Records of South Carolina: Documents Relating to Indian Affairs, 1754–1765* (Columbia: South Carolina Archives Department, 1970; hereafter cited as SCIA), 62; Kathryn E. Holland Braund, *Deerskins & Duffels: Creek Indian Trade with Anglo-America, 1685–1815* (Lincoln: University of Nebraska Press, 1993), 143–44. For the leading diplomatic role of the village of Okchai among the Upper Creeks at this time see Joshua A. Piker, "'White & Clean' & Contested: Creek Towns and Trading Paths in the Aftermath of the Seven Years' War," *Ethnohistory* 50, no. 2 (Spring 2003): 315–47. See also Steven Hahn, *The Invention of the Creek Nation* (Lincoln: University of Nebraska Press, 2004), 218–28.

11. For the Alabamas acting as intermediaries between French and British interests in Indian Country in 1715 and as early as 1709, see Hahn, *The Invention of the Creek Nation*, 79, 86. For a history of the Alabama Indians and their villages around

Fort Toulouse, see Sheri Marie Shuck-Hall, *Journey to the West: The Alabama and Coushatta Indians* (Norman: University of Oklahoma Press, 2008), 32, 54–63, 77, 93–94; and Patricia Kay Galloway, "Four Ages of Alibamon Mingo, *fl.* 1700–1766," *Journal of Mississippi History* 65, no. 4 (2003): 331–32. On the symbolism of rivers among southeastern Indians see Charles Hudson, *The Southeastern Indians* (Knoxville: University of Tennessee Press, 1976), 128, 172–73, 355, 416. For a general history of Fort Toulouse, see Daniel H. Thomas, *Fort Toulouse: The French Outpost at the Alabamas on the Coosa* (Tuscaloosa: University of Alabama Press, 1989).

12. *MPA:FD*, 5:157, 170.

13. *MPA:FD*, 154–57; *SCIA*, 66–67; James Glen to Lords Commissioners for Trade April 14, 1756, Records in British Public Record Office Relating to South Carolina, 1663–1782 (Columbia: South Carolina Archives Department, microfilm; hereafter cited as Records Relating to South Carolina), reel 9:52–56; William Henry Lyttelton to Lords Commissioners for Trade, October 17, 1756, Records Relating to South Carolina, 9:154–57; Daniel Pepper to Lyttelton, November 30, 1756, December 21, 1756, and December 23, 1756, all in *SCIA*, 295–301.

14. *MPA:FD*, 5:155–59.

15. One such Eastern Division Choctaw chief of the mid-eighteenth century was named Alibamon Mingo, who possibly possessed Alabama Indian ancestry, as his name means "chief among the Alabamas," although he also identified himself as a member of the Choctaw Inhulahta ethnic group that dominated the Eastern Division. Alibamon Mingo famously told French officials in 1738 that the Alabamas "consider me their chief." The existing records are unclear about who led the Choctaws to the Alabama villages in the 1750s, but it is probable that Alibamon Mingo either participated or at least tacitly agreed to the new diplomatic effort performed by his Eastern Division colleagues. Alibamon Mingo quote: *MPA:FD*, 4:163. See also Galloway, "Four Ages of Alibamon Mingo," 321–42. On the Eastern Division's relationship with the Alabamas, see Galloway, *Choctaw Genesis*, 311–13; and Galloway, "Confederacy as a Solution to Chiefdom Dissolution: Historical Evidence in the Choctaw Case," in *The Forgotten Centuries: Indians and Europeans in the American South, 1521–1704*, ed. Charles Hudson and Carmen Tesser (Athens: University of Georgia Press, 1994), 393–420. On the Eastern Division's pro-French stance, see Galloway, "Choctaw Factionalism and Civil War," 289–327; Galloway, "'So Many Little Republics': British Negotiations with the Choctaw Confederacy, 1765," *Ethnohistory* 41 (1994): 522–23; Galloway, *Choctaw Genesis*, 323; and *MPA:FD*, 5:61.

16. Raymond Demeré to Lyttelton, November 25, 1756, Records Relating to South Carolina, 9:226–27.

17. *SCIA*, 261–62. For an earlier example of British rumor-based fears of Cherokee intentions, see Gregory Evans Dowd, "The Panic of 1751: The Significance of Rumors on the South Carolina–Cherokee Frontier," *William and Mary Quarterly* 53, no. 3 (July 1996): 527–60. Sometime in 1753 the Cherokees, probably the chief Attakullakulla, had sent a letter to Kerlérec inquiring about an alliance with France but nothing came of the notion at that time and no Cherokees visited French Louisiana; see *MPA:FD*, 5:144,151n.6.

18. Raymond Demeré to Lyttelton, November 25, 1756, Records Relating to South Carolina, 9:228–29; *SCIA*, 294–97, 378, 387, 420–21. Hahn speculates that the Mortar may have been a nativistic leader seeking a multitribal Indian alliance against European, particularly British, domination in *The Invention of the Creek Nation*, 250–53, but I have placed the dominant motivation for most of the South's Native groups in support of this international cooperation on the need for consistent European (especially British) trade. The interpretations are not mutually exclusive.

19. John Richard Alden, *John Stuart and the Southern Colonial Frontier: A Study of Indian Relations, War, Trade, and Land Problems in the Southern Wilderness, 1754–1775* (Ann Arbor: University of Michigan Press, 1944), 96. See also Gregory Evans Dowd, *War under Heaven: Pontiac, the Indian Nations, and the British Empire* (Baltimore MD: Johns Hopkins University Press, 2002), 27.

20. *MPA:FD*, 5:182–83. See also *MPA:FD*, 5:179–81, 220–22.

21. *MPA:FD*, 5:189. See also *MPA:FD*, 5:191, 194–98, 222–23.

22. Alden, *John Stuart and the Southern Colonial Frontier*, 92–93.

23. *SCIA*, 354, 364, 370, 378–79, 390, 420.

24. *SCIA*, 420, quotes: 423, 424. For the French garrison trading for British goods, see Shuck-Hall, *Journey to the West*, 93; Edmond Atkin, *The Appalachian Indian Frontier: The Edmond Atkin Report and Plan of 1755*, ed. Wilbur R. Jacobs (Lincoln: University of Nebraska Press, 1967), 63–64. See also Alden, *John Stuart and the Southern Colonial Frontier*, 97.

25. John Buckles to John Brown, June 8, 1759, William Henry Lyttelton Papers, William L. Clements Library, University of Michigan, Ann Arbor. I thank the Clements Library for awarding me a Price Research Fellowship in 1997 that enabled me to examine the Lyttelton Papers.

26. British fur trader Jerome Courtonne visited the Chickasaw villages from September 1756 until the end of May 1757 and recorded numerous battles between the Choctaws and Chickasaws, *SCIA*, 413–17.

27. British trader John Buckles lived with the Chickasaws and left two journals covering the periods from May 1757 to April 1759 that chronicled the constant Choctaw–Chickasaw assaults, *SCIA*, 458–61; Records Relating to South Carolina, 9:230–31, quotes on 231.

28. The Chakchiumas had traditionally lived between the northern edge of Choctaw country and the southern edge of Chickasaw territory but had also lived farther west in the Yazoo River basin in an apparent attempt to escape fighting between the Choctaws and Chickasaws in the late seventeenth century. For a brief, recent history of the Chakchiumas, see Patricia Galloway, "Chakchiuma," in *Handbook of North American Indians: Volume 14: Southeast*, ed. Raymond D. Fogelson (Washington DC: Smithsonian Institution, 2004), 496–98; see also Galloway, *Choctaw Genesis*, 193–96; Atkinson, *Splendid Land, Splendid People*, 14, 16; and Jay K. Johnson et al., "Measuring Chickasaw Adaptation on the Western Frontier of the Colonial South: A Correlation of Documentary and Archaeological Data," *Southeastern Archaeology* 27, no. 1 (2008): 1–30.

29. *SCIA*, 415.

30. Horatio Cushman, the son of missionaries to the Mississippi Choctaws, described an apocryphal story of the Choctaws and Chickasaws uniting to destroy the Chakchiumas and leaving only one female survivor who mothered children among the Choctaws. H. B. Cushman, *History of the Choctaw, Chickasaw, and Natchez Indians* (orig. pub. 1899; Norman: University of Oklahoma Press, 1999), 187–90. See also MPA:FD, 5:62–63; Adair, *History of the American Indians*, 322. Robbie Ethridge argues persuasively that the ancestral Chakchiumas comprised part of the Chicaza chiefdom that encountered the De Soto expedition and from which the Chickasaws are also descended, Robbie Ethridge, *From Chicaza to Chickasaw: The European Invasion and the Transformation of the Mississippian World, 1540–1715* (Chapel Hill: University of North Carolina Press, 2010), 77, 229. The various creation and migration stories of the Choctaws and Chickasaws often include the Chakchiumas as a related, sometimes conjoined, people who chose to live independently at some point in the precontact past before (re)amalgamating with the Choctaws and Chickasaws in the eighteenth century. For Chakchiumas living among the Quapaws, see SCIA, 415.

31. Records Relating to South Carolina, 9:232–34.

32. Records Relating to South Carolina, 9:234.

33. For the traditional cultural ties between the Western Division and the Chickasaws see Galloway, *Choctaw Genesis*, 311–13; and Galloway, "Confederacy as a Solution to Chiefdom Dissolution," 393–420.

34. For the Chakchiuma background of Shumaka, her son Robert Cole, and her grandson Coleman Cole, see their famous legal depositions provided in 1837/38 as Choctaws remaining in Mississippi sought deeds to the land they had been promised in the Dancing Rabbit Creek Removal Treaty of 1830. The Choctaw Nation of Indians vs. the United States, National Archives and Records Administration, Record Group 75, Entry 270 Evidence, 1837–38, U.S. Court of Claims, no. 12742; transcripts also in Piepenbrink Collection, Oklahoma Historical Society Research Division, Oklahoma City, folder 10, two bound volumes. See also Adair, *History of the American Indians*, 354; O'Brien, *Choctaws in a Revolutionary Age*, 34, 96, 104.

35. Records Relating to South Carolina, 9:191.

36. John Buckles and Chickasaw Chiefs to John Brown, June 8, 1759, Lyttelton Papers.

37. Wendy Cegielski and Brad R. Lieb, "Hina' Falaa, 'The Long Path': An Analysis of Chickasaw Settlement Using GIS in Northeast Mississippi, 1650–1840," *Native South* 4 (2011): 24–54; however, note that the authors credit the end of the Seven Years' War and the removal of the French from the region in 1763 rather than Native actions and peace in 1759 as the cause of this more dispersed settlement pattern.

38. Treaty of Friendship and Commerce, July 18, 1759, Lyttelton Papers.

39. Atkin to John Buckles, July 29, 1759, Lyttelton Papers; Atkin to Jerome Courtonne, John Brown, and John Heyarider [traders among the Chickasaws], September 20, 1759, Lyttelton Papers; Alden, *John Stuart and the Southern Colonial Frontier*, 98; David H. Corkran, The *Creek Frontier, 1540–1783* (Norman: University of Oklahoma Press, 1967), 202.

40. MPA:FD, 5:541–42.

41. Conferences with 73 Chactaw Head Warriors, October 25–November 1, 1759, Lyttelton Papers; Allen D. Candler, ed., *The Colonial Records of the State of Georgia* (Atlanta GA: Franklin-Turner Co., 1907), 8:394–98.

42. Examples of French and British excessive optimism and unfounded fears about the influence of each other in southern Indian affairs during the Seven Years' War abound. See the journals of Louis Antoine de Bougainville, captain in the French military and aide-de-camp to the Marquis de Montcalm. Captain de Bougainville was convinced that Choctaw forces were soon to join the French military in Detroit in 1757, while the next year he expressed dismay that British Indian agent Sir William Johnson had marched to Lake Champlain with hundreds of Indians, including Choctaws. The Choctaws seem to have engaged in neither action. Edward P. Hamilton, ed., *Adventure in the Wilderness: The American Journals of Louis Antoine de Bougainville, 1756–1760* (Norman: University of Oklahoma Press, 1964), 89, 119, 180, 196, 232. Andrew Lewis wrote to Governor Dinwiddie of Virginia in 1756 that all Indians in the South were joining the French and would soon attack the British, Lewis to Dinwiddie, October 11, 1756, British Colonial Record Office, Class 5 files, vol. 48, also found in Randolph Boehm, ed., British Colonial Office, French and Indian War, 1754–1763 (microfilm, Frederick MD: University Publications of America), reel 2. For an example of a historian uncritically accepting such rumors as fact, see William Nester, *The First Global War: Britain, France, and the Fate of North America, 1756–1775* (Westport CT: Praeger, 2000), 193 (Nester describes "hundreds" of Choctaw warriors joining British forces in Pennsylvania).

Four

Cherokee and Christian Expressions of Spirituality through First Parents

Eve and Selu

ROWENA MCCLINTON

The diaries of the Moravian Springplace Mission to the Cherokees are replete with descriptions of Cherokee and Christian spiritual beliefs and practices. This chapter addresses the contact experiences between Moravians, a Christian group originally from central Europe, and the Cherokees, a southeastern tribe. As we will see, tensions arose when Cherokees and Moravians, a highly regimented and zealous mission group that wanted to spread the Gospel to the "forgotten peoples of the world," questioned each other about their spiritual and cultural moorings.[1]

In Genesis, a story emerges in the paradise called the Garden of Eden. The fall of man came when Adam was all alone. God took Adam's rib to carve out a helpmate named Eve to join Adam in the Garden. God warned Eve not to eat fruit from the tree of knowledge of good and evil for it embodied the secrets to life belonging only to God. Eve, tempted by the subtlety of a serpent, ate the fruit and encouraged Adam to do the same. Since Eve challenged God's authority, God became angry and punished Adam by making his descendants work by the "sweat of their brows" and Eve and her descendants by causing childbirth to be painful. Suddenly, Adam and Eve felt guilt and shame for their nakedness. God clothed them and then drove them from the Garden.[2]

Eve's disobedience doomed her forever as an evil temptress inferior to her counterpart Adam. Eve was deemed the promulgator of guilt and sin until the advent of Christ, whose martyrdom redeemed humanity's fall from grace. According to the New Testament authors, Christ took on the sins of the world; and his death and suffering on the cross atoned for the sins of individuals willing to accept his grace. The fall continued to plague humankind, however, because most could never be worthy of Christ's sufferings, or would refuse to accept his grace, or would fail to live a guilt-free life.

The Judeo-Christian character of Eve can be contrasted with her Cherokee counterpart, Selu, the tribe's first female parent. Selu was the giver of corn, the producer of vegetable food, and one of life's creators. Cherokees were animists and believed that all rocks, trees, animals, and humans had souls embodying real life-giving forces. Humans struggled to maintain balance and order in this universe. Selu was a prominent figure in understanding the Cherokee need for universal balance, and her significance lay not in her responsibility for human decline but in her power to procreate and replenish the earth through her fertility.[3]

The story of Selu involved elements that many Christians considered heathenish, lustful, and sinful. The Judeo-Christian idea of a woman bearing responsibility for humanity's evil, on the other hand, was anathema to Cherokee cosmology. The Cherokees had no concept of sin. Noted ethnohistorian James P. Ronda investigated how Christian missionaries inflicted the concepts of sin and guilt on Indian societies and showed that these Christian concepts were both unintelligible and meaningless to Native peoples. As one Huron man asked, how could he repent when he had never seen sin? Likely, Cherokees asked the same question. Similarly, some potential converts rejected the notion of a heaven because the missionaries pictured the dreary place without grain fields or sexual activity. The prospect of an afterlife without marriage or labor was an unpleasant destiny for Cherokees and other Natives of the Eastern Woodlands.[4]

Cherokees first heard the stories about the fall of man and the New Testament redeemer when they began to encounter Europeans. Cherokee visitors to the Springplace Mission, which the Moravians established in 1801 in present-day northwest Georgia, were told these stories many times by Moravian missionaries. They even saw paintings of the crucifixion hanging on the walls of mission houses and sometimes questioned whether Jesus's blood could have fallen over all the earth.[5]

Many Cherokees frequented Springplace because a nonviolent religious group had finally opened a school to teach Cherokee children the "arts of civilization." President George Washington and his secretary of war, Henry Knox, had originated the civilization program to encourage Indians to embrace an Anglo-American farming lifestyle. The plan ignored what we think of today as the separation of church and state, for missionaries were paid by the federal government to minister to the Indians. Government-financed missionaries fostered Western-style education, tried to convert indigenous peoples to Christianity, and even attempted to alter gender roles to mirror Anglo-American ones. Missionaries and other agents of change encouraged Cherokee males to abandon hunting and become farmers.[6]

Traditionally, Cherokee women were the agriculturalists in their society, a role established by Selu. It was her example that taught Cherokee women to plant and harvest the fields. Under the civilization program, the United States asked women to vacate their time-honored place as agriculturalists, move into the home, and fulfill domestic chores such as weaving, cooking, and carding cotton.[7]

Early nineteenth-century Cherokee females resisted the U.S. effort to transform their gender responsibilities and faced constant criticism from missionaries and U.S. policy makers. Albert Gallatin, who served as secretary of state under President Thomas Jefferson, viewed Cherokee females as impediments to civilization. The real problem with Indians, Gallatin believed, was that women did the farming instead of the men. Although many men and families embraced the civilization program, most Cherokee women did not abandon the fields. They continued to plant and harvest their crops, despite the instruction of the American agents and the Moravians.[8]

Moravian missionaries also failed in their attempts to convince Cherokees they should embrace the stories of the fall of man, the evil of Eve, and the precepts of guilt and sin. In contrast to the shame that Christians experienced from the legacy of Eve's nakedness, Cherokees actually flaunted their bodies while attending ball play, a game where bystanders bet anything and everything on their chosen side. Cherokees bathed in the nude in the limestone springs near the mission to cleanse themselves before and after ball play and often walked right by Springplace on their way to a ball field. Cherokee players and bystanders in those days considered ball play to be a communal and intimate gathering and a significant ritual of cultural revitalization. Missionary Anna Rosina Gambold, a careful observer and recorder of Cherokee customs (usually in a disparaging fashion) wrote: "Oh, it is a quite unholy thing, the ball play here in this country, and the longer the worse! One is just barely over when a new one is arranged. It is very difficult for us, when it is held close to us, because the Indians, who gather for it, always stop in here and make our children want to attend it as well." She continued, "Old gray-headed men and women as well as a considerable number of children came with great pomp from all corners and occupied our yard and house. We hear several shots and wild screaming. At twilight most came back here and pass by quietly. Yet young and old gambled away all their valuables, even the clothing off their backs. Several came to demand food and also stayed over night."[9]

Other ancient customs irritated the missionaries. The Moravians did not like the fact, for example, that Cherokees did not necessarily live in nuclear families. Women tended to live with female relatives while men stayed in council houses except when hunting. Furthermore, Cherokee females held significant command in family life, which, of course, was in direct opposition to patriarchal Judeo-Christian practices. In 1820 Moravians noted that Cherokees so revered their maternal relatives that "the family tree rests on them; the father counts for little or nothing and is able to exercise no more authority on the children than what the mother . . . at least tacitly . . . concedes." Matriarchy was also especially embedded in ancient arts of healing. Even Moravian convert and Second Principal Chief Charles Hicks confessed to Gambold that he could not interfere with "heathen" treatment on his grandson by several old women using magic because only the mother and the mother's side could govern the boy.[10]

The practice of matrilineality often surfaced in the Springplace Mission school, affirming what Theda Perdue discovered in her seminal work, *Cherokee Women: Gender and Culture Change,*

1700–1835. Cherokee fathers brought their children to mission schools, and mothers removed them. A Cherokee woman named Polly removed her daughter, Dorcas, from Springplace because she said Dorcas had learned enough English, and she did not want her to learn any more about the Bible. Rattling Gourd, Dorcas's father, had brought her to Springplace, and told Gambold that he was embarrassed to show his face to her again. Gambold exclaimed: "The poor man! We really understood him. It was not *his* fault, rather the *mother*'s, who made their lives painful until she fetched the girl against his will."[11]

The ways in which some Cherokee men retold origin stories during this time period showcased the Cherokees' reverence for women. To the missionaries' chagrin, Cherokees had their own first parents, Selu and Kanati, who had lived in the sky before Europeans came to the "New World." An elderly venerable leader and storyteller named the Elk described Selu's restorative powers in an origin story:

> You said that you white people desired *more* land from the Indians: now I will inform you of our ancestry. At first there was a man and a woman on the earth. They had two sons, who made an attempt on the life of their mother on the pretext that she was a sorceress because she procured sufficient food for them without planting and they could not discover where she got it. And this was her way: she went out and quickly returned with the necessary provisions. The bad intentions of the sons against the mother was finally found out, and she talked this over with them and requested they stop, because she would not stay with them much longer but would go into the sky; they would never see her again. However, she would attentively watch all of their behavior. If they resolved to be *evil*, gloom would surround them. Soon thereafter she left her sons and quickly rose into the heights.[12]

Unlike Christianity, where the martyr for humanity, Jesus, was a man, in the Cherokee worldview, as the Elk pointed out, Selu, the female, was the martyr and progenitor of Cherokee spirituality. The Elk's narrative also reflected the importance of the vegetable kingdom in the story of Selu, whose two sons attempted to kill her because they did not understand how she could produce corn from her armpits. Anthropologist Raymond D. Fogelson contends that the two sons were terrified; they saw their mother in this primal scene and became frightened because they could not comprehend what they witnessed. In her association with the vegetable realm, Selu embodied maternal sources of fear and hope: fear that they might lack food if she disappeared and the hope that she would return and that her breasts would continue to feed her children. In this story, corn therefore symbolized mother's milk; and Cherokees interchanged the sacred properties of corn and mother's breast milk. In concluding her discussion of the Elk, Anna Rosina described how "The Elk and his companions sat there fully caught in a wind and firmly resolute that no one should take away their beliefs." She recorded: "It is remarkable how this nation has open ears for such fairy tales and imaginations gone wild."[13]

When Moravian missionaries came into the Cherokee Nation, they encountered a people with a highly stratified priestly class. Unlike Christians who depended on Christ to mitigate or forgive wrongs, Cherokees hired persons who had supernatural powers to negotiate conflicts. These conjurors and shamans represented a surviving segment of a complex religious system. Their expertise was held by very few Cherokees, and a candidate had to undergo intense training to learn formulas and incantations and master ways to right a wrong or diffuse the cause of distress. As a result, conjurors played a major role in maintaining societal peace and ancestral religion.[14]

A woman named Dawnee of Oostanaula, a town at the confluence of the Oostanaula and Etowah Rivers, was one of the wives of Upper Town Cherokee leader James Vann. She perceived that missionaries had mistreated her child Robin and resorted to traditional ways to diffuse the conflict: she hired a conjuror. Dawnee had brought Robin to the mission school in the fall of 1815 with the hope that he would reap the benefits of a "civilized" life. She wanted him to learn English so he could negotiate with encroaching settlers and help his nation retain its ancestral lands.[15]

According to Gambold, "[Dawnee] arrived after the children had already gone to bed, late in the night. The next day, Dawnee left with the excuse that she had left something in The Trunk's house in the Mission neighborhood. She said she merely wanted to take her son there. But we soon discovered that she had brought a conjuror with her and had left him in the house in order for him to perform magic on her son. Such things happen from time to time but are kept very secret from us so that we find out about it only accidentally." Gambold wrote that Dawnee "was really an ignorant heathen." When Robin "had complained to her about our bad treatment," Dawnee had become "enraged against us" and came and took Robin away.[16]

The efficacy of a conjuror was due partly to the secrecy surrounding their actions. As Gambold noted, "such things happened from time to time but were kept secret from us." Ethnohistorian James Axtell has argued that Indians used secrecy as a weapon to diffuse conflict and disagreements with outsiders.[17] Theda Perdue's work suggests that hiring the conjuror allowed Dawnee to assuage her own psychological tension in volatile periods of sociopolitical turmoil. Conjurors also had the power to "fix" or "victimize" the person or persons who had caused Robin's suffering.[18]

Noted Cherokee scholars, Jack and Anna Gritts Kilpatrick, unearthed an overlooked type of conjuror, the one who could remove an unpleasing neighbor or member of a household. Perhaps this was Dawnee's intention. Dawnee, thinking the missionaries had caused her son unhappiness, acted within societal norms and employed the conjuror to protect her son from what anthropologist Lucy Mair refers to as "unneighborly persons." Mair describes the "unneighborly person" as "the one whom one would not wish to resemble and also the one whom one should avoid offending."[19] Similarly, Cherokee anthropologist Robert Thomas noted that among conservative Cherokees scrupulous attention had to be given to maintaining "harmonious interpersonal relationships . . . by avoiding giving offense or the negative side."[20]

Dawnee exerted her own influence by observing the "harmony" ethic that required her to maintain a sense of balance and order in the community. Cherokee scholar Fred Gearing points out that a corollary to the Cherokee harmony ideal is that "direct, open conflict is injurious to one's reputation."[21] Dawnee resorted to the indirect means of attack—procuring a conjuror—because, as Gearing maintains, it was a weapon that could be used as a way to confront an antagonist and still avoid "open face-to-face clashes."[22]

According to the Kilpatricks, the conjuror learned special types of incantations to cast a spell. Perhaps the conjuror only had in mind to get the missionaries out of the nation and recited incantations to make them very sad. Gambold mentioned that the conjuror lingered nearby at The Trunk's, the neighbor's house; in the woods; and along the lane bordering the mission premises. The Kilpatricks pointed out that if the incantations were effective, the intended target would move on to friendlier spiritual climates and be relieved of melancholy.[23]

Since Gambold stated that the practice of procuring conjurors in and around the mission was fairly common, it seems plausible that the conjuror hired by Dawnee wanted the victims to experience no actual harm, but to feel loneliness and rejection. The conjuror probably wanted Robin to assist him by obtaining mental pictures of the missionaries. So Gambold had misunderstood what the conjuror was actually doing with Robin in The Trunk's house. She thought he had performed "magic" on Robin; instead, the conjuror had likely asked Robin to produce a description of the missionaries to aid in his ability to remove the missionaries. The conjuror could later recall their images, enhancing the temporary spell of rejection and causing them to move away.[24]

White persons were particularly earmarked as "unneighborly," and ridding the nation of "unneighborliness" was not out of the ordinary. In this case, the conjuror seldom required the name or matriarchal family connection of the victim, but only the mental picture. A white person would be fair game because they knew no antidote; they would be more vulnerable to the full force of the sorcery than an Indian. Naturally, Dawnee subscribed to such practices because they reflected ancient Cherokee ethics and her own sense of what it meant to be a female in Cherokee society.[25]

Perdue explained that "conjuring was a way for females to express traditional familial relationships and exercise their own prerogatives." Conjurors provided crucial rituals for Indians seeking control over or knowledge of the invisible world. This was quite different from the way white Americans thought about the spirit world. The tree of knowledge of good and evil in the Garden of Eden and the subtle serpent that caused Eve to sin held no meaning for the Cherokees. For Cherokees, secret knowledge was to be used, not avoided. The conjuror used his secrets to right a wrong, to avoid face-to-face confrontation, and to cast spells on persons considered harmful to society. His goal was to restore order and balance.[26]

Though they were naïve of Cherokee beliefs, the Moravian missionaries did display a certain degree of tolerance in that they welcomed many parents and relatives of Cherokee students to Springplace, fed them, and even offered them places to stay. However, they also denigrated Cherokee women for their honored place in the family. Perhaps Moravians thought if they insinuated themselves into Cherokee families, they would understand and learn about Cherokees' emotions and fears, and consequently, they would be more successful in fostering patriarchal families.

The examples of Polly Rattling Gourd and Dawnee Vann demonstrated Cherokee women's strength and the persistence in their beliefs when facing missionaries who wanted them to adopt Western habits and force them to abandon time-honored matriarchal customs. Just as the Elk had done, they upheld time-honored Cherokee origin explanations. As Theda Perdue put it, "Selu met Eve, but she did not surrender." Cherokee women continued to do the things that Cherokee women had always done, just as men continued to do the things that they had always done. Men continued to revere the female as the disciplinarian of the family. Selu, the Mother of the Nation, had warned fellow Cherokees to dispel "evil" introductions into their culture. For instance, traditionally, Cherokees did not apply corporal punishment for wrongs incurred. Instead, ostracism was their effective mode of punishment. Chief Koychezetel (Warrior's Nephew) rejected the alien method of punishment. He came to Springplace Mission with the following news from the Cherokee Council: "Also your Mother [of the Nation] is not pleased that you punish each other severely. Yes, you whip until blood flows." Warrior's Nephew focused on Selu as the Mother of the Nation and the one who protected customs sacrosanct to Cherokee heritage.[27]

We may draw two conclusions from these episodes: first, perhaps, as strangers in the Cherokee Nation, missionaries caused women to intensify their matriarchal roles in the Cherokee family life. Threads of independence and self-determination surfaced in these encounters. Cherokee women did champion their way of life and actually preserved their places as heads of families and their children.

Second, Cherokee men, such as the Elk, viewed women as sacred to their society. They did not look upon women as evil, as fostered by Judeo-Christian beliefs and personified in Eve, but rather as vegetable providers and healers. Charles Hicks, for instance, deferred to the elderly women of his community to use traditional methods to heal his grandson, and he did not interfere in their treatment.

In *Cherokee Women*, Perdue explained how Selu, the Mother of the Cherokee Nation, metaphorically met Eve when whites moved into the Cherokee Nation. Although Selu was introduced to Judeo-Christian ways and Western notions of right and wrong, as Mother of the Nation she did not surrender her time-honored traditional role. Selu, as the first female Cherokee mother, had intrinsic qualities of sensitivity, discipline, and hard work; these attributes went beyond Eve's feelings of guilt and sin. Finally, Selu defined her own sense of sexuality, and it was one that defied the shame represented by the story of Eve.

Notes

1. Rowena McClinton, *The Moravian Springplace Mission to the Cherokees, 1805–1813 and 1814–1821*, 2 vols. (Lincoln: University of Nebraska Press, 2007).

2. Genesis 2:4–3:24.

3. James Mooney, ed., "Kana'ti And Selu: The Origin of Game and Corn," in *Myths of the Cherokee*, 19th Annual Report of the Bureau of American Ethnology, 1897–98, part 1 (1900), 242–49. For further study of the Cherokee cosmic world, see Charles Hudson, *Elements of Southeastern Indian Religion* (Leiden: E. J. Brill Press, 1984), 1–15. For a critical analysis of Hudson's paradigm of oppositional forces in traditional Cherokee society, see Mary C. Churchill, "Purity and Pollution: Unearthing an Oppositional Paradigm in the Study of Cherokee Religious Traditions," in

Native American Spirituality: A Critical Reader, ed. Lee Irwin (Lincoln: University of Nebraska Press, 2000), 205–35.

4. James P. Ronda, "We Are Well as We Are: An Indian Critique of Seventeenth-Century Christian Missions," *William and Mary Quarterly,* 3rd ser., vol. 34 (January 1977): 68–70; Theda Perdue, *Cherokee Women: Gender and Culture Change, 1700–1835* (Lincoln: University of Nebraska Press, 1988), 171.

5. A Cherokee chief, The Bird, questioned missionaries John and Anna Rosina Gambold if a human being could hold enough blood to flow over the entire earth. McClinton, *Moravian Springplace Mission,* 1:292. Colonial historians have written quite persuasively on the significance of blood in Moravian proselytization. See, for example, Craig D. Atwood, "Sleeping in the Arms of Christ: Sanctifying Sexuality in the Eighteenth-Century Moravian Church," *Journal of the History of Sexuality* 8 (1997): 25–51; Atwood, "The Passion of the Christ and Christian Devotion from a Moravian Perspective," *Covenant Quarterly* 73 (2005): 16–28; Jane T. Merritt, "Dreaming of the Savior's Blood: Moravians and the Indian Great Awakening in Pennsylvania," *William and Mary Quarterly,* 3rd ser., 54 (1997): 723–46; Rachel Wheeler, "'Der Schönste Schmuck': Mahican Appropriations of Moravian Blood and Wounds Theology," *Covenant Quarterly* 63 (2005): 20–34; Karl Westmeier, "Out of a Distant Past: A Challenge for Modern Mission from a Diary of Colonial New York," *Transactions of the Moravian Historical Society* 27 (1991): 67–86. For a discussion of violence toward Moravians in Pennsylvania as a result of "blood theology," see Aaron Fogleman, "Jesus Is Female: The Moravian Challenge in the German Communities of British North America," *William and Mary Quarterly* 3rd ser., 60 (2003): 295–332.

6. Francis Paul Prucha, *The Great Father: The United States Government and American Indians* (Lincoln: University of Nebraska Press, 1984), 135–58.

7. Perdue, *Cherokee Women,* 115–34.

8. Perdue, *Cherokee Women,* 115–34, Gallatin comment at 189.

9. McClinton, *Moravian Springplace Mission,* 1:453; 2:74. Anna Rosina mentions the frequency of ball play the years following the 1814 Creek War. See also McClinton, "The Moravian Missionaries of Bethlehem and Salem," in *Ethnographies and Exchanges: Native Americans, Moravians, and Catholics in Early North America,* ed. A. G. Roeber (University Park: Pennsylvania State University Press, 2008), 115–24.

10. McClinton, *Moravian Springplace Mission,* 1:36 and 2:59; John Gambold to Jacob Van Vleck, July 1, 1820, Moravian Archives Salem, North Carolina; Perdue, *Cherokee Women,* 183.

11. Perdue, *Cherokee Women,* 172–75; McClinton, *Moravian Springplace Mission,* 2:103.

12. McClinton, *Moravian Springplace Mission,* 2:86, 87, and 514, n. 60 and 61. The Elk story held further relevance for the Cherokees because he explained the significance of Cherokee attachment to land and the source of food. Later, Swimmer explained to ethnologist James Mooney that the first man and woman, Kanati and Selu, held the secrets to the origin of the hunt for game and the mystery surrounding the growing of corn. The story implied that the "bad intention" was her boys' threat on her life because they thought she was a sorceress. The Elk is mentioned in William G. McLoughlin, *Cherokee Renascence in the New Republic* (Prince-

ton NJ: Princeton University Press, 1986), 176, 177; McLoughlin, "The Cherokees' Use of Christianity," in *The Cherokees and Christianity, 1794–1870: Essays on Acculturation and Cultural Persistence*, ed. Walter Conser (Athens: University of Georgia Press, 1994), 168–69; and Claudio Saunt, "Telling Stories: The Political Uses of Myth and History in the Cherokee and Creek Nations," *Journal of American History* 93, no. 3 (2006): 673–98.

13. Raymond D. Fogelson, "A Re-look at the Cherokee Green Corn Ceremony" (paper presented at the annual meeting of the Southern Anthropological Society, Asheville, North Carolina, April 4–7, 2002); McClinton, *Moravian Springplace Mission*, 2:87.

14. Lee Irwin, "Cherokee Healing: Myth, Dreams, and Medicine," *American Indian Quarterly* 16 (Spring 1992): 245; Raymond D. Fogelson, "Change, Persistence, and Accommodation in Cherokee Medico–Magical Beliefs," in *Symposium on Cherokee and Iroquois Culture*, ed. John Gulick and William N. Fenton, Bureau of American Ethnology Bulletin 180 (Washington DC: Government Printing Office, 1961), 215, 216; Fogelson, "The Conjuror in Eastern Cherokee Society," *Journal of Cherokee Studies* 5 (1980): 60–87; James Mooney, "Myths of the Cherokee and Sacred Formulas of the Cherokee: Nineteenth Annual Report, 1897–1898" (Washington DC: Bureau of American Ethnology, 1900; repr., New York: Johnson Reprint Corporation, 1970), 250–52.

15. McClinton, *Moravian Springplace Mission*, 2:116. Patron to the Moravians, James Vann was widely known for his entrepreneurial skills and as a longtime resident of the same area. Born in 1768, Vann's exact heritage is uncertain; his mother was Cherokee, member of the Blind Savannah clan. His father first built a trading post near the Chattahoochee River and then moved this post farther into the Cherokee Nation near the Conasauga River. By 1809 this area became known as Vannsville, but early in the 1800s Vann in his correspondence refers to the area as Diamond Hill. William G. McLoughlin, "James Vann: Intemperate Patriot, 1768–1809," in *The Cherokee Ghost Dance: Essays on the Southeastern Indians, 1789–1861* (Macon GA: Mercer University Press, 1984), 39–72; Whitfield–Murray Historical Society, *Murray County's Indian Heritage* (Fernandina Beach FL: Wolfe Publishing, 1987; repr., 1997), 3. For the most recent study of interracial cooperation with emphasis on settler expansion creating a racially tense landscape, refer to Jane T. Merritt, *At the Crossroads: Indians and Empires on a Mid-Atlantic Frontier, 1700–1763* (Chapel Hill: University of North Carolina Press, 2003). Chapter 4, "Mission Community Network," includes a study of Moravian mission communities among the Mahicans and Delawares.

16. McClinton, *Moravian Springplace Mission*, 2:240.

17. In Native society, this "secret weapon" was a form of politeness and thus reinforced Native attachment to communal life. To the chagrin of missionaries, Axtell divulges how Natives could even totally reject the Christian message and in their disapproval reveal that they who had the least contact with Christian preaching and action displayed even more integrity than Englishmen. James Axtell, *The Invasion Within: The Contest of Cultures in Colonial North America* (New York: Oxford University Press, 1985), 19, 331–33.

18. Perdue, *Cherokee Women*, 182–83; Albert J. Raboteau, *Slave Religion: The Invisible Institution in the Antebellum South* (New York: Oxford University Press, 1978; repr., 1980), 276. The concept of suffering in a Christian sense would have come from feelings of guilt. Indians were a shame-oriented society as opposed to a guilt-ridden one. Charles Hudson, *The Southeastern Indians* (Knoxville: University of Tennessee Press, 1976), 121–25.

19. Jack Frederick Kilpatrick and Anna Gritts Kilpatrick, *Run Toward the Nightland: Magic of the Oklahoma Cherokees* (Dallas TX: Southern Methodist University Press, 1967), 173–74; Lucy Mair, *Witchcraft* (New York: McGraw-Hill, 1969), 202; McClinton, *Moravian Springplace Mission*, 2:517. Anthropologist Monica Wilson points out that the more tangible "unneighborly person behaves badly in the accepted cultural context," and in this case, the resulting response, hiring a conjuror, represents the missionaries' failure to appropriate the correct Cherokee societal obligation. Monica Wilson, *Rituals of Kinship among the Nyakyusa* (London: Oxford University Press for International African Institute, 1957), 14.

20. Alan Kilpatrick, *The Night Has a Naked Soul: Witchcraft and Sorcery among the Western Cherokee* (Syracuse NY: Syracuse University Press, 1997), 126; Robert K. Thomas, "Cherokee Values and World View," research paper, 1958, Papers Based on Research of the Cross-Cultural Laboratory of the Institute for Research in Social Science, North Carolina Collection, Wilson Library, University of North Carolina, Chapel Hill, 1.

21. Fred Gearing, "Priests and Warriors: Social Structures for Cherokee Politics in the 18th Century," Memoir 93 (American Anthropological Association, vol. 64, no. 5, pt. 2., 1962), 31. For further study of the Cherokee cosmic world, see Fogelson, "Change, Persistence, and Accommodation in Cherokee Medico–Magical Beliefs," 215, 216; and Fogelson, "The Conjuror in Eastern Cherokee Society," 60–87; Hudson, *Elements of Southeastern Indian Religion*, 1–15; Kilpatrick, *The Night Has a Naked Soul;* Perdue, *Cherokee Women*, 36–38; and *Moravian Springplace Mission*, 2:517.

22. Kilpatrick, *The Night Has a Naked Soul*, 126. The exact nature of the "fix" is unknown. Sometimes shamans hid along a trail and waited for the victim to spit. After they gathered the saliva, conjurors employed the correct formula to cause a fatal sickness. Sometimes the practitioner produced powerful spells to steal a person's soul or to "ravish" it by inducing suffering for six or seven months before dying. One shamanistic category concerned those individuals who could use their skills and knowledge to harm other people. The most notorious causes of disease were those begun by these infamous practitioners, who were "of a different mind"; they could cause illness or even death through uncommon formulaic utterances. Irwin, "Cherokee Healing: Myth, Dreams, and Medicine," 24; McClinton, *Moravian Springplace Mission*, 2:517.

23. The Kilpatricks recorded that the hired conjuror advances about halfway and blows the smoke toward the undesirable ones' house. Kilpatrick and Kilpatrick, *Run Toward the Nightland*, 173–74.

24. Kilpatrick and Kilpatrick, *Run Toward the Nightland*, 173–74.

25. Kilpatrick and Kilpatrick, *Run Toward the Nightland*, 174.

26. Theda Perdue, *The Cherokee* (New York: Chelsea House Publishers, 1989), 183; Peter Benes, "Fortune Teller, Wise-Men, and Magical Healers in New England, 1644–1850," in *Wonders of the Invisible World: 1600–1900,* ed. Peter Benes (Boston MA: Boston University Press, 1995), 127–48.

27. Perdue, *Cherokee Women,* 184; Gregory Evans Dowd, "Gift Giving and the Cherokee–British Alliance," in *Contact Points: American Frontiers from the Mohawk Valley to the Mississippi, 1750–1830,* ed. Andrew R. L. Cayton and Fredrika J. Teute (Chapel Hill: University of North Carolina Press, 1998), 127–31. For British attitudes toward corporal punishment, see Lawrence Stone, *The Crisis of the Aristocracy, 1558–1641* (Oxford: Clarendon Press, 1965).

Five

Andrew Jackson's Indian Son

Native Captives and American Empire

CHRISTINA SNYDER

On April 8, 1818, Andrew Jackson wrote a letter to his wife Rachel in which he delighted in recounting the bloody conclusion of the First Seminole War. During his invasion of the Mikasuki towns, Jackson claimed to have found "upwards of fifty fresh scalps from the infant to the aged matron." He called Mikasuki and San Marcos de Apalachee "Sodom and Gomorrow," rejoicing in their destruction. Triumphantly, Jackson reported that Hillis Hadjo and Homathle Miko had been hanged that very morning, and that Alexander Arbuthnot and Robert Ambrister awaited the trial that would be a sham. The letter ends on a jarring note of paternal affection; Andrew bade Rachel to "Kiss my Two sons for me." The Jacksons had no biological children. By "sons," Andrew meant his grandnephew Andrew Jackson Hutchings as well as his nephew and heir, whom he called Andrew Jackson Junior. A third Andrew, Andrew Jackson Donelson, also a nephew, attended West Point by this time. The "Andrews," as Jackson called them, were doubtlessly his favorites, but within his household was another child he often called a "son"—a Creek Indian boy named Lyncoya.[1]

From Mary Rowlandson's narrative to James Fenimore Cooper's *The Last of the Mohicans*, American history and mythology abounds with the captivity narratives of whites taken by Indians. Generations of white Americans have used such stories for purposes ranging from propaganda to self-definition. Less well-known are the stories of Indian war captives forced to live and labor in white households. Lyncoya resided with America's most famous Indian-fighter, who likely took the child for political and personal reasons, but this Creek boy was hardly alone in his fate; throughout the colonial period and well into the nineteenth century, whites held Indian captives in states ranging from slavery to nominal kinship. In North American history, we usually associate interracial marriage, métissage, and inclusive adoption with Spanish and French colonialism, but these practices were also common in the borderlands between Anglo-America and Indian nations. This essay focuses on how and why southern whites captured Native Americans and what these diverse captivity practices reveal about creolization, kinship, and the nature of empire.[2]

Recent scholarship has uncovered the profound role that one aspect of this captivity spectrum—slavery—played in the foundation of American colonies ranging from New Spain to New England to Louisiana. In the South, the Indian slave trade reached its zenith between 1670 and 1715, during which time Carolina traders acquired about 25,000 Native American slaves, most of whom were sold to New England or the Caribbean. During the Yamasee War of 1715 to 1717, a diverse group of Native nations, including the Yamasees, Lower Creeks, Savannahs, and Apalachees, struck out against South Carolina for its abusive trade practices. Destroying outlying plantations, the Yamasees and their allies killed about four hundred colonists—7 percent of Carolina's white population. Such devastation led many Carolinians to question the wisdom of trafficking in Indian slaves. As significant as the Yamasee War was, however, it did not destroy the Indian slave trade. In fact, South Carolina's enslaved Indian population did not peak until 1724, when two thousand Native people labored under white masters. Among southern colonies, only Florida, Virginia, and Louisiana ever attempted to outlaw Indian slavery or to distinguish it in any way from black slavery.[3]

Until the Yamasee War, Indian warriors acquired most Native captives while whites acted as middlemen and eventual masters, but, as the eighteenth century wore on, whites became the primary captors of Indian slaves. An account of the 1776 retaliatory expedition against the Cherokees dramatized how the desire for both retaliation and profit drove whites' demand for Indian captives. In 1776, seeking revenge for raids committed by the militant Chickamauga faction of the Cherokees, militias from several colonies set out on a scorched-earth campaign designed to bring the entire Cherokee Nation to its knees. Serving under Brigadier General Griffith Rutherford, Captain William Moore commanded a portion of the North Carolina soldiers. In early November, the expedition captured two Cherokee women and a boy. Clearly uneasy about the capture of noncombatants, Moore and some other officers declared that the three Indians should be held in prison until the Continental Congress could decide their fate. The soldiers disagreed; according to Moore, "the Greater Part Swore Bloodily that if they were not Sold for Slaves upon the Spot, they would kill and Scalp them Immediately." Moore conceded to the demands of the mob, and the women and boy were auctioned off to the soldiers for a total of 242 pounds. Moore's men were not the only ones who captured Cherokees in 1776: William Dells, who served under Colonel William Christian, reported that in addition to cattle, horses, "Dear Skins and other Rich plunder," his party took over fifty captives, mostly Indians but also whites and African Americans who lived in Cherokee country.[4]

Among the Cherokees captured in 1776 was an eight-year-old girl taken near Field Town on the Seneca River. When Colonel William Christian and his men approached the town, most Cherokees fled, but the girl and her mother, Olufletoy, were left behind. The militia later boasted that they held their guns over Olufletoy's head to frighten her. They took the child and then killed Olufletoy. The girl, thereafter called "Nancy," was carried to Virginia, where she became a slave and passed through the hands of several masters. The documentary record surrounding Nancy's enslavement reveals how easily Virginia statutes prohibiting Indian slavery were evaded. Her second bill of sale, drawn up by William Kennedy, described Nancy as "a Negro Girl, mixture of the Indian Breed." Nancy's third master, John Fulton, settled on a different heritage, claiming that Nancy came from the "East Indies." (Nancy later countered this narrative, saying "that she never saw any waters larger than the Tennessee & Clinch rivers.") By 1801 Nancy was living in eastern Tennessee, near the Cherokee Nation. Hearing of their relative's return, the Cherokees demanded her liberation, saying that Nancy "belong[ed] to their nation" and was "a native of their country." Longtime trader William Whiteside confirmed Nancy's account, saying she was "taken by the Americans in war but notwithstanding she had been sold as a slave several times." Federal Indian agent Return Josiah Meigs called Nancy's enslavement a "base act," concluding that "her undisguised narrative cannot be doubted." Meigs attempted to pressure John Fulton into liberating Nancy, but Fulton sold her away to yet another master. In 1808, over thirty years after her capture, Nancy remained a slave, and by this time, so did her children and grandchildren.[5]

Captive-exchange figured prominently in treaty negotiations during this period, but Native leaders objected that Anglo-Americans, who frequently retained Indian war captives, failed to comply. In 1786 Cherokee chiefs protested to South Carolina officials that Brigadier General Andrew Williamson of the town of Ninety Six held two Cherokee children "in Slavery." Williamson had a long history of holding Indians as slaves. In 1772, a "half Indian Man, named Frank," ran away from Williamson's cattle ranch in the Carolina borderlands, probably toward Indian Country "to pass for a Freeman." Williamson had also commanded South Carolina troops during the 1776 Cherokee expedition, during which he and his men had taken several Native captives. The South Carolina General Assembly, following the post-Yamasee War logic that Indian slavery endangered the colony, ordered Williamson to give up his captives, but it is unclear whether the general complied. Elsewhere, those holding captives from the 1776 expedition were recalcitrant. James Miller of North Carolina refused to relinquish a Cherokee boy, and another captive, an adult woman, died in the household of General Griffith Rutherford shortly before her brother arrived to redeem her.[6]

During the American Revolution, factions from several southern Indian nations took an active role against the rebels, combating the white settlements that grew at an alarming rate even before the United States declared independence. Settlers responded in kind, and in the southern borderlands the war devolved into a series of bloody skirmishes over land, property, and captives. In a March 1781 campaign against the Chickamaugas, Colonel John Sevier and his men killed fifty men and took fifty women and children captive; ten of the captives lived with Sevier for three years before being ransomed. During the peace talks that followed, Chickamaugas demanded the return of their kin. Sevier claimed, "I am not afraid to fight with men, but I never hurt women & children, they are innocent harmless Beings; It is true I took some of them Prisoners, but it was only with a view to exchange for our People you have as Prisoners. I have used them well, kept them at my own House, and treated them as my own Children." Colonel William Christian echoed Sevier, "We hate Slavery, and have no desire to keep your People[.] [A]ll we want is our own." Of course, most southerners had no such aversion to slavery, and many continued to take Indian slaves without any intention of ransoming them for white prisoners.[7]

The Treaty of Paris awarded a vast swath of eastern North America to the United States, but Native people—who had not been invited to Paris—mostly regarded it as a fraudulent compact. In his memoirs of early Georgia, former governor George Gilmer reflected, "Independence, which secured peace to the other States, gave no peace to Georgia. . . . The frontiers were too extensive to be defended by its scattered inhabitants." In truth, the same could be said of the entire region. In the absence of a strong state or, in the words of a contemporary, "any competent authority from the United States," whites living in the borderlands took matters into their own hands, using squatting, intimidation, and violence to acquire Indian land. According to one Georgia woman, "The doctrine in her neighbourhood was, let us kill the Indians, bring on a war, and we shall get land." Thus began another decade of border wars, during which Indian captive-taking became a matter of course. In 1792 governor of the Southwest Territory William Blount advised Brigadier General James Robertson, who was then fighting Native militants, "You may give orders to all excursive parties, to consider all Creeks and Cherokees found North of the [treaty] line as enemies but women and children on all occasions are to be spared *except that they may be made prisoners.*" Similarly, Winthrop Sargent, first territorial governor of Mississippi, threatened the Choctaws, "If you wage war with the People of our Territories . . . we will destroy your Fields, and little Stock, and make Captives your Wives and Children." Creek warrior John Galphin, no stranger to captive-taking himself, explained that Creek men were afraid to leave their villages because "the Americans mite take the oportunity of Cuming into our towns & Carry of[f] our Wom[e]n & Children."[8]

Wherever warfare occurred, captivity followed. In 1792, when Cherokee subagent John D. Chisholm tried to redeem recently captured Indian slaves held in Kentucky, captors refused and threatened to kill their prisoners if Chisholm tried to take them by force. The following year, in what one American critic described as a typical "sham campaign," a group of Georgia men went to a Creek town on the Chattahoochee where "they killd six warriors, took six prisoners, they being Women & Children, with a good deal of plunder, laid waste the town." During their attacks against the Chickamauga towns of Running Water and Nickajack in 1794, American militiamen killed fifty-five warriors and captured about twenty women and children. At the Tellico Blockhouse treaty in 1795, Chickamaugas clamored to redeem their kin. Militiamen had either taken these captives back to their homes or sold them to others, and the Chickamauga prisoners were now scattered throughout the South, living in Tennessee, Kentucky, Virginia, Georgia, and South Carolina. One chief, the Crier of Nickajack, brought a young African American girl to negotiations "expressly for the purpose of recovering in exchange his daughter now a Prisonner at Kentuckey." The Treaty of Tellico Blockhouse concluded the post-Revolutionary border wars, but in the next major conflict, the Red Stick War of 1813–1814, whites resumed taking Native captives. At the Battle of Horseshoe Bend alone, American forces and their Indian allies took an astonishing number of captives—353 women and children and 3 warriors. Although federal removal policy had expelled most Indians from the region by 1840, dozens remained enslaved under white masters. A Creek man, Ward Cochamy, at great personal risk, made it his mission to secure freedom for as many as possible. By 1848, he had liberated sixty-five Indian slaves, but reported that at least one hundred Creeks remained enslaved in Alabama alone. Although threatened by their "would-be masters," Cochamy vowed, "I shall get them yet."[9]

The enslavement of Indians continued into the nineteenth century, but slavery represented one extreme of a broad spectrum of captivity. Some Native people experienced more temporary states of bondage. During negotiations between Chickamauga chief John Watts (or New Tassel) and territorial governor William Blount, Watts demanded the return of "a person of my own blood among the white people. . . . He was carried off when a small boy & committed to the care of Col. Anderson . . . and we lately heard he was there working." This may have been the same boy referred to in another document as "Thomas," who was forced to labor on the farm of a local militia officer until reaching adulthood. Thomas endured a kind of indentured servitude, and eventually managed to return to his village of Sumack and find his kin. When a Mohawk named John Norton traversed Cherokee country from 1809 to 1810, he met a woman who had endured a similar experience. She "had been taken prisoner by the Virginians at a very early age" and "brought up and detained by them until lately." Norton could tell that the woman had endured an extensive apprenticeship in "the useful labours of females" and was fluent in English, but "perfectly ignorant of her native language."[10]

Some Anglo-Americans, including Andrew Jackson, incorporated Indian war captives into their households, calling them kin. Jackson had captured Lyncoya during the Red Stick War in November 1813. Commanding the Tennessee militia, General Jackson ordered John Coffee to destroy the Creek town of Tallushatchee. Fire and bullets took many Creek lives that day. Participant Davy Crockett remembered that Creek women, seeing no escape, clung to the Tennessee militiamen. He interpreted their cries as pleas for captivity rather than death. Of the men, Crockett recalled, "We . . . shot them like dogs." In all, Jackson's troops killed 186 people and took 84 women and children captive. Among these captives was an infant boy, whose family supposedly had died. Initially, Jackson gave the boy to Colonel Leroy Pope and his family, asking them to care for the baby until he could arrange for transport to the Hermitage. Leroy's daughter Maria Pope dressed the infant like a doll and named him "Lyncoya." "Lyncoya" comes not from the Muskogee tongue of the

Creeks, but rather from young Maria Pope's imagination: she must have thought that "Lyncoya" sounded like an Indian name.

Jackson decided that he and his wife should "adopt him as one of our family." In a letter to his father, Andrew Jackson Jr. claimed that Rachel treated baby Lyncoya "as well as aney pearson on Earth Could." However, Jackson also once referred to Lyncoya as a "pet" for Andrew Jackson Jr., and the boy was one of several Indian children who had lived in the Jackson household. During the Red Stick War, Jackson captured another Creek boy, named him Charley, and offered him as a playmate for Andrew Jackson Donelson. Lyncoya was intended as a replacement for Theodore, another captured Indian boy, who died in the spring of 1814. Andrew Jackson Jr. threw a fit when his own playmate died and coveted Charley. According to Rachel, "he dont like the other Andrew to have the little Indian boy. . . . I told him we Could not keepe so maney." Seeking to pacify Junior, Andrew described Lyncoya as "about the size of theodore and much like him." Although Lyncoya lived at the Hermitage much longer and was called a "son" by the Jacksons, he, like Theodore and Charley before him, would never become one of the Andrews. The Jacksons' mixed feelings toward Lyncoya are emblematic of the larger world they inhabited—intimate with Native people, but also locked in a violent conflict over land, sovereignty, and the future of the continent.[11]

Growing up at the Hermitage, Lyncoya was reared in an ambiguous state of captivity. In his youth Lyncoya went to the same country school that the Andrews attended. By this time, Lyncoya was the plantation's sole Indian occupant, and Jackson feared that the boy might become "like a lost sheep without a shepherd." Jackson advised his wife to dissuade Lyncoya from associating with the slaves. This was a common refrain among planters, but Jackson may have feared that Lyncoya, as an Indian, was more susceptible to their "corrupting influence." Once, when Lyncoya apparently ventured out to the slave quarters for too long, Andrew thanked Rachel for "taking poor little Lyncoya home & cloathing him—I have been much hurt to see him there with the negroes." Despite the fact that Lyncoya's Indianness marked him as different, Jackson also identified with him as a fellow orphan.

He once told his wife, "When I reflect that he as to his relations is so much like myself I feel an unusual sympathy for him." Correspondence between Andrew and Rachel depict the Jacksons as an affectionate family with the future president as benevolent patriarch. From his Senate seat in Washington, Andrew bade his wife to "tell Lyncoya to read his book and be a good boy and obey you in all things." One wonders, however, whether Andrew Jackson's parenting also tested one of his earlier axioms: in a letter to Tennessee governor William Blount, Jackson had declared "fear is better than love with an indian."[12]

In a letter that Lyncoya penned to Andrew Jackson, the ten-year-old wrote of Jackson's paternalism toward Indians, saying that other Native people, including those from the "woods," called him "father." But Lyncoya distinguished between metaphorical and substantive kinship, saying that these other Indians had not "gathered strength from your table, nor rest[ed] under your roof." The boy recounted how "you placed me on your knee and learned me the talk of your Andrews." Optimistic about his own exceptionalism—the possibility of his inclusion in American society—Lyncoya suggested that to succeed, a man did not need "white skin," "but to be just, to [avoid] only evil actions, and to do good, is to be the *bigerest* of men." As Lyncoya explained, he tried to act as a companion to his brothers, a peer to his classmates, and a loyal son. By fulfilling the cultural expectations of his adoptive society, he hoped his father would not "feel a blush" when he told others "*this is the Indian boy I . . . raised.*"[13]

As Lyncoya grew, Jackson schemed to have the boy admitted to West Point, which he regarded as the premiere institution of higher learning in the United States. Jackson's desire for Lyncoya to pursue a career in the military reflected another commonality between these two orphans: they both came from martial peoples who valued masculine honor accrued through warfare. And, though a lofty aim, Lyncoya's admission was not out of the question. Fellow Creek David Moniac, admitted in 1817, was the first person of color to attend West Point. Moniac went on to become a major in the U.S. Army, and he died leading troops into battle against the Seminoles in 1836. A number of young Indian men followed Moniac to West Point, but Lyncoya was not among them. Jackson, supposedly thwarted by political rivals in the War Department, failed to secure Lyncoya's admission. Lyncoya instead ran errands and delivered letters for his father, and he also trained to become a saddler. Although Jackson himself had considered this career path in the poverty of his youth, it was hardly an appropriate choice for a planter's son. As historian Lorri Glover has demonstrated, members of elite southern families generally "shunned jobs that appeared even tangentially servile." Despite his education and his father's connections, Lyncoya's race limited his opportunities. Sadly, Lyncoya had little chance to explore life outside of the Hermitage. He died at age sixteen on July 1, 1828, after a bout of illness. His obituary reported, "By the general and Mrs. Jackson he was mourned as a favorite son, and they always spoke of him with paternal affection."[14]

While seemingly incongruous with his Indian policy, Jackson's adoption of Lyncoya reflected his belief that the sovereignty of Native nations was far more dangerous than Indian individuals. He saw southern Indian nations, in particular, as troubling because they were among the continent's most populous and still controlled much of the richest land in the South. Jackson feared that the southern nations would ally with European powers to compromise America's imperial ambitions. Jackson campaigned on a promise to secure U.S. expansion by removing Indians from the East, justifying this policy change by citing new "scientific" evidence coming out of phrenology. Jackson argued that Indians could not survive "in the midst of another and superior race." According to Jackson, Indians "have neither the intelligence, the industry, the moral habits, nor the desire of improvement which are essential to any favorable change in their condition." But even the ardent proponent of Indian removal had difficulty reconciling the rigid racial ideology he promoted publicly with his everyday behavior at home.[15]

Jackson shared this conundrum with dozens of other white families in the southern borderlands who adopted Indian women and children. In 1801, when Cherokee leaders pressed their federal agent, Return J. Meigs, to recover their people held captive by whites, Meigs reported that "those persons or some of them are unwilling to be given up, that they are unwilling to live with the Indians." When Tennessee governor John Sevier attempted to redeem Cherokee captives to satisfy the Treaty of Tellico Blockhouse, a captor named Allen Gillespie contacted him: "I do confess that there is an Indian boy in my possession now but I do not consider him a prisoner." Gillespie continued, "I have had the boy at school almost two years now and he is so attached to me." Four years earlier, Gillespie had seen a war party composed of Creeks and Chickamaugas kill one of his biological sons and take another captive. Gillespie claimed that Chickamauga chief John Watts, as well as one of the boy's kin, had given Gillespie the Indian child, presumably to compensate for his murdered son. In this case, Chickamaugas extended a form of indigenous justice to a white neighbor, who accepted it. Loath to give up his adopted son, Gillespie told Sevier that he would turn the boy over "if nothing else would please the Indians." Like Gillespie, an Alabama planter named John P. Booth argued that he had genuinely adopted an Indian child. Objecting vehemently to the accusation that he held the Creek girl in slavery, Booth railed, "As to her treatment, I can assure you, that so far from being regarded as a *Slave*, she is not permitted to associate with my negroes, more than my own children."[16]

American captors also incorporated Indian women into their families through marriage. Richard "Dick" Findleston, for example, claimed a Cherokee woman as his "wife," and the couple had a son together. Formerly a resident of the multiethnic Mississippi River trading town of Kaskaskia, Findleston fought under George Rogers Clark during the American Revolution. He later moved south and served as a spy and scout for the Tennessee militia during the Chickamauga Wars. He almost certainly captured his future wife in one of these campaigns. While some scholars have assumed that Findleston was white (presumably because he became a U.S. citizen), primary sources reveal that Findleston was clearly of both European and Native ancestry, himself a son of America's borderlands. Although Cherokee leaders initially attempted to redeem Findleston's wife, they ultimately concluded that she wished to remain with her new husband. According to Governor Blount, "the Nation are content she should stay with him." The Findlestons were not an isolated case. During the spring of 1803, as Pennsylvanian James Patriot Wilson traveled across the southern interior, he observed that intermarriage between white men and Indian women was quite common in the borderlands separating the Cherokee Nation from the United States. While it is impossible to divine the origins of these sorts of relationships, at least some Americans did adopt Indian captivity practices, absorbing war captives—especially women and children—into their households.[17]

Adoptive white parents claimed that they could offer Indian children a better life, one with more education, greater material comforts, and exposure to the blessings of "civilization." In a case strongly reminiscent of Jackson's, a Tennessean named William Wynne adopted a Creek girl during the Red Stick War. Wynne, a surgeon in the militia, claimed that the girl's father was killed during the war and that her mother had been executed as a witch. This may have been the case; some Red Stick prophets did engage in witch hunting, singling out those who seemed too friendly to Americans or their culture. An examination of other cases, however, reveals that the discovery of unfit Indian relatives is a trope constructed by whites to justify the capture of Native children. After the Battle of Tallushatchee, Jackson declared that Lyncoya was "the only branch of his family left," and, when Jackson's Creek interpreter asked if others in the village would care for him, they reportedly "would have nothing to do with him but wanted him to be killed." Jackson felt compelled by "Charity and christianity" to adopt the boy. John Booth, the Alabama planter who adopted an eleven-year-old Creek girl, claimed that he found her wandering in the woods, left behind by relatives who had immigrated to Indian Territory. Frontier historian Lyman Draper, who interviewed many veterans of the Chickamauga Wars, recorded the story of an Indian mother and child during the Battle of Nickajack in 1794. Militiamen were rowing the pair away from the battle in a canoe when the Chickamauga woman suddenly threw her child overboard: "she made off, & *dove*, keeping under as long as she could, then r[o]se & d[o]ve again . . . she escaped under a volley of bullets" but "her child sunk in the river." At Nickajack, Draper recorded, Colonel

William Whitley saved several other Indian children from such a fate by bringing them back with him to Kentucky. Drawing on the doctrine of just war, captors like Wynne, Jackson, Booth, and Whitley must have reasoned that captivity was a small price to pay for a chance at "civilized" life and eternal salvation.[18]

For hundreds of years, the South was a borderlands region, where diverse populations of settlers, slaves, and Indians lived in close proximity. As in other borderlands, ideas, technology, and even people moved between the porous bounds that separated colonial and indigenous societies. Warfare, in particular, occasioned some of the heaviest trafficking. This creolization began in the sixteenth century, when Hernando de Soto's soldiers discarded their heavy chain mail in favor of Native armor made from woven cane, and when they forced hundreds of Indians—mostly women—to serve as sexual partners and servants. Although scalping was unknown to sixteenth-century Europeans (who preferred to sever entire heads), colonists quickly adopted the practice and even innovated, adding ears and eyes to their menagerie of war trophies. Euro-Americans also borrowed methods of execution from Indians. In a gruesome divide-and-rule strategy used during the 1729–1731 war between the Natchez Indians and French Louisiana, colonial officials handed three enslaved Africans who had aided the Natchez over to Choctaw warriors. Employing their usual method of executing captured warriors, the Choctaws burned the enslaved men alive on a public square in New Orleans. A Jesuit observer believed that the execution had succeeded in "inspir[ing] all the Negroes with a new horror of the Savages," but he fretted over the fact that "our own people, it is said, begin to be accustomed to this barbarous spectacle." Carolinians took a more active role in the ritual deaths of several captured Indians during the Tuscarora War of 1711–1715. In January of 1712, colonial commander John Barnwell invaded Tuscarora territory, and his army, largely composed of allied Indian warriors, took hundreds captive. On at least two occasions, Barnwell ordered soldiers to torture and burn captured Indians alive, and, after the capture of Narhantes Fort, white troops from South Carolina reportedly "cooked the flesh of an Indian in good condition and ate it." Captivity was part of a much broader exchange of martial values in the American borderlands, where ritualized violence became a mutually intelligible language.[19]

To cast themselves as civilizers in North America, whites chose to forget their own lust for torture, war trophies, and captives, yet they could not completely disavow a kind of cultural kinship that bound them to southern Indians. Like Spaniards, who distinguished *indios bárbaros* from *indios de razón*, nineteenth-century Americans separated Cherokees, Creeks, Choctaws, Chickasaws, and Seminoles from other Indians by calling them "the Five Civilized Tribes." This designation reflected the settled life and agricultural productivity that had characterized southern Indian societies for hundreds of years, as well as trends toward commercial ranching, black slavery, and political centralization that began in the late eighteenth century.

The Five Tribes also believed that their culture and history distinguished them from other Native peoples. Cherokee chief Doublehead, for example, called Native peoples of the trans-Mississippi west "the western wild Indians." Native leaders, however, generally eschewed such loaded terms, and instead referred to southern Indians collectively as "the Southern Nations," or, because most considered the Seminoles part of the Creek Nation, "the Four Nations." Part of that distinctiveness came from a creolized culture born of centuries of exchange with Europeans and Africans. When a federal Indian agent tried to persuade Bloody Fellow, a former Chickamauga war chief, to remove west, Bloody Fellow responded that "he had no inclination to leave the country of his birth. Even should the habits & customs of the Cherokees give place to the habits & customs of the whites, or even should they themselves become white by intermarriage not a drop of Indian blood would be lost; it would be spread more widely but not lost. He was for preserving them together as a people, regardless of complexion." Even as whites and Indians increasingly relied on racial idioms to define themselves against one another, they recognized that a shared past and generations of captivity and intermarriage bound them together.[20]

Lyncoya's captivity came at the apex of cultural exchange between Indians and whites in the South, shortly before removal expelled most of the region's Native people. When the Red Stick

War began in 1813, Andrew Jackson spoke of a need to fulfill the "*lex taliones*" or law of retaliation. Jackson echoed southern Indians' notion of "crying blood," which held that the souls of the dead cried out, animating their kin to seek vengeance. In fact, Jackson considered the massacre at Tallushatchee, in which Lyncoya was captured, direct retaliation for "the destruction of Fort Mims," a Red Stick victory that took the lives of some three hundred Americans and rival Creeks. The vengeance continued at Horseshoe Bend, where according to one white veteran of the battle, whites took gruesome war trophies: "Many of the Tennessee soldiers cut long strips of skin from the bodies of the dead Indians and with these made bridle reins." Lyncoya's captivity points to the paradox of removal; even as imperial America sought to break the power of Native nations and seize their land, the absorption of Indian culture—and even Indian individuals—continued.[21]

Few American historians have taken a critical look at white kinship practices in the colonial and early national South. Why do we write about Indian "kinship" and white "families"? In part, this is a legacy of a disciplinary divide: to generalize, historians often naturalize the paternal, nuclear family; ethnohistorians, borrowing from anthropology, have invested great energy in studying expansive kinship networks. These divergences have affected not just our semantics, but, far more importantly, the kinds of questions that we ask as historians. A recent anthology of European kinship practices warns, "The old story of the rise of the nuclear family and the decline of the importance of kinship is not simply innocent. It has been used as the model that all modernizing economies and societies are held up to. . . . The history of the family is part of the history of the rise of the Western individual, cut loose from the responsibilities of kin, and cut out for the heroic task of building the self-generating economy." Indians and settlers lived not in oppositional realms, but were instead intimately connected, and over time borrowed much from one another. Even as the United States expanded, beneficiaries like the Jacksons maintained broad and flexible notions of kinship, a necessity in the face of such high mortality rates. In fact, white descent reckoning had much in common with Indian practices. Joan Cashin, one of the few historians to analyze this trend, has argued, "The planter family had a nuclear core of parents and children, but . . . its borders were permeable and its structure was elastic." Households often included extended family as well as "fictive kin": in the words of Carolyn Billingsley, "those whose kinship ties are not biologically or legally based but who, for a variety of reasons, are treated and named as kin." In contrast to the rugged individuals of American myth, settlers, like their Native neighbors, relied on an expansive and dynamic network of kin to support them by providing labor, fulfilling social obligations, and generating political capital.[22]

Some whites even recognized kin across color lines. Consider, for example, Amanda America Dickson, an African American woman in Georgia who inherited—and, perhaps more significantly, retained—her white father's $500,000 estate. Like Amanda's father David, Kentuckian Richard Mentor Johnson, vice president under Martin Van Buren, also had a long-term relationship with an enslaved woman. Johnson and his slave Julia Chinn had two daughters, Imogene and Adaline, whom Johnson emancipated, educated, and financially supported.[23]

Like their Native neighbors, white men incorporated captive women and children into their own households in various capacities. White captors, like southern Indians, often called these captives of color "kin." Kinship, however, did not mean equality. As scholars of captivity have suggested, the language of kinship can express "the closeness of a relationship" but also "authority and subordination."[24]

Lyncoya's 1828 obituary in the *U.S. Telegraph* depicted him as a feral child, a wild boy tolerated and even indulged by the Jacksons. Drawing on popular and enduring Indian stereotypes, the article claimed that Lyncoya fashioned himself a bow without ever having seen one before: "Whether from immediate instinct, or from a predisposition to imitate Indian manners, he was in the habit of dressing his head with all the feathers he could pick up in the yard—and amusing himself *constantly* with his little bow—

differing in this from civilized children, who change their amusements and toys with a sort of capricious variety." Like his stoic and doomed Indian brethren, Lyncoya died with "the uncomplaining fortitude of his race." This article, reprinted in newspapers throughout the United States, would shape how subsequent generations thought about Andrew Jackson's Indian son, if they thought about him at all. Lyncoya became a curiosity, a footnote, an instructive and counterintuitive point of reflection on Jackson's character.[25]

Lyncoya's story, though spare and marginalized by historians and Jackson biographers, is of major importance, for it exposes the cultural exchanges and social complexity that characterized borderland regions. The United States was not exceptional among empires, for Americans, like their Spanish and French counterparts, captured, married, adopted, and had children with indigenous people. A far cry from the self-made men of American myth, settlers eagerly benefited from Native epistemologies, and they relied on a surprisingly expansive and diverse web of kin to sustain them. Well into the nineteenth century, settlers, like Indians, sought out war captives, who served in capacities ranging from slave to spouse. Families selectively absorbed a diverse range of foreign people, many of whom were neither full kin nor chattel, but something in-between. Seeking to distance "white" civility from Indian savagery, Lyncoya's obituary depicted him as inherently different, exotic, and incapable of change. Following removal, American elites became more invested in codifying a simplified racial binary: black versus white, slave versus free. The cotton curtain and, later, Jim Crow laws obscured but could not erase the region's diversity. In a 1996 poll, sociologist John Shelton Reed found that 40 percent of southerners claimed to have Indian ancestry, while only about half that number recognized Confederate kin.[26] Perhaps the memory of captives such as Lyncoya, Findleston's wife, Wynne's Creek girl, and Gillespie's Cherokee boy are behind the ever-persistent myth of the Cherokee grandmother. In expelling most Indians from the region, whites engaged in their own mythmaking, drawing upon real or imagined family members, and casting themselves as the new native people of the land.

Notes

1. Quotations from Andrew Jackson to Rachel Jackson, April 8, 1818, *Correspondence of Andrew Jackson*, ed. John Spencer Bassett (Washington DC: Carnegie Institute, 1926–35), 2:357–58. For Lyncoya as "son," see, for example, Andrew Jackson to James Gadsden, May 2, 1822, *The Papers of Andrew Jackson, Volume V: 1821–1824*, ed. Harold D. Moser, David R. Hoth, and George H. Hoemann (Knoxville: University of Tennessee Press, 1984), 180. Michael P. Rogin interpreted Jackson's "Kiss my two sons" here to mean Andrew Jackson Donelson and Lyncoya. Rogin, *Fathers and Children: Andrew Jackson and the Subjugation of the American Indian* (New York: Vintage, 1975), 199. Jackson's correspondence, however, usually paired the two resident Andrews and singled out Lyncoya. See, for example, Andrew Jackson to Andrew Jackson Donelson, January 18, 1824, *Papers of Andrew Jackson*, 5:340.

2. On captivity, see Gary Ebersole, *Captured by Texts: Puritan to Postmodern Images of Indian Captivity* (Charlottesville: University Press of Virginia, 1995); June Namias, *White Captives: Gender and Ethnicity on the American Frontier* (Chapel Hill: University of North Carolina Press, 1993); Richard Slotkin, *Regeneration through Violence: The Mythology of the American Frontier, 1600–1860* (Middletown CT: Wesleyan University Press, 1973), chapter 5; Pauline Turner Strong, *Captive Selves, Captivating Others: The Politics and Poetics of Colonial American Captivity Narratives* (Boulder: University of Colorado Press, 2000). For French and Spanish imperialism, see James F. Brooks, *Captives and Cousins: Slavery, Kinship, and Community in the Southwest Borderlands* (Chapel Hill: University of North Carolina Press, 2001); Kathleen DuVal, "Indian Intermarriage and Métissage in Colonial Louisiana," *William and Mary Quarterly*, 3rd ser., vol. 65 (April 2008): 267–304; Ramón A. Gutiérrez, *When Jesus Came, the Corn Mothers Went Away: Marriage, Sexuality, and Power in New Mexico, 1500–1845* (Stanford CT: Stanford University Press, 1991); Jennifer Spear, *Race, Sex, and Social Order in Early New Orleans* (Baltimore MD: Johns Hopkins University Press, 2008).

3. Juliana Barr, "From Captives to Slaves: Commodifying Indian Women in the Borderlands," *Journal of American History* 92 (June 2005): 19–46; Brooks, *Captives and Cousins*; Alan Gallay, *The Indian Slave Trade: The Rise of English Empire in the American South, 1670–1717* (New Haven CT: Yale University Press, 2002); Brett Rushforth, "'A Little Flesh We Offer You': The Origins of Indian Slavery in New France," *The William and Mary Quarterly*, 3rd ser., vol. 60 (October 2003): 777–808; Christina Snyder, *Slavery in Indian Country: The Changing Face of Captivity in Early America* (Cambridge MA: Harvard University Press, 2010), chapter 2; Almon Wheeler Lauber, "Indian Slavery in Colonial Times within the Present Limits of the United States" in *Studies in History, Economics, and Public Law* 54 (1913): 300–310, 564–68.

4. Captain William Moore to Brigadier General Rutherford, November 18, 1776, folder 1, Griffith Rutherford Collection, Southern Historical Collection, Louis Round Wilson Special Collections Library, University of North Carolina at Chapel Hill; William Dells Journal, August 29–September 30, 1776, Arthur Campbell Papers, Filson Historical Society, Louisville, Kentucky.

5. Bill of Sale, copy, April 2, 1778, reel 5, microcopy 208, Cherokee Agency, Letters Received, Office of Indian Affairs, National Archives, Washington DC; Testi-

mony of the Cherokee Chiefs, October 28, 1808, Cherokee Agency, Letters Received; Narrative of Nancy, November 24, 1801, Cherokee Agency, Letters Received; Misc. Notes from the Cherokee Agency, n.d., Cherokee Agency, Letters Received; Return J. Meigs to John Sevier, July 14, 1801, reel 2, no. 2, John Sevier Papers, First Administration, Governors' Papers, Tennessee State Library and Archives, Nashville.

6. Report of the Committee Respecting . . . the Cherokee orphans, 1786, series s165009, item 173, Governors' Messages, South Carolina Department of Archives and History, Columbia; Andrew Pickens to William Moultrie, January 6, 1786, item 378, Governors' Messages; Journal of the proceedings of the commissioners appointed to treat with the southern Indians, bin 61, folder 6, document 1, Telamon Cuyler Collection, Hargrett Rare Books and Manuscripts Library, Digital Library of Georgia; *South Carolina Gazette* (Charleston), April 12, 1773; A. S. Salley Jr., ed., *Journal of the General Assembly of South Carolina: September 17, 1776–October 20, 1776* (Columbia: Historical Commission of South Carolina, 1909), 60–61; William Sharpe to Waightstill Avery, November 3, 1777, 1KK36–39, North Carolina Papers, Lyman Copeland Draper Manuscript Collection, microfilm copy, State Historical Society of Wisconsin, Madison.

7. Talk of John Sevier to Cherokee Warriors and Chiefs, July 28, 1781, 1XX48, Tennessee Papers, Draper Collection; Talk of William Christian to Cherokee Warriors and Chiefs, July 26, 1781, 1XX46, Tennessee Papers, Draper Collection.

8. George R. Gilmer, *Sketches of Some of the First Settlers of Upper Georgia, of the Cherokees, and the Author* (1855; repr., Baltimore MD: Genealogical Publishing Company, 1970), 251; Esteban Miró to Don Antonio Valdes, June 15, 1788, Pontalba Papers, Temple Bodley Collection, Filson Historical Society; H. Thomas Foster II, ed., *Collected Works of Benjamin Hawkins, 1796–1810* (Tuscaloosa: University of Alabama Press, 2003), 102; William Blount to James Robertson, October 7, 1792, reel 801, James Robertson Papers, Tennessee State Library and Archives, emphasis mine; Winthrop Sargent to Timothy Pickering, February 10, 1800, in *The Mississippi Territorial Archives, 1798–1803*, ed. Dunbar Rowland (Nashville TN: Brandon Printing Company, 1905), 206; John Galphin to unknown [William Panton?], September 18, 1794, section 29, reel 43, document 59, East Florida Papers, P. K. Yonge Library of Florida History, Department of Special and Area Collections, George A. Smathers Libraries, University of Florida, Gainesville.

9. First quotation from William Martin to Joseph Martin, October 27, 1793, 2XX40, Tennessee Papers, Draper Collection; second quotation from Tellico Blockhouse Treaty Negotiations, December 28, 1794–January 3, 1795, reel 801, Robertson Papers; third quotation from Ward Co-cha-my to Commissioner of Indian Affairs, July 16, 1848, in Grant Foreman, *Indian Removal: The Emigration of the Five Civilized Tribes of Indians* (Norman: University of Oklahoma Press, 1972), 190n35; Henry Knox to William Blount, August 15, 1792, in *The Territorial Papers of the United States: The Territory South of the River Ohio, 1790–1796*, ed. Clarence Edwin Carter (Washington DC: Government Printing Office, 1936), 4:162; *Knoxville Gazette* (TN), September 26, 1794; John Haywood, *Civil and Political History of the State of Tennessee from Its Earliest Settlement up to the Year 1796* (1823; repr., New York: Arno Press, 1971), 98;

Blount to Secretary of War, September 22, 1794, *Territorial Papers, Territory South of the Ohio*, 4:356; Journal of the proceedings of the commissioners appointed to treat with the southern Indians, Cuyler Collection; Blount to Robertson, March 8, 1794, reel 801, Robertson Papers; Blount to Robertson, April 15, 1794, Robertson Papers; Blount to Robertson, November 12, 1794, Robertson Papers; Robert V. Remini, *Andrew Jackson and His Indian Wars* (New York: Viking, 2001), 79. Other examples of Indian slaves include an Indian girl aged between ten and twelve supposedly held by William Whiteside in Kentucky (the same man who supported Nancy's case for freedom) and "two young Indian lads or rather young men held as slaves by a Colonel Davies in the Neighborhood of Knoxville." Benjamin Logan to Governor Randolph, September 24, 1787, folder 515, Benjamin Logan Correspondence, Bullitt Family Papers–Oxmoor Collection, Filson Historical Society; Return J. Meigs to John Sevier, July 14, 1801, Sevier Papers.

 10. Minutes of a talk between John Watts and William Blount, 1792, box 16, w-17, Tennessee Historical Society Miscellaneous Files, Tennessee State Library and Archives; Carl F. Klink and James J. Talman, eds., *The Journal of Major John Norton, 1809–1816* (Toronto ON: The Champlain Society, 1970), 153; Nathaniel J. Sheidley, "Unruly Men: Indians, Settlers, and the Ethos of Frontier Patriarchy in the Upper Tennessee Watershed, 1763–1815" (PhD diss., Princeton University, 1999), 114.

 11. James A. Shackford and Stanley J. Folmsbee, eds., *A Narrative of the Life of David Crockett of the State of Tennessee* (Knoxville: University of Tennessee Press, 1973), 88, first quotation on 75; Andrew Jackson to Rachel Jackson, December 19, 1813, *The Papers of Andrew Jackson, Volume 2: 1804–1813*, ed. Harold D. Moser and Sharon MacPherson (Knoxville: University of Tennessee Press, 1984), 494–95, second quotation on 495; third quotation from Andrew Jackson Jr. to Jackson, April 8, 1814, The Papers of Andrew Jackson, Library of Congress, Washington DC, reel 10; fourth quotation from Rachel Jackson to Andrew Jackson, March 21, 1814, *Correspondence of Andrew Jackson*, 1:482–83; fifth quotation from Andrew Jackson to Rachel Jackson, March 4, 1814, "Letters of Andrew Jackson," *Huntington Library Bulletin* 3 (February 1933): 115–16; Andrew Jackson to Rachel Jackson, November 4, 1813, *Papers of Andrew Jackson*, 2:444; Andrew Jackson to Rachel Jackson, May 8, 1814, *The Papers of Andrew Jackson: Volume 3, 1814–1815*, ed. Harold D. Moser, David R. Hoth, Sharon MacPherson, and John H. Reinbold (Knoxville: University of Tennessee Press, 1984), 71; Robert V. Remini, *Andrew Jackson and the Course of American Empire, 1767–1821* (New York: Harper & Row, 1977), 193; Robert V. Remini, *Andrew Jackson and the Course of American Freedom, 1822–1832* (New York: Harper & Row, 1981), 395n8; Andrew Jackson to Rachel Jackson, February 21, 1814, *Papers of Andrew Jackson*, 3:35; Andrew Jackson to Rachel Jackson, April 7, 1814, *Papers of Andrew Jackson*, 3:59.

 12. Andrew Jackson to Rachel Jackson, September 18, 1816, *The Papers of Andrew Jackson, Volume IV: 1816–1820*, ed. Harold D. Moser, David R. Hoth, and George H. Hoemann (Knoxville: University of Tennessee Press, 1984), 62; Andrew Jackson to Rachel Jackson, December 29, 1813, *Papers of Andrew Jackson*, 2:516; Andrew Jackson to Rachel Jackson, December 28, 1823, *Correspondence of Andrew Jackson*, 3:220; Andrew Jackson to William Blount, July 3, 1812, *Papers of Andrew Jackson*, 2:307. On

slaves supposedly corrupting children, see Lorri Glover, *Southern Sons: Becoming Men in the New Nation* (Baltimore MD: Johns Hopkins University Press, 2007), chapter 7.

13. Lyncoya to Andrew Jackson, copy, December 29, 1823, box 6, no. 28, Sir Emil Hurja Collection, Tennessee State Library and Archives, courtesy of the Tennessee Historical Society.

14. Glover, *Southern Sons*, 151–55, first quotation on p. 151; second quotation from *U.S. Telegraph* (Washington DC), July 3, 1828; John K. Mahon, *History of the Second Seminole War, 1835–1842* (Gainesville: University of Florida Press, 1985), 185; Andrew Jackson to Rachel Jackson, December 7, 1823, *Papers of Andrew Jackson*, 5:322; Andrew Jackson to Felix Grundy, 1826, roll 2, folder 152, William C. Cook War of 1812 in the South Collection, Historic New Orleans Collection, New Orleans, Louisiana; Mark R. Cheathem, *Old Hickory's Nephew: The Political and Private Struggles of Andrew Jackson Donelson* (Baton Rouge: Louisiana State University Press, 2007), 14–15; Remini, *Jackson and the Course of American Freedom*, 3–5.

15. Remini, *Andrew Jackson and His Indian Wars*, 85, 121, 211, 237; Andrew Jackson, Fifth Annual Message to Congress, December 3, 1833, *Compilation of the Messages and Papers of the Presidents, 1789–1897* (New York: Bureau of National Literature, 1897), 3:33.

16. Meigs to Sevier, July 14, 1801, Sevier Papers; Allen Gillespie to John Sevier, December 14, 1796, oversize letterbook Q-39, Sevier Papers; John P. Booth to John Bell, May 30, 1841, reel 240, frames 137–39, microcopy 234, Letters Received, Office of Indian Affairs; Haywood, *Civil and Political History*, 264–65.

17. Quotation from Blount to Robertson, November 12, 1794, reel 801, Robertson Papers; Blount to the Secretary of War, October 10, 1792, *Territorial Papers, Territory South of the Ohio*, 4:197, 110n43; Petition on behalf of William Hodge to Governor James Jackson, bin 44, folder 5, document 2, Cuyler Collection; Sheidley, "Unruly Men," 160; James Patriot Wilson to Patrick Wilson, April 1803, American Philosophical Society, Philadelphia, Pennsylvania. John Haywood's papers contain another account of a Cherokee boy adopted by John Shannon in 1793. Along with other militiamen, Shannon attacked a camp, killing some and taking others prisoner. The boy, then a teenager, lived with Shannon for several years. After he was redeemed, he sometimes visited his former captor. Miscellaneous Notes, folder 4, document 3, John Haywood Papers, Tennessee State Library and Archives, Nashville. In another episode during the Patriot War, an officer requested to adopt an Alachua Seminole boy after troops killed the boy's father. Smith to Flournoy, February 24, 1813, box 14, T. Frederick Davis Collection, P. K. Yonge Library. See also John Thaddeus Ellisor, "The Second Creek War: The Unexplored Conflict" (PhD diss., University of Tennessee, 1996), 363–64.

18. First quotation from Andrew Jackson to Rachel Jackson, December 19, 1813, *Correspondence of Andrew Jackson*, 1:400–401; second quotation from "Nickajack Battle," 29s98, Draper's Notes, Draper Collection; Andrew Jackson to William Wynne, July 22, 1814, Cook War of 1812 in the South Collection; George Stiggins, *Creek Indian History: A Historical Narrative of the Genealogy, Traditions, and Downfall of the Ispocoga or Creek Indian Tribe of Indians*, ed. Virginia Pounds Brown (Birmingham AL: Birming-

ham Public Library Press, 1989), 88, 93; John P. Booth to John Bell, May 30, 1841, reel 240, frames 137–39, microcopy 234, Letters Received, Office of Indian Affairs.

19. First quotation from Mathurin le Petit to Père d'Avaugour, July 12, 1730, in *The Jesuit Relations and Allied Documents, Travels, and Explorations of the Jesuit Missionaries in New France: 1610–1791*, ed. Reuben Gold Thwaites (Cleveland OH: Burrows Brothers, 1896–1901), 68:199; second quotation from "Narrative by Christoph von Graffenried concerning his voyage to North Carolina and the founding of New Bern," in *Colonial Records of North Carolina*, ed. William L. Saunders (Raleigh NC: P. M. Hale, 1886–1890), 1:954; James Axtell and William Sturtevant, "The Unkindest Cut, or Who Invented Scalping," *William and Mary Quarterly*, 3rd ser., vol. 37 (July 1980): 451–72; Elliott J. Gorn, "'Gouge and Bite, Pull Hair and Scratch': The Social Significance of Fighting in the Southern Backcountry," *The American Historical Review* 90 (February 1985): 18–43; Chapman J. Milling, *Red Carolinians* (Chapel Hill: University of North Carolina Press, 1940), 120.

20. First quotation from Doublehead to Return J. Meigs, November 20, 1802, reel 1, microcopy 208, Cherokee Agency, Letters Received, Office of Indian Affairs; Bloody Fellow quotation from Miscellaneous Notes, reel 1, vol. 2, p. 23, John Howard Payne Papers, microfilm copy, Edward E. Ayers Manuscript Collection, Newberry Library, Chicago. See also Sheidley, "Unruly Men," 8.

On southern Indians' self-conception see, for example, Speech of John Watts, in William Blount to Henry Knox, November 8, 1792, William Blount Letters, Filson Historical Society; Talk of Mad Dog [Efau Hadjo] to James Burgess and the Seminoles, August 2, 1798, box 1, Marie Taylor Greenslade Papers, P. K. Yonge Library, courtesy of the Florida Historical Society; Talk of the Choctaw Kings, Headmen, and Warriors to Mad Dog, White Lieutenant, Nine Hadjo and Apoyl of the Hickory Ground and all their elder brothers the Creeks in general, June 10, 1795, reel 801, Robertson Papers.

21. Andrew Jackson to Governor Holmes, April 18, 1814, Mrs. Dunbar Rowland Papers: Correspondence and Papers Concerning the Mississippi Territory in the War of 1812, typescript, Mississippi Department of Archives and History, Jackson, 1:462; Jackson to Blount, *Papers of Andrew Jackson*, 2:444; for bridle reins, see H. S. Halbert and T. H. Ball, *The Creek War of 1813 and 1814*, ed. Frank L. Owsley Jr. (1895; repr., Tuscaloosa: University of Alabama Press, 1969), 276–77. In a similar trophy-taking incident, John O'Fallon, who saw Tecumseh's dead body at the Battle of the Thames, reported that strips of skin had been cut from the warrior's thighs. John O'Fallon to William Henry Harrison, April 21, 1834, folder 4, John O'Fallon Papers, Filson Historical Society.

22. David Warren Sabean and Simon Teuscher, "Kinship in Europe: A New Approach to Long-Term Development," in *Kinship in Europe: Approaches to Long-Term Development (1300–1900)*, ed. David Warren Sabean, Simon Teuscher, and John Mathieu (New York: Berghahn Books, 2007), quotation on p. 23; Joan E. Cashin, "The Structure of Antebellum Planter Families: 'The Ties that Bound us Was Strong," *Journal of Southern History* 56 (February 1990): 55–70, quotation on p. 56; Carolyn Earle Billingsley, *Communities of Kinship: Antebellum Families and the Set-*

tlement of the Cotton Frontier (Athens: University of Georgia Press, 2004), quotation on p. 20; Jane Censer Turner, *North Carolina Planters and Their Children, 1800–1860* (Baton Rouge: Louisiana State University Press, 1984), chapter 2; Melissa L. Meyer and Kerwin Lee Klein, "Native American Studies and the End of Ethnohistory," in *Studying Native America: Problems and Prospects,* ed. Russell Thornton (Madison: University of Wisconsin Press, 1998), 182–216; Richard White, *The Middle Ground: Indians, Empires, and Republics in the Great Lakes Region, 1650–1815* (New York: Cambridge University Press, 1991); Daniel K. Richter, *Facing East from Indian Country: A Native History of Early America* (Cambridge MA: Harvard University Press, 2001); Nancy Shoemaker, *A Strange Likeness: Becoming Red and White in Eighteenth-Century North America* (New York: Oxford University Press, 2004).

23. Kent Leslie Anderson, *Woman of Color, Daughter of Privilege: Amanda America Dickson, 1846–1893* (Athens: University of Georgia Press, 1995); Richard M. Johnson to Thomas Henderson, January 13, 1826, folder 2, Thomas Henderson Papers, Filson Historical Society; Johnson to Henderson, February 26, 1836, folder 10, Henderson Papers.

24. Catherine M. Cameron, "Captives and Culture Change," *Current Anthropology* 52 (2011): 183.

25. Quotations from *U.S. Telegraph,* July 3, 1828. For Lyncoya references, see, for example, John William Ward, *Andrew Jackson: Symbol for an Age* (New York: Oxford University Press, 1962), 197–98; Rogin, *Fathers and Children,* 189; Remini, *Andrew Jackson and the Course of American Freedom,* 3–4, 144; Remini, *Andrew Jackson and His Indian Wars,* 64–65, 214–15.

26. John Shelton Reed, "The Cherokee Princess in the Family Tree," *Southern Cultures* 3 (Spring 1997): 111–13.

Six

Inevitability and the Southern Opposition to Indian Removal

TIM ALAN GARRISON

In 1830 the U.S. Congress passed the Indian Removal Act, which gave the president the authority to exchange federal territory west of the Mississippi River for the homelands of the tribes residing in the existing states. In the bill, Congress appropriated $500,000 to relocate those tribes that surrendered their lands in the East to their new homes. By 1843 the United States had relocated all of the major tribal nations from the southern states to what is now eastern Oklahoma. Almost all of the tribal nations in the northern United States were also pushed across the great river. Thousands died and tens of thousands were displaced by this national "Indian Removal policy."[1]

Over the years I have had opportunities to offer many lectures on the history of the removal policy. Provoked by my criticism of the policy, on several occasions a member of the audience has sidled up to me after the talk and asked a loaded question: "Wasn't removal inevitable?" This sense of inevitability is not uncommon, and scholars down through the years have expressed the opinion that, sooner or later, the Indian tribes in the East would have been pushed to the West or annihilated. For example, in *A Constitutional History of Georgia*, the state's most respected political scientist at its publication, Albert Berry Saye, wrote, "Finally, in 1835, the Cherokees bowed to the *inevitable* and agreed to a treaty with the United States whereby they gave up the last of their Georgia lands in exchange for $5,000,000 and territory in the west." The late Robert Remini, the former historian of the House of Representatives and the renowned author of many volumes on the life of Andrew Jackson, announced in his study of the Tennessee president's relations with Indians: "To his dying day on June 8, 1845, Andrew Jackson genuinely believed that what he had accomplished rescued these people from *inevitable* annihilation. And although that statement sounds monstrous, and although no one in the modern world wishes to accept or believe it, that is exactly what he did. He saved the Five Civilized Nations from probable extinction." This fatalistic presumption that the Indians were disappearing, which was also common among nineteenth-century American intellectuals, was, by the way, one of the paternalistic justifications that some removal advocates offered for the Indian expulsion. Personally, I am agnostic on the issue of whether or not the indigenous peoples would have been eradicated but for their removal. I am not particularly fond of the counterfactual daydreaming required by this specific inquiry. However, the question of the "inevitability" of removal does raise an historical issue that piques my interest. It seems to me that "inevitability" hinged on removal's popularity as public policy in the South. So, just how popular was the removal policy, and to what degree was there opposition to it, among white southerners?[2]

Conventional narratives of the Indian removal point out that individuals and philanthropic and religious groups from the North raised a powerful opposition to the policy.[3] Of course, the most significant resistance came from the targets and victims of removal themselves. The vast majority of southern Indians did not want to be removed from their homelands and carted up, marched, or floated hundreds of miles to a mysterious destination; and they did what they could to oppose the policy.[4] The southern nations resisted in their own ways. The Seminoles fought a long, bitter war to avoid relocation; the Creeks also turned to violent opposition in 1836. Others used nonviolent means of resistance. Political leaders such as Tishomingo (Chickasaw), Levi Colbert (Chickasaw), David Folsom (Choctaw), John Ross (Cherokee), and many other Native leaders lobbied in vain to forestall their peoples' relocation; sadly, the American officials who mattered generally refused to take their entreaties as seriously as they deserved. Ross and the Cherokees also tried to use the American legal system to thwart their removal. Many Native women added their voice to the resistance by writing memorials and signing petitions against expulsion.[5] Many indigenous individuals and their families resisted with their feet; small groups of Cherokees escaped into the mountains and numbers of Choctaws and Seminoles slipped off into the swamps to avoid capture and relocation.[6]

Thousands of non-Indian Americans supported the Native opposition to removal, and it is true that the vast majority of them lived north of the Mason-Dixon line. American missionaries, including those working for the American Board of Commissioners for Foreign Missions and other ministers and lay Christians from across the northern United States organized their congregations against the removal policy and lobbied to turn the government against it. Women in the North, some of whom were becoming engaged in the abolitionist movement and would later lead the fight for women's rights, joined their Native sisters and sent memorials to Congress protesting the policy. Their remonstrations flowed in with the dozens of anti-removal petitions from towns across the North. Jeremiah Evarts, under the pseudonym of "William Penn," attempted to foment public opposition to removal by writing and publishing scholarly polemics against the policy. Individual congressmen took up Evarts's arguments and offered vocal opposition in the federal legislature. Theodore Frelinghuysen of New Jersey, Peleg Sprague of Maine, and several others from the North fought heroically, but in futility, to kill the Indian removal bill.[7]

While scholars have described this opposition in the North and dramatized the resistance of American Indians and their leaders, very few have examined the views of those who rejected removal in the South. In the absence of political polling, which was not contrived until the twentieth century, we have no way of knowing quantitatively, beyond counting legislative votes, the level of public support for, or opposition to, the expulsion of the tribes. We can only gauge, in a very general fashion, the enfranchised citizenry's views on the subject. One interested in this question has only the limited available commentary of the literate political and social elite and the words of those who published disagreements in contemporary newspapers. Sadly, few of those papers survived the erosion of time and apathy and made their way into southern archives. Still, we can ask, was there opposition among the "white" political, social, and cultural leadership in the region? Were there material numbers of politicians, clergymen, journalists, or respected members of the public who criticized or opposed the removal policy?[8]

To measure the character of the opposition, I looked for commentary during the critical period of 1827–1833. During this time, two developments laid the legal and political foundation for the expulsion of the southern tribal nations: 1) the efforts of the legislatures in Georgia, Alabama, Mississippi, and Tennessee to extend their state's jurisdiction over the tribes within their borders; and 2) Jackson's removal bill. I concentrated on these "extension states," for this is where the political power for removal emerged, and looked for opposition among the extant newspapers, among the votes and speeches in the state and federal legislatures, and among the judicial decisions that sanctioned or challenged aspects of the removal policy. What I found was a *very* limited but courageous and articulate opposition.

State Extension Laws

Removal had been an idea in incubation since Thomas Jefferson proposed it in 1776. Only in the early 1820s, however, did southern legislators, primarily in Georgia, attempt to force the United States to adopt relocation as a formal policy. On July 26, 1827, the Cherokee Nation adopted a republican constitution, which reaffirmed their position that their people constituted a sovereign nation that would not abandon its territory. The Georgia legislature responded by passing an act purporting to extend the state's jurisdiction over the Cherokee Nation. In 1828 Georgia followed up its opening salvo by declaring null and void the laws and political institutions of the tribe. Following Georgia's lead, the legislatures of Alabama (1829), Mississippi (1830), and Tennessee (1833) also extended their jurisdiction over Indian land within their borders. These acts challenged the historical understanding of the appropriate relationships among the states, the federal government, and the tribal nations. Federalists and their philosophical descendants had maintained that the national government possessed plenary authority over relations with the Indian tribes, a position John Marshall and the U.S. Supreme Court later sanctioned in *Worcester v. Georgia* (1832). Southern states' rights ideologues, on the other hand, declared that the states held constitutional authority over all relations with the tribes save commerce and the power to impose state jurisdiction over individual Indians within their borders.[9]

While Georgia's most invasive extension law passed by a wide majority of twenty-seven to eleven, it is noteworthy that there was a material opposition to the act. Unfortunately, state legislative records from the era do not include records of the debates, so we can only speculate about the reasons for dissent. The opposition, for instance, could have been related simply to Georgia's own peculiar party rivalries. However, some objections were based on principle. In 1829 the Georgia legislature approved another extension law that criminalized the act of encouraging the Cherokees not to remove and gave the state the power to arrest individuals in the Cherokee Nation. The law also required Georgia courts to treat the laws of the Cherokee Nation "as if the same had never existed." The law passed by voice vote in the state senate, but in the state house, forty-eight members opposed the seventy who enacted the law. On November 23, 1830, one of the dissidents, William Schley, condemned the state's attacks on the Cherokees: "The Indians have a natural right to the occupancy of all the lands within their boundaries, and . . . may enjoy that right undisturbed until they shall voluntarily relinquish it." One suspects that there existed a spectrum of removal advocates in the legislature and that the more thoughtful among them bridled at the radical nature of extension.[10]

It is significant to recall that the controversy over the tariff of 1828 was raging at the same time as the removal crisis. As historians have noted, Jackson deftly supported states' rights on the removal question while he worked to vanquish the nullifiers in South Carolina. John Howard, a member of the Georgia legislature from Baldwin, pointed out that his state's extension law was a de facto exercise of John C. Calhoun's radical constitutional theory. Howard wrote that nullification "has been done more than once, and strange to tell, it has not only been done by this Legislature, but by the very men who are now denouncing the doctrine as *baneful*." "Every man who voted for the Indian bill is a nullifier," he declared. Howard then moved to the status of the Indian nations: "The United States government have solemnly by several treaties guaranteed to the Cherokee Nation all the lands which they claim within the jurisdictional limits of Georgia." Howard complained that Georgia "entirely disregarded" the "solemn treaties," which the Constitution held to be "the paramount laws of the land." The extension legislation was "in direct violation of these treaties," he said, "and in utter contempt of the injunction of Congress." Of course, while critics of the tariff were willing to use the state extension of jurisdiction over the tribes as evidence of their opponents' duplicity, this does not necessarily mean that they genuinely opposed relocation of the tribes. Still, Howard's argument does boldly reference the sacred nature of the U.S.-Cherokee treaties, a point proremoval Georgians found infuriating.[11]

Alabama's bill to extend jurisdiction over the tribes in the state was also more complicated than a simple rubber stamp of proremoval wishes. The act passed only by an eleven-to-eight count in the state senate. The Mississippi legislature took two years to adopt an extension law after one was introduced in 1828, suggesting that the bill there faced considerable opposition. According to one scholar, however, this dissent was rather self-interested. The bill encountered opposition from the representatives of the older, more established counties in the state who feared that opening up the lands of the Chickasaw and Choctaw Nations for white settlement would result in the creation of new legislative seats that would undermine their political power. The speculators among their constituents worried, similarly, that opening up those lands would create an oversupply of available land and diminish real estate values within their realms.[12]

In Tennessee the bill to extend jurisdiction passed by a vote of twenty-four to fifteen in the state house. According to one source, the bill "met with considerable opposition, upon the grounds that the Cherokees were, in accordance with existing treaties under the constitution, a *quasi* independent nation, and could not rightfully be subjected to the jurisdiction of the state."

It thus appears that there existed in all of the extension states the kind of principled opposition that might have served the Indian nations well if it could have been mustered by an influential leader in a more orderly and constructive fashion.[13]

The judiciaries of the extension states, with only a few exceptions, upheld the acts of their legislatures. One trial court judge in Alabama did condemn his state's extension law. In 1833 state authorities in St. Clair indicted Scott Mankiller, a Cherokee man, for the murder of his brother, Buck. The judge in the case released Mankiller, finding that the killing occurred within the Cherokee Nation and beyond Alabama's jurisdiction. In repudiating the state's extension law, the judge noted that Alabama had entered the Union with full knowledge of the treaties the federal government had negotiated with the tribes in the state. Those treaties, he pointed out, were a part of the supreme law of the land as it was defined in Article VI of the U.S. Constitution. The state, he concluded, had exceeded its authority when it arrested Mankiller. The Alabama Supreme Court had, however, already affirmed the constitutionality of the extension statute.[14]

Perhaps the most articulate critic of the removal policy among southern jurists was a justice on the Tennessee Supreme Court named Jacob Peck. In 1833 Tennessee authorities arrested two Cherokee men, James Foreman and Anderson Springston, and charged them with the murder of John "Chief Jack" Walker Jr., a highly regarded Cherokee legislator and partisan of the emerging "Treaty Party" that was calling on the Cherokee government to sign a removal treaty.[15] The killing had occurred in the Cherokee Nation, and the attorney for Foreman and Springston argued that the law extending the state's jurisdiction over the tribe's land was unconstitutional. When the trial judge agreed, the prosecution appealed the jurisdiction question to the state supreme court.

At the time that court consisted of three judges. John Catron, the chief judge and a protégé of Andrew Jackson, voted to uphold the Tennessee extension law and scoffed at the idea that the Cherokee people constituted a sovereign nation. Judge Nathan Green accepted the idea, espoused by John Marshall in *Cherokee Nation v. Georgia*, that the tribe was a "domestic, dependent nation" that retained some powers of self-government. However, he believed that the hostilities that had developed among the Cherokees, and between Cherokees and whites within the Cherokee Nation, required Tennessee to extend its criminal jurisdiction over the tribe. The votes of Catron and Green were sufficient to uphold the Tennessee extension law.

Jacob Peck's instincts about the extension law, on the other hand, were contrary to the views of his colleagues on the bench, to those of his state's governor, and to those of most of the Tennessee public; and he bravely chose to dissent. For the previous fifty years, he wrote, the United States had acknowledged the sovereignty of the Cherokee Nation and the states had accepted that precedent. Now, Peck complained, his state was in the control of states' rights radicals who threatened to destroy the precarious balance of federalism and the delicate relationships between the United States and the Indian nations. The Cherokee Nation was an independent, sovereign state, Peck argued, and the Tennessee extension statute was an unconstitutional attack on the Cherokees and intruded on their treaty relationship with the U.S. government. These treaties, moreover, proved that the Cherokees possessed essential elements of national sovereignty: territorial boundaries, the power to determine who could enter or live within their nation's borders, and unilateral jurisdiction over crimes committed in their territory. The Contract and Supremacy Clauses of the U.S. Constitution, Peck added, prohibited Tennessee from infringing on the rights acknowledged in those treaties.[16]

Peck's decision was particularly courageous in light of the sentiment of the voting public in Tennessee. However, by 1835, when he expressed his views, the removal express had essentially cleared the station. White southerners notoriously despised being lectured to by what they perceived to be hypocritical moralists from the Northeast, a region that had already exterminated or removed its Native residents. Here, however, was one of their own, defending the right of the Indian nations to retain their lands and govern themselves as they wished. One wonders what might have happened if passionate defenses of indigenous sovereignty by southern intellectuals such as Peck had appeared in southern newspapers at the time Congress was debating the

Indian removal bill. Peck's position, however, was generally anomalous in the South.

Private criticism of state action was also quite rare. Opposition to Georgia's extension legislation, however, did surface in *Nile's Weekly Register* when Robert Campbell, a lawyer from Savannah, offered to fund a petition against his state's general assembly. He declared, "In modern times in civilized countries there is no instance of expelling the members of a whole nation from their homes or driving an entire population from its native country." The state's efforts, he predicted accurately, "will bring enduring shame to Georgia's posterity." (As historian Mary Hershberger discovered, Campbell and other opponents of removal in Georgia kept northern newspapers apprised of the state's actions.) Only in Savannah, apparently, did newspapers in the state publish this kind of critique. To the west the *Auburn Free Press* and the *Cahawba Press and Alabama State Intelligencer* actually printed editorials condemning removal as an immoral policy that required the American government to take advantage of the tribes and welch on the promises made to them in several treaties. Again though, these were rare cries of protest in another state dead set on removal.[17] According to one historian who reviewed the papers of Mississippi, *The Natchez* was the only newspaper in the state to "have consistently supported the claims of the Indians to their lands in the East." The editor of *The Natchez* maintained that the Indians in Mississippi did not want to leave their homes, that the tribes were sovereign nations holding legitimate title to their lands, and that the state's extension law intruded on the federal government's constitutional responsibility over Indian affairs. Moreover, *The Natchez* said, Mississippi was using the extension laws to disenfranchise Indians and define them as an inferior caste. The vast majority in the extension-state South, however, cared deeply about white political equality but expressed little concern about the property and political rights of their Native neighbors.[18]

The Indian Removal Act

In 1829 Andrew Jackson's allies in Congress introduced the bill that would empower the president to implement his removal policy. The measure was received with acclamation by most whites in the extension states and pursued with gusto by their representatives in Congress. Still, the bill passed the House of Representatives by a very slender margin: 102–97. If three of the nays had voted to the contrary, in other words, the bill would have gone down in defeat. The Senate vote was relatively close as well: 28–19. One could argue, therefore, that the policy that today seems so inevitable in hindsight was a much closer run thing in 1830.[19]

The opposition to the bill in the South, and particularly in the extension states, was limited. The records of Congress are replete with petitions opposing the bill or calling for its repeal after it had passed; almost every single one of them originated from the North, from New England west to Ohio. Very few white southerners expressed concerns about removal to the Office of Indian Affairs or to their legislators or governors. We know that there were some—for the lack of a better descriptive—people of conscience in the extension states, so it is surprising that the congressional record is bereft of *any* remonstrance from the region. Perhaps groups led by dissenting individuals such as Robert Campbell, the Savannah lawyer mentioned above, did, in fact, present memorials, letters, or petitions opposing removal to their representatives and senators. It is unlikely, however, that their congressmen would have presented them to their respective deliberative bodies. Why would they have passed on statements opposing their own point of view or the wishes of a vast majority of their constituents?[20]

While the votes on the bill were relatively close, there was general unanimity among the southern representatives, and particularly among those from the extension states. According to one count, southern senators approved the bill by fourteen to three; western senators voted nine to three in favor; and northeasterners voted against by a count of thirteen to five. All of the senators from the states that extended jurisdiction, it is worth pointing out, voted for the removal bill. The situation in the House was much more complex. A number of southerners who considered themselves opponents of Jackson or who have been classified by historians and political scientists as "anti-Jacksonians" voted against the bill, including William Armstrong of Virginia; James Clark and Robert P. Letcher of Kentucky; Edmund Deberry and Lewis Williams of North Carolina; Philip Doddridge, Lewis Maxwell, Charles F. Mercer, and John Taliaferro of Virginia; and Edward D. White of Louisiana. Of course, the fact that Jackson's adversaries or disciples of Henry Clay would vote against Jacksonian legislation is not particularly surprising. However, it is noteworthy that several congressmen who have traditionally been considered as "Jackson men" opposed the removal bill, including Daniel L. Barringer, Edward B. Dudley, and Augustine H. Shepperd of North Carolina and Thomas Chilton and John Kincaid of Kentucky. (All five of them, by the way, subsequently became disillusioned with Jacksonianism and joined the Whig Party.)[21]

Not one of the dissidents mentioned above, however, hailed from a state that extended its jurisdiction over the Indian tribes. Only one congressman from those states opposed the removal bill, and that was, famously, David Crockett of Tennessee's ninth district. Crockett had entered Congress as a supporter of Jackson, but the Indian removal bill turned him against the president. Crockett condemned the bill in the House debate on May 19, 1830, after saying that he doubted another man within "500 miles of his residence would give a similar vote." He said that he was aware that "he had his constituents to settle with" but that he also had "a settlement to make at the bar of his God." He would do "what his conscience dictated would be just and right," he declared, "be the consequences what they might." He would have loved to have voted with his party, and with his colleagues from the West and the South, he said, but decided that "he would never let party govern him in a question of this great consequence."

Crockett then addressed the substance of his disfavor. He stated that "he had always viewed the native Indian tribes of this country as a sovereign people." "They had been recognized as such from the very foundation of this government," he asserted, "and the United States were bound by treaty to protect them." Crockett pointed out that the Indians did not want to leave their homeland. He knew many Cherokees who opposed removal, and one had told him, "No. We will take death here at our homes. Let them come and tomahawk us here at home; we are willing to die, but never to remove."

Crockett pointed out that his congressional district bordered the Chickasaw Nation, that he "knew many of their tribe," and that "nothing should ever induce him to vote to drive them west of the Mississippi." Furthermore, he knew nothing of the country where they were being asked to move. He would support appropriations for expeditions for the Chickasaws and the other tribes to inspect the lands the government had set aside for them in the West. "And when this had been done, and a fair and free treaty had been made with the tribes," he explained, "if they were desirous of removing, he would vote an appropriation of any sum necessary." Otherwise, he would not "vote one cent" for removal. He would not, moreover, put half a million dollars into the hands of the president "to be used in a manner to which nobody could foresee, and which Congress was not to control." In his peroration, Crockett said that "if he should be the only member of that House who voted against the bill, and the only man in the United States who disapproved it, he would still vote against it." As reward for his courage, Crockett's constituents turned him out at the next election.[22]

Although few in the extension states opposed the Indian Removal Act, at least one raised concerns about the headlong rush to expedite the expulsion of the tribes. At the end of 1830 the Georgia General Assembly passed legislation requiring the survey and subdivision of Cherokee territory and the distribution of it to white Georgians in a lottery. In subsequent months the state sent surveyors into the Cherokee Nation to prepare for the mass expropriation.[23]

In January of 1832 the *Milledgeville Recorder*, a paper that supported Jackson, published a remarkable condemnation of the impending land grab. First, the editor warned that the state's actions might damage the political standing of the president, who was supported by both of the political factions in the state. "What motive could induce those of both parties, who vie with each other in the expression of their veneration and attachment for Gen. Jackson, to pass *prematurely* an act for the survey and occupancy of the Cherokee country—a measure not in accordance with the strict rule of right—of doubtful, if not of dangerous policy; and which must greatly embarrass President

Jackson, if it does not injure his popularity, and hazard the loss of his election." Although the editor's point was to protect the president rather than prevent the removal of the Cherokees, it was one of the few public voices in the extension states to call for deliberate action. The editor apparently feared a repetition of the fiasco in South Carolina, where rabid states' rights partisans were abandoning their affinity for Jackson to pursue Calhoun's revolutionary theory of nullification.

The Milledgeville paper then condemned Wilson Lumpkin, the Georgia governor, for refusing to veto the survey and lottery act. Lumpkin was not, like the Founders, devoted to the "good of the Republic." Rather, he belonged to "that order of Modern Patriots, whose love of country consists in self-aggrandizement—who prop up an ephemeral, worthless popularity by doing whatever the whim of the people." The *Recorder* suggested that Lumpkin was the most noteworthy example in a state where citizens were drunk with the expectations of speculative profit. The editor reminded readers that the Georgia state seal included the motto "Justice, Wisdom, Moderation" and wondered whether the words represented "a *fact*, or . . . a mere *mockery*." Was it "cue of the attributes of *Justice* or of *Wisdom*," he wrote, "to get possession of lands or money, *per fas aut nefas?—by means fair or foul?*" The editor believed the state and its people had debased themselves in their hysterical grasping after Cherokee land. After suggesting that "*honesty is the best policy,*" he asked: "Is it honest then to seize on, and take by force, a piece of property that pleases our fancy but does not exactly belong to us?" The state, he complained, was pursuing a policy of "*might gives right,*" which "is the maxim of the ambitious unprincipled politician, but not of an honest, pious man."

States' rights removal activists had been arguing in their speeches, memorials, and legal briefs that, contrary to the overwhelming visible evidence, Indians in the South were nomadic peoples, that they did not practice agriculture, and that they therefore lacked a legal claim to their lands. The title of the states, they maintained, was superior to all others, including that of the United States. The Milledgeville editor repudiated this notion and offered an acknowledgment of Indian title that was exceptional in the extension states. "The Aborigines of the country," he wrote, still held "some rights in the soil of their native land, derived from the laws of Nature and of Nations—from being the first and only possessors." He agreed that the states "have a kind of reversionary claim to these Indian lands" that was "clear and indisputable." However, the state's claim to the Cherokees' lands would only ripen "whenever the Government of the U. States can purchase, as she is bound to do, for our use" the Indian title.

The editor then compared the state's trespasses on the Cherokees to the Spanish conquest of Native America. "The Spaniards were once the most chivalrous, warlike, enterprising people in all Europe," he wrote. "Instead of treating the Aborigines or Indians with some degree of justice and humanity, . . . they took away their lands by force, without paying any thing for them, and hunted the poor natives with blood-hounds." He then suggested that Georgia was in danger of constructing its own Black Legend: "Shall we Georgians imitate the example of these cruel Spaniards? God forbid!" He added that "as a punishment for their sins, [the Spanish] are become a proud, lazy, miserable race" and had "lost all their energy of character, and their ancient glory as a Nation." "Some ascribe this change to the discovery of the mines of Mexico and Peru," he observed, "if this be so, let us be wary of the Cherokee Gold Mines." The editor, however, had his own explanation for the decline of Spanish hegemony: "I attribute the degradation of old Spain and her once valiant sons . . . as a manifestation of the Divine wrath—as a punishment from Heaven for the injustice and cruelty practised on the Indians. . . . Let us profit by a knowledge of their fate." The *Milledgeville Recorder* then called for patience: "Let us be content to wait a few years longer for these Cherokee lands. We shall then get them, by purchase, made by the [federal] Government for our use, honestly and honorably, fairly. . . . Let us get the Cherokee country, not by *force* or *fraud*, but honestly, that we may enjoy our inheritance with a good conscience, and sustain our character, as individuals and as a State, free from reproach."[24]

The editor of the *Recorder* had at least one like-minded ally in the Georgia legislature. In a state senate debate on a resolution to finalize the sale of the Cherokee lottery lands to white Georgians, Josiah S. Patterson of Early County bemoaned the fact that, "they have given us the brightest empire in the world. We have taken their lands, their mountains, their streams." In return, he said, "we have given them our vices." "We talk of giving them a fair equivalent, but posterity will condemn us as unjust and untrue," he warned. "I tremble for my country, when I remember that God is just." These were outnumbered voices of restraint crying in a wilderness of self-interested speculators, men on the make, and racial fanatics.[25]

With the enactment of the removal bill, the Jackson administration immediately began to try to persuade and coerce the southern tribes into signing treaties that would result in their relocation. What little opposition to removal that had existed among white southerners faded as the years passed, as the southern Indian nations submitted to removal treaties, and as relocation became a fait accompli.

In the end the political resistance against removal in the extension states was weak, unorganized, and poorly led. In 1830 Charles Wilkes of Natchez probably identified why the idea of removal became federal policy that year. Wilkes said that he had discovered that "many were disposed to raise their voices in favor of this removal law." And, he added, "although many felt an interest" in defending the Indians from removal, "few were willing to step forward as the public champions of the poor children of the forest." Indeed, while there were individual acts of political courage, such as the one evinced by Crockett, what was missing was transcendent leadership in the South capable of challenging Jackson face-to-face on the policy and a concomitant ability to build an effective opposition to it. Such a countervailing force might have been able to offer Jackson and the removal advocates a compromise: the establishment of indigenous national enclaves (or what we now call reservations) on or within the general vicinity of the tribes' homelands.[26]

As I noted at the outset, however, my aim here was not to try to imagine a more sanguine counterfactual history of the removal crisis. Rather, my objective was to point out that a small measure of opposition existed in the South and, in the end, to lament that it never acquired traction in the region. Removal was not predestined or inevitable. However, it must have felt that way to those who opposed it in the South.

Notes

1. For a history of the development of the removal policy, see Tim Alan Garrison, *The Legal Ideology of Removal: The Southern Judiciary and the Sovereignty of Native American Nations* (Athens: University of Georgia Press, 2002), 13–33.

2. Albert Berry Saye, *A Constitutional History of Georgia, 1732–1968* (Athens: University of Georgia Press, 1970), 205; Robert V. Remini, *Andrew Jackson and His Indian Wars* (New York: Viking Penguin, 2001), 281; Reginald Horsman, *Race and Manifest Destiny: The Origins of Racial Anglo-Saxonism* (Cambridge MA: Harvard University Press, 1981), 189–207.

3. For an example of this narrative, see Francis Paul Prucha, *The Great Father: The United States Government and the American Indian* (Lincoln: University of Nebraska Press, 1984), 204–5.

4. The Indian nations in the North also resisted removal. However, this chapter focuses on the resistance in the South.

5. For the Second Seminole War, see John K. Mahon, *History of the Second Seminole War, 1835–1842* (Gainesville: University of Florida Press, 1967). For the Creek Removal Crisis, see Michael D. Green, *The Politics of Indian Removal: Creek Government and Society in Crisis* (Lincoln: University of Nebraska Press, 1982). For the Cherokee opposition, see Gary E. Moulton, *John Ross: Cherokee Chief* (Athens: University of Georgia Press, 1982), 34–105; Walter H. Conser Jr., "John Ross and the Cherokee Resistance Campaign, 1833–1838," *Journal of Southern History* 44, no. 2 (May 1978): 191–212; and Garrison, *Legal Ideology of Removal.* For Choctaw resistance, see James Taylor Carson, *Searching for the Bright Path: The Mississippi Choctaws from Prehistory to Removal* (Lincoln: University of Nebraska Press, 1999), 112–26. For Chickasaw resistance, see Cecil L. Summers, *Chief Tishomingo: A History of the Chickasaw Indians and Some Historical Events of Their Era* (Amory MS: Amory Advertiser, 1974), 116–25. For resistance by Cherokee women, see Tiya Miles, "'Circular Reasoning': Recentering Cherokee Women in the Antiremoval Campaigns," *American Quarterly* 61, no. 2 (June 2009): 221–43; Theda Perdue, *Cherokee Women* (Lincoln: University of Nebraska Press, 1998), 156–57; and Theda Perdue and Michael D. Green, *The Cherokee Removal: A Brief History with Documents* (Boston MA: Bedford/St. Martin's, 2005), 133–34.

6. These resisters and their children and grandchildren remained in their isolated hideaways until their descendants reemerged and constructed their own national polities. For the establishment of the Eastern Band of Cherokee Indians, see John R. Finger, *The Eastern Band of Cherokees, 1819–1900* (Knoxville: University of Tennessee Press, 1984) and *Cherokee Americans: The Eastern Band of Cherokees in the Twentieth Century* (Lincoln: University of Nebraska Press, 1991). For the Seminoles, see the works of Harry A. Kersey Jr. For the Mississippi Choctaws, see Samuel J. Wells and Roseanna Tubby, *After Removal: The Choctaw in Mississippi* (Jackson: University of Mississippi Press, 1986).

7. William G. McLoughlin, *Cherokees and Missionaries, 1789–1839* (New Haven CT: Yale University Press, 1984), 239–334, and *Cherokee Renascence in the New Republic* (Princeton NJ: Princeton University Press, 1986), 428–47; Mary Hershberger, "Mobilizing Women, Anticipating Abolition: The Struggle against Indian Removal in the 1830s," *The Journal of American History* 86, no. 1 (June 1999): 15–40; Alisse Portnoy, *Their Right to Speak: Women's Activism in the Indian and Slave Debates* (Cambridge MA: Harvard University Press, 2009); John A. Andrew III, *From Revivals to Removal: Jeremiah Evarts, the Cherokee Nation, and the Search for the Soul of America* (Athens: University of Georgia Press, 2007); Prucha, *The Great Father*, 200–208.

8. Mark R. Leutbecker examined the opposition in the newspapers in Alabama and Mississippi in a few pages of "Some Public Views on Indian Removal in the South, 1820–1840" (MA thesis, Louisiana State University, 1973). Ronald N. Satz, in *American Indian Policy in the Jacksonian Era* (Lincoln: University of Nebraska Press, 1975), 20–31, touched tangentially on the attitudes of southern males. Michael Paul Rogin explored the psyches of Jackson and his followers in *Fathers and Children: Andrew Jackson and the Subjugation of the American Indian* (New York: Alfred A. Knopf, 1971). Many scholars, including Thomas Gossett and Reginald Horsmen, have examined the racial views of nineteenth-century white southerners. A passel of law professors comprising a list that is too long to mention here, and even a sitting U.S. Supreme Court justice, have examined the Cherokee cases in detail. Some of these works make references to how white southern men thought about the removal policy. However, they have not looked closely at those who opposed removal in the region.

9. Thomas Jefferson to Edmund Pendleton, August 13, 1776, *The Papers of Thomas Jefferson*, ed. Julian P. Boyd, 25 vols. (Princeton NJ: Princeton University Press, 1950–1992) 1:494; *Acts of the General Assembly of the State of Georgia*, December 26, 1827 (Milledgeville GA: Camak and Ragland, 1828), 99–101; *Acts of the General Assembly of the State of Georgia*, December 20, 1828 (Milledgeville GA: Camak and Ragland, 1829), 87–89; *Acts of the General Assembly of the State of Georgia*, December 19, 1829 (Milledgeville GA: Camak and Ragland, 1830), 270; *Journal of the Senate of the State of Georgia*, December 16, 1829 (Milledgeville GA: Camak and Ragland, 1830), 269; *Journal of the House of Representatives of the State of Georgia*, December 11, 1829 (Milledgeville GA: Camak and Ragland, 1830), 247; *Georgia Messenger*, November 27, 1830; *Records of the States of the United States of America, Alabama, B.I. 1823–1833*, 223–25; *Public Acts Passed at the First Session of the Twentieth General Assembly of the State of Tennessee, 1833* (Nashville TN: Allen A. Hall and F. S. Heiskell, 1833), 10–12; Garrison, *Legal Ideology of Removal*, 13–24; McLoughlin, *Cherokee Renascence*, 394–401; Theodore Henley Jack, "Sectionalism and Party Politics in Alabama, 1819–1842" (PhD diss., University of Chicago, 1919), 37–54.

10. *Acts of the General Assembly of the State of Georgia*, December 19, 1829, 270; *Journal of the Senate of the State of Georgia*, December 16, 1829, 269; *Journal of the House of Representatives of the State of Georgia*, December 11, 1829, 247; *Georgia Messenger*, November 27, 1830.

11. William H. Freehling, *Prelude to Civil War: The Nullification Controversy in South Carolina, 1816–1836* (New York: Harper and Row, 1966), 232–34; *Georgia Journal* (Milledgeville), January 20, 1831, 3.

12. Unfortunately for the author of this chapter, the act passed by voice vote in the state house, so we cannot know how many or who exactly opposed the law in that assembly. *Records of the States, Alabama,* 223–25; Edwin A. Miles, *Jacksonian Democracy in Mississippi* (New York: De Capo Press, 1970), 24–25, 161.

13. *General Assembly of the State of Tennessee, 1833,* 10–12; *American Railroad Journal and Advocate of Internal Improvements* 2, no. 45 (November 9, 1833): 718; *Richmond Enquirer,* November 8, 1833. For Jacksonian-era politics in Tennessee, see Jonathan M. Atkins, *Parties, Politics, and the Sectional Conflict in Tennessee, 1832–1861* (Knoxville: University of Tennessee Press, 1997), chapters 1 and 2.

14. "Indians in Alabama," *Richmond Enquirer,* October 22, 1833; Caldwell v. Forman, 6 Stewart and Potter 327 (Ala. 1831).

15. For my account of the murder of Chief Jack Walker, see Garrison, *Legal Ideology of Removal,* 198–233.

16. Tennessee v. Forman, 204–6, 207, 211–29.

17. Hershberger, "Mobilizing Women," 23. Mark R. Leutbecker wrote that "opposition to Indian removal in Alabama and Georgia in the form of the printed word was almost non-existent." "Some Public Views on Indian Removal," 175, 182–84.

18. The extension legislation, for instance, proscribed Choctaws and Chickasaws from serving on juries and from testifying in court. Leutbecker, "Some Public Views on Indian Removal," 175–82, citing *The Natchez,* February 13, April 3, May 8, and September 18, 1830.

19. For a history of the bill, see Satz, *American Indian Policy in the Jacksonian Era,* 9–63.

20. Leutbecker, "Some Public Views on Indian Removal," 191. I did not find a single memorial from an extension state, even though, as Wilson Lumpkin reported, "thousands" of petitions with "millions" of signatures poured into Congress. Wilson Lumpkin, *The Removal of the Cherokee Indians from Georgia,* 2 vols. (New York: Dodd, Mead and Company, 1907), 1:47.

21. Alfred A. Cave, "Abuse of Power: Andrew Jackson and the Indian Removal Act of 1830," *The Historian* 65, no. 6: 1330–53; Kenneth Penn Davis, "Ousting the Cherokees from Georgia" (MA thesis, Georgia State College, 1968), 49–50n19; *Journal of the House of Representatives of the United States, 1829–1830,* May 26, 1830 (Washington DC: Duff Green, 1830), 730; *Journal of the Senate of the United States of America, 1789–1873,* April 24, 1830 (Washington DC: Duff Green, 1830), 268.

22. Jeremiah Evarts, ed., "A Sketch of the Remarks of the Hon. David Crockett," in *Speeches on the Passage of the Bill for the Removal of the Indians* (Boston MA: Perkins and Marvin, 1830), 251; James R. Boylston and Allen J. Wiener, *David Crockett in Congress: The Rise and Fall of the Poor Man's Friend* (Houston TX: Bright Sky Press, 2009), 65–75. One of Crockett's biographers argued that by this point the congressman had split with Jackson and was in the middle of a flirtation with the Whig Party. Crockett may have opposed the removal bill, under this theory, as a politi-

cal strike against Jackson. James Atkins Shackford, *David Crockett: The Man and the Legend* (Chapel Hill: University of North Carolina Press, 1956), 116–36. In my view, the motivations were not mutually exclusive.

23. *Acts of the General Assembly of the State of Georgia,* December 21, 22, and 23, 1830 (Milledgeville GA: Camak and Ragland, 1831).

24. *Columbus (GA) Enquirer,* January 7, 1832, republishing an editorial by the *Milledgeville (GA) Recorder,* 2.

25. Mary Young, "Racism in Red and Black: Indians and Other Free People of Color in Georgia Law, Politics, and Removal Policy," in *Georgia Historical Quarterly* 73, no. 3 (Fall 1989): 517.

26. Charles Wilkes, *The Natchez,* April 3, 1830, quoted in Leutbecker, "Some Public Views on Removal," 192.

Seven

An Absolute and Unconditional Pardon
Nineteenth-Century Cherokee Indigenous Justice

JULIE L. REED

By the end of 1839, the bulk of the Cherokees who had resisted removal, experienced incarceration in internment camps in Tennessee and Georgia, and marched nine hundred miles to the west arrived in Indian Territory widowed, orphaned, indigent, sick, weak, exploited, grieving, and politically divided. The best estimates place the number of Cherokee deaths that resulted from the removal process at approximately 25 percent of the total population.[1] Those numbers suggest every Cherokee family lost a family member or a neighbor as a direct result of removal. Applying traditional law, only recently dislodged by national laws, the individuals or their respective clans who signed the removal treaty bore responsibility for the lives lost. The political centralization process that had taken place over the previous generation, in part to fend off removal, masked and muted older understandings of social policy still practiced and transported west in families. Clan law expected those responsible to make amends with their lives in order to restore balance and for those lost to move on to the Darkening Land. The demographic disaster and social rupture created by removal exposed the ways grieving survivors struggled to reconcile newer national social policy related to wrongdoing and homicide with an older system governed by kinship responsibilities and clan law to deal with political, economic, and family trauma. In June of 1839 those Cherokees subjected to forced removal, including Principal Chief John Ross's son, whose mother and clan kin Quatie died during removal, planned the executions of key Removal Treaty signers. The younger Ross remained with his father while others carried out the coordinated executions of Elias Boudinot, John Ridge, and Major Ridge that month. Treaty signer Stand Watie, a family member of the Ridges and Boudinot, only escaped execution through advance warning.[2] Over seventy-five individuals participated in the executions, slightly more than the total number who signed the removal treaty. The catastrophic loss faced by the Cherokees demanded a legal response, but as removal and its aftershocks suggest, the extension of Cherokee national laws did not ensure the erasure of traditional practices.

This chapter describes how, over the course of the nineteenth century, Cherokee people rejected, interpreted, navigated, used, and reconciled national policies governing amnesty and pardon with older legal theory that had established procedures to restore wrongdoers and those wronged to each other. The introduction of an executive pardon applicable to all criminal cases, even homicide, violated traditional legal precedents, but it also provided a new bureaucratic procedure through which Cherokee people and the U.S. government interacted with the Cherokee Nation. Examining the use of amnesty and pardon applications provides another means of understanding how older legal theory, gender, race, class, and sovereignty intertwined to determine whose wrongdoing could be absolved, under what conditions, and according to whom, as well as how this changed over time. As the Cherokee Nation centralized, it excluded women from the formal political and democratic processes previously available to them under traditional social policy. This created a conspicuously gendered legal space dominated by men. However, Cherokee people's use of the executive pardon provided a new legal arena where women participated and asserted political rights. Cherokee people were not the only ones making use of the pardon as a bureaucratic mechanism. Because the Cherokee Nation regularly confronted jurisdictional issues with federal courts and established compacts with neighboring Native nations, the bureaucratic use of the executive pardon provides additional insight into questions of race and sovereignty in Indian Territory.

Throughout most of the eighteenth century, rather than meting out "justice," penalties for clan or community violations aimed to restore temporal and cosmic balance. Legal obligations were clear.

Town elders publicly announced the law that reminded everyone of their duties and responsibilities to each other at annual ceremonies. Clans and towns had until the time of the Green Corn Ceremony to administer punishments in all cases except homicide. Preparations for the Green Corn ritualism required individual and community purifications; everyone went "to water" in the river and received medicinal roots to continue purification rituals at home. Men hunted and gathered wood; women prepared food; everyone fasted, including children. Buildings were repaired. Homes were cleaned. The Sacred Fire polluted by the wrongdoing of the previous year was reignited. All was made anew.

Community restoration through ceremonies reinforced the importance of all members of society. Daily responsibilities and ceremonial preparations balanced the labor and contributions of men and women, old and young; everyone had an equal responsibility to the health and well-being of the entire community. Oral traditions emphasized an egalitarian view of community and valued the contributions that all Cherokee people had made and should continue to make, regardless of age, ability, or gender. All members of the community had abilities and an obligation to contribute to the well-being of their families and their community. This renewal included restoration of Cherokee people to one another. No one could participate in the ceremony if anger or hostilities remained.[3] Cherokee livelihood, food, homes, and communities depended on the ability of Cherokee people to pardon offenses and move into the future restored.

The Cherokee Nation's social policies, including how it responded to wrongdoing, underwent rapid change from 1800 to 1830, when the Indian Removal Act passed. It moved from an older system that privileged the local community and the wronged clan's authority to determine the appropriate punishment for a wrongdoer to a constitutional republic in 1827, bound by obligations to citizens. The first written law in 1808 extended a pardon to officers of the Nation for homicides committed while carrying out their official duties. An 1810 law criminalized the killing of one brother by another, whereas older law granted clans the ability to pardon a brother.[4] Both of these laws attempted to shift how Cherokees conceived of pardonable offenses. Crimes and restoration were no longer matters managed by clans and communities; they were crimes that harmed the Nation and challenged its national authority. These changes occurred, in part, so that Cherokees could better defend against attacks on their communal landholdings by the surrounding American states and the U.S. government. The national system included local and district courts and a national supreme court complete with judges, juries, and lawyers.

A full pardon of the treaty signers was not an option by traditional or national social policy. Traditional social policy used annual ceremonies to restore all people to one another, purify the spaces Cherokee people occupied, and set aside all wrongs committed the previous year. The single exception to the wrongs annual ceremonies righted was homicide. Traditional law did allow those who committed homicide to seek a temporary respite in refuge towns, but land losses in the East followed by the removal of Cherokee people from their homelands placed refuge towns nine hundred miles away and under the control of non-Cherokees.[5] There were no refuge towns in Indian Territory in the West. In Indian Territory just after removal, homicide required those clans whose members were responsible, directly or indirectly, to forfeit their lives to restore balance to the world and quiet the blood of the deceased. The extralegal processes that led to the executions hearkened back to older Cherokee legal practices when community members, not national officers, enforced the law.

National leaders justified the executioners' actions against the Treaty Party members as based on national law that barred individual Cherokees from ceding land that belonged to and protected the social well-being of all Cherokee people. Contributing to the extralegal process, no unified court system yet existed in the West in June 1839 to carry out the formal procedures to charge and try treaty signers for their national crimes. Less than three months after the executions and after Cherokee men passed an Act of Union and wrote a new constitution to govern all Cherokees in the West, the National Council passed legislation allowing citizens of districts to petition the principal chief for the release or acquittal of those found guilty of murder.[6] Not only did this continue a centralizing process, it introduced a legal mechanism that might have mediated the events that led to the executions of Major Ridge, John Ridge, and Elias Boudinot.

Despite this legal reform, the loss and sorrow federal removal policy had instigated continued to manifest itself through Cherokee men's violent acts against other Cherokee men. From 1839 to 1846 officials' abilities to discern between criminal activity and political violence became difficult. In many ways, these actions can be understood as a legitimate psychological response to group trauma. In 1843 Stand Watie killed Cherokee James Foreman, who was linked to the killing of his brother, cousin, and uncle. Watie stood trial and was found not guilty on the grounds of self-defense. In 1845 Watie's brother Thomas was killed during ongoing reprisals.[7] Because of the violence, the Cherokee council reestablished the light horse, the Cherokee Nation police, which Treaty Party members viewed less as a police force and more as an arm of the executive branch to put down political detractors.

In the aftermath of removal and civil strife, the Cherokee Nation included an amnesty provision in the Treaty of 1846 to reconcile the Treaty Party and the National Party. It granted amnesty for all "offenses and crimes committed by a citizen or citizens of the Cherokee Nation against the nation, or against an individual or individuals." It invited those who had sought refuge outside the Nation to return to their homes so that they could "unite in enforcing the laws against all future offenders."[8]

Amnesty, in theory, made homicide a pardonable offense on a massive scale. The internal use of amnesty that followed the Cherokees' civil war performed a similar function to those previously provided by annual ceremonies, but amnesty distorted the once-egalitarian processes by excluding women, elders, and children. It ignored those individuals' demands, voices, expectations, and importance to community restoration. The U.S. Civil War, as it played out in Indian Territory, suggests the amnesty issued in 1846 could not provide long-term internal stability and may not have fulfilled the needs of those governed by older social policy.

Just fifteen years after the civil conflict that followed removal came to a close, Cherokee families yet again faced the harsh realities of a divided nation. Other scholars have examined the events that led to the Cherokees' participation in the U.S. Civil War in detail.[9] Briefly outlined, Principal Chief John Ross hoped to avoid participation in the Civil War, but pressure mounted early when Texas and Arkansas seceded from the Union in February and May of 1861 respectively. The federal Indian agent resigned his post and joined the Confederacy. The Confederacy appointed Albert Pike, an Arkansas attorney who had represented the Creek, Choctaw, and Chickasaw nations, as its Commissioner of Indian Affairs; it then authorized him to negotiate generous treaties with the tribes.[10]

When the federal government withdrew troops from Indian Territory and sporadically paid its annuities, it left tribes militarily and economically vulnerable. The Creek, Choctaw, and Chickasaw nations all signed treaties with the Confederacy in early July 1861 and the Seminoles signed their treaty August 1. Stand Watie viewed an alliance with the Confederacy as an opportunity to supplant Ross's leadership. When the Confederacy commissioned Stand Watie as a colonel, it undermined the Nation's ability to maintain its official neutrality. In October 1861 the Cherokee Nation was the last of the Five Tribes to conclude an alliance with the Confederacy. The Cherokee units segregated into Ross and Watie supporters. Later, most Ross supporters joined Indian Home Guard units in support of the Union.

Cherokee women's activities and choices during the war suggest the possibility that the "amnesty" issued in 1846 by and for men did not necessarily fulfill some women's spiritual and legal expectations for the losses they endured. Carolyn Johnston submits that women who raided the homes of other women during the Civil War were possibly applying a traditional social policy that required wealth be redistributed and shared, especially during times of deprivation. She also suggests traditionally minded women were acting out angst over growing racial and class divides in the Cherokee Nation.[11] A third possibility is that women's exclusion from the 1846 effort at community reconciliation left the world out of balance for those women who adhered to traditional social policy. Susan Riley, who was four years old when the war began, described her mother's experiences with other women during the war and noted, "the women belonging to the Pins [Cherokee traditionalists also known as Keetoowahs] were just as bad, if not worse, than the men, as they ransacked the house."[12]

Regardless of what guided women's actions, multiple views on morality and community ethics coupled with shifting approaches to how and when to pardon offenses and restore the community left women without formal spaces to renew their relationships with one another in the post-removal era.

The U.S. Civil War destroyed the political unity Ross sought to maintain and the "strife among [Cherokee people]" he had hoped to avoid.[13] At the close of the war two Cherokee governments existed and both sent delegations to meet with federal officials to negotiate a treaty. After protracted negotiations, the United States signed a new treaty with the delegation led by Principal Chief John Ross that included concessions for the southern Cherokee delegation led by Stand Watie.[14]

The Treaty of 1866 that reestablished the terms of the nation-to-nation relationship between the United States and the Cherokee Nation included an amnesty provision that performed a civil and international function. Article II offered amnesty on behalf of the United States and the Cherokee Nation "for all crimes and misdemeanors committed by one Cherokee on the person or property of another Cherokee, or of a citizen of the United States, prior to the fourth day of July, eighteen hundred and sixty-six; and no right of action arising out of wrongs committed in aid or in the suppression of the rebellion shall be prosecuted or maintained in the courts of the United States or in the courts of the Cherokee Nation."[15] U.S. and Cherokee Nation officials granted amnesty to all those who committed offenses during wartime, including the women who raided the homes of other Cherokee people and the women who failed to abide by a community ethic that required everyone, including those with the most, to share their resources with others.

The Cherokee Nation's pardon process became far more salient following the Civil War because of the legal reforms it enacted. By 1873 the Nation moved forward with plans to build a prison it had negotiated decades earlier, but had been unable to achieve due to budget constraints.[16] The following year the council approved its New Codes, which maintained use of the executive pardon based on "such conditions and restrictions as [the executive] may think proper."[17] In anticipation of the prison sentences that would replace the use of the lash to punish offenders, the executive gained the ability to commute the prison sentences for anyone convicted of a crime.[18]

The Cherokee Nation's legal reforms coupled with the introduction of the prison reflected similar trends in the United States, but deviated from a traditional system that privileged freedom of movement and the autonomy of Cherokee people. Confinement ended the relative immediacy of punishments that had been inflicted before the Civil War and limited the ability of the incarcerated to fulfill their familial and community obligations. External threats levied by territorializers, speculators, reformers, and politicians led many to see the prison as a necessary evil.[19]

Appeals for pardon became a means for Cherokee people to communicate their expectations for legal reforms with the Nation. For example, in 1895, Cherokee petitioners sought an "unconditional pardon" for James Peacock, who was convicted by the Cherokee courts of attempted murder. Applications for pardon usually came from a single community group on behalf of an incarcerated individual. In the James Peacock case, however, competing appeals arrived at the executive branch. The petitioners for pardon invoked arguments that favored families headed by economically independent men. Petitioners argued Peacock needed to care for his blind wife and child and attend to his farm. He headed his family, his wife and children were dependent on him, and he was solely responsible for their livelihood. Another group of citizens presented a petition that "respectfully asked that no clemency be shown to James Peacock, a convict in the National Prison" for what they described as one of "the most treacherous and atrocious crimes ever committed in the Cherokee Nation by a human by attempting to steal the lives of a man and wife while peacefully sleeping in their own house, by chopping them with an axe and then leaving them for dead."[20] The circumstances of the case were in fact quite different from other cases. Most attempted murder and murder cases involved whiskey and/or money. This case involved neither.

The competing arguments framed by the petitioners revealed the extent to which families who adhered to traditional social welfare practices tenuously supported the Nation's reforms. Petitioners who objected to Peacock's pardon invoked older systems of community responsibilities that favored the wronged party above the wrongdoer and provided protection to its members. They asked "in justice to our laws, and to his victims" that Peacock be denied a pardon. They supported the current system of justice because Peacock's conviction performed the function of a traditional social service system. If that system failed, they feared, "neighborhood trouble" could arise.[21] The veiled threat implied that the older system of blood vengeance could and would be employed if the national system of courts, juries, jails, and pardons failed.

Petitioners opposing Peacock's pardon also described the use of *gadugi*, cooperative labor by men and women in the community, to protect its members. Peacock's wife, they said, had "always" called upon her "friends for protection," which implied that kinship and reciprocity supported and protected the woman more than her husband. Petitioners suggested that her husband was actually a threat to her; they insisted that the woman would need even more assistance if the executive granted clemency.[22] Her community, not her husband, provided her care and protection. The community, therefore, consented to the Cherokee Nation's institutional social services based on the Nation's ability to uphold and support traditional social service principles, including its responsibility to protect its members.

Throughout the nineteenth century, U.S. citizens' requests for and the president's use of the executive pardon had increased. In 1896, 64 percent of all federal prisoners received a pardon, some of whom had not even applied for one. Some of this is explained by the limited use of parole or probation as options for release. The absence of federal facilities and the need to house federal prisoners in state institutions offer another reason for its prevalence.[23]

By the late nineteenth century many Cherokee leaders articulated similar justifications for pardons as those living in the United States. But others articulated the Cherokee peoples' use of the pardon as one that extended from their traditional social service system and a different philosophical worldview than those reflected in United States legal systems.[24] Traditional social services functioned at their best when they achieved restorative balance, not retributive justice.[25] The sheer number of pardon applications, over 240 applications in the Cherokee Nation papers alone, reveal the willingness of Cherokee communities to excuse convicted criminals, yet they also reveal the debates within the community over who could be restored and who could not and under what conditions.[26]

Almost universally, Cherokees embraced the use of an executive pardon in the post–Civil War period, but how they navigated the process reflected their everyday reliance on national versus traditional social service systems. Cherokee people adapted the use of a pardon process to conform to their particular social service worldviews, but how Cherokee people applied for pardons within the community adhered to gendered patterns, some of which they deployed outside the Cherokee Nation as well. Most petitions for pardon came from men in the community who sought to correct some legal error. The second most common appeal came from attorneys on behalf of women who sought pardons for family members. Cherokee men and women utilized the pardon process based on the social service needs of their families and communities.

In their appeals for pardons, men tended to challenge the legality of trials, points of law, and unethical or problematic actions of jurors. The people who presented such appeals often included the signatures of hundreds of men from the appellants' community to support their claims.[27] Petitions from leading men did not guarantee one's release. In October of 1893, for example, the *Advocate* reported that "a strong petition was presented to the Chief for commutation of the sentence of Sam Mayes who was hung yesterday."[28] But such petitions often succeeded. For example, Chief Clerk of the Senate L. B. Bell visited Principal Chief Oochalata with a petition for executive clemency on behalf of John Still.[29] The courts had convicted Still of the murder of Edwin Downing and sentenced him to seven years of hard labor. The petition carried by Bell claimed that juror Moses

Fields was "not of lawful age." Therefore, the court convicted Still based on an illegal trial. Jennie Stinson, an adoptive mother who "raised the said Moses Fields from infancy," testified that he was between the age of nineteen and twenty at the date of the trial rather than twenty-one, the age required of jurors.[30] Based on her affidavit and a petition from "a large number of responsible citizens," the executive council "unanimously advised the unconditional pardon of the said John Still." Less than eight weeks after the conviction, Principal Chief Oochalata Charles Thompson set John Still free.[31]

Despite nineteenth-century changes that had excluded Cherokee women from political office and service on juries, women used the pardon to appeal to forms of justice that existed before written laws, modern courts, and the use of a prison. Women used appeals much as they had petitions during the removal era; they invoked their matrilineal rights as mothers and sisters, but applications for pardon also reflected the willingness of many women to advocate for their husbands. In 1882 the wife of Sam Beaver told Principal Chief Dennis Bushyhead that her husband was crippled and could "only be a burden on the prison keepers."[32] For Beaver, imprisonment did not provide justice. To achieve justice, traditional Cherokee people sought a restoration of balance. The jailors, in a sense, were being punished for Beaver's crime; this did not achieve balance. A wrongdoer must pay for his crimes, but not at the expense of another.

William Grapes's mother combined older interpretations of Cherokee legal thinking with the newer goals promoted by reformers when she argued for her son's pardon. During his arrest he was "shot several times and crippled for life." For his mother, this was "punishment enough" and "such a severe lesson that he would be a reformed man if given another chance."[33] Traditionally, Cherokee people did not seek punishments; they sought a restoration of both temporal and cosmic order. The injuries of these men balanced their crime; the addition of prison terms amounted to overkill.

Appeals for pardons also exposed the complex negotiations produced by intertribal compacts, race, and sovereignty in Indian Territory. In 1880 officials of the district court at Fort Smith wrote Principal Chief Bushyhead to seek a pardon for Jeff Marshall, "a negro" convicted of larceny in 1879, so that he could testify in a federal case against "a gang of thieves" accused of robbing railroad company trains.[34] Without Marshall, the court had not been able to "procure sufficient proof to convict them." On its surface, this case was a routine bureaucratic negotiation between two sovereign bodies. Marshall was a Creek Nation citizen subject to the laws of the Cherokee Nation by virtue of an 1843 intertribal compact, but the federal court and railroad corporations needed his assistance.[35] Jeff Marshall fully understood the importance of his testimony and leveraged the U.S. court against the Cherokee Nation.

The Marshall case reveals how issues of law, race, intertribal politics, and sovereignty collided as the Cherokee Nation navigated what threatened to provide further ammunition for outsiders to attack Native nations' rights to exist. The Marshall case followed two significant events. First, in 1878, the Senate Committee on Territories began holding hearings to disuss the extension of U.S. jurisdiction over Indian Territory. In order to bolster support from railroad officials and the few Indian Territory citizens in favor of territorialization, the Committee chose to hold their meetings in railroad towns in Indian Territory, infuriating Cherokee people and national officials. The locations encouraged the participation and highlighted the voices of a Cherokee minority in favor of territorialization. Efforts to build railroads and territory measures increasingly went hand-in-hand. Most Cherokees felt no sympathy for the owners when individuals robbed the railroads.

The second event involved intertribal disputes over cattle theft between African-Creeks and Cherokees along the Cherokee-Creek border, where Jeff Marshall had lived. Many of the Cherokees involved were members of former slaveholding families and the families of intermarried white men. As the violence escalated on both sides, Cherokee vigilantes took direct aim at African-Creek light horse. In 1880 Cherokees seized two African-Creeks and lynched them. A gun battle followed, resulting in Cherokee men's deaths. Cherokee Nation citizens argued that the Creek Nation failed to police its border towns.[36]

Creek Nation residents worried that African-Creeks could not possibly receive fair trials in the Cherokee district courts. This climate likely contributed to Marshall's refusal to testify without the pardon and explains the reluctance of his family, who were also witnesses, to do the same.

Becoming desperate, the U.S. district court offered to exchange "twelve Creek negroes" accused of robberies, possibly the crimes on the Cherokee-Creek border, and held at Fort Smith on other charges in exchange for Marshall's testimony.[37] The Cherokee Nation refused the swap. Instead, when Marshall's sentence expired on November 10, 1881, the Cherokee Nation released Marshall with his new suit of clothes and his five-dollar cash payment as it did for other Cherokee citizens.[38] Despite racial tensions between the Creeks and Cherokees, protecting tribal sovereignty trumped the interests of the federal courts doing the bidding of railroads.

By the late 1880s federal Indian policy shifted. Increasingly, politicians lobbied by railroads, speculators, and progressive northeastern reformers favored the allotment of communally held lands into individually owned tracts and U.S. territorialization of Indian Territory. Despite successfully lobbying Congress for an exemption to the Dawes Allotment Act in 1887, the Cherokee Nation was subjected to allotment and its courts were dissolved when the federal government passed the Curtis Act in 1898.

Yet the question of what to do with those already incarcerated in the Cherokee national prison remained. By 1900 the Cherokee Nation and the federal government had reached an impasse over what to do about the prison. The federal government broadly criticized the prison's operations, from its architecture to its budget, but offered no concrete solution or additional funding to address these problems. Despite the president's disapproval, on January 18, 1900, Principal Chief Samuel Mayes granted an "absolute and unconditional pardon to all persons who have been heretofore convicted in the courts of the Cherokee Nation of a violation of Cherokee law." The pardon also extended to "all other persons . . . convicted or indicted by the courts of the Cherokee Nation" the restoration of their "full rights of citizenship."[39]

In a final act of sovereign authority and in anticipation of allotment, the Cherokee Nation used its executive pardon to restore Cherokee people to their families and community. The centralizing political processes that had occurred over the previous century had erased the universal political and democratic participation previously exercised by Cherokee people. For the individuals pardoned, it restored their personal autonomy, a crucial factor for better managing the allotment process, which would prove to be a legally, socially, economically, and personally denigrating process for most Cherokee people. Ironically, the introduction of the executive pardon represented a continuation of centralizing efforts as it simultaneously added an avenue for those who lacked political rights, namely women, to exercise their political voice. Though amnesty and the pardon were engineered with the support of U.S. officials to manage internal civil strife and its larger impacts, as Jeff Marshall's case made clear, Cherokee officials used the power of the executive pardon and its national institutions as sovereign diplomatic tools, intertribally and with the federal government. Symbolically, that final pardon, more than any other, stood to accomplish what the annual ceremonies had also aimed to achieve. Any chance Cherokees had at facing down allotment collectively required internal anger and hostilities to be washed away.[40] Achieving a world as close to balanced as possible was paramount; Cherokee livelihood, food, homes, and communities depended on the ability of Cherokee people to pardon offenses and attempt to move into the future restored to one another.

Notes

1. Demographer Russell Thornton generally accepts approximately four thousand deaths, but he argues the numbers have to include the numbers lost because of the disruption to normal family life cycles. Cherokee population was on an upswing before removal. Removal, therefore, did not just take the lives of those who died, but those who should have been born had removal and the civil war that followed not disrupted their parents' and grandparents' lives. Russell Thornton, *The Cherokees: A Population History* (Lincoln: University of Nebraska Press, 1990), 47–78. John Ross lost his wife Quatie from pneumonia during removal. Thurman Wilkins, *Cherokee Tragedy: The Story of the Ridge Family and the Decimation of a People* (New York: Macmillan, 1970), 327–28. The Beaver, a disabled War of 1812 pensioner, died during

removal. Beaver, War of 1812 Pension and Bounty Land Warrant Application Files, compiled ca. 1871–ca. 1900, documenting the period 1812–ca. 1900, Record Group 75 (hereafter cited as RG75) M208, National Archives and Records Administration, Washington DC (hereafter cited as NARA).

2. Michelle Daniel, "From Blood Feud to Jury System: The Metamorphosis of Cherokee Law from 1750 to 1840," *American Indian Quarterly* (Spring 1987): 113–14.

3. Charles Hudson, *The Southeastern Indians* (Knoxville: University of Tennessee Press, 1976), 367–70.

4. Cherokee Nation, *Laws of the Cherokee Nation: Adopted by the Council at Various Periods [1808–1835] Printed for the Benefit of the Nation* (Cherokee Advocate Office, 1852; hereafter cited as LCN), 3–4.

5. James Mooney and Cary Michael Carney, *Historical Sketch of the Cherokee* (New Brunswick NJ: Aldine Transaction, 2005), 215–16.

6. LCN, 4, 5–15, 17–18.

7. W. Craig Gaines, *The Confederate Cherokees: John Drew's Regiment of Mounted Rifles* (Baton Rouge: Louisiana State University Press, 1989), 5.

8. The treaty reads, "Amnesty is hereby declared by the United States and the Cherokee Nation for all crimes and misdemeanors committed by one Cherokee on the person or property of another Cherokee, or of a citizen of the United States . . . and no right of action arising out of wrongs committed in aid or in the suppression of the rebellion shall be prosecuted or maintained in the courts of the United States or in the courts of the Cherokee Nation." "Treaty with the Cherokee, 1846, Article 2," in Charles J. Kappler, ed., *Indian Affairs Laws and Treaties* (Washington DC: Government Printing Office, 1904), 562.

9. For a more detailed explanation of the events see, Annie Heloise Abel, *The American Indian in the Civil War, 1862–1865* (Lincoln: University of Nebraska Press, 1919); Clarissa W. Confer, *The Cherokee Nation in the Civil War* (Norman: University of Oklahoma Press, 2012); William G. McLoughlin, *After the Trail of Tears: The Cherokees' Struggle for Sovereignty, 1839–1880,* 1st ed. (Chapel Hill: University of North Carolina Press, 1994), 121–254.

10. Gaines, *The Confederate Cherokees*, 7–10; Confer, *The Cherokee Nation in the Civil War*; Laurence M. Hauptman, *Between Two Fires* (New York: The Free Press, 1995), 41–65.

11. Carolyn Ross Johnston, *Cherokee Women in Crisis: Trail of Tears, Civil War, and Allotment, 1838–1907* (Tuscaloosa: University of Alabama Press, 2003), 87–89.

12. "Interview with Mrs. Susan Riley," 35:64, Indian Pioneer Papers, Western History Collections, University of Oklahoma, Norman, Oklahoma (hereafter cited as WHC).

13. Ross and Joseph Vann to John Drew, July 2, 1861, John Ross Papers, Gilcrease Museum, Tulsa, Oklahoma.

14. "Treaty with the Cherokee, 1866," in Kappler, *Indian Affairs Laws and Treaties,* 950.

15. "Treaty with the Cherokee, 1866, Article 2," in Kappler, *Indian Affairs Laws and Treaties,* 942–43.

16. McLoughlin, *After the Trail of Tears,* 80.

17. *Cherokee Nation, Constitution and Laws of the Cherokee Nation* (first published Philadelphia, 1875; repr., Ithaca NY: Cornell University Library, 2009), 29–35.

18. "Duties of the Principal Chief," *Constitution and Laws of the Cherokee Nation*, 41.

19. McLoughlin, *After the Trail of Tears*, 102–10.

20. Petition for Pardon of James Peacock Confined in the National Prison, March 6, 1895, microfilm roll 90, Cherokee Nation Records, Oklahoma History Center, Oklahoma City OK (hereafter cited as CHN 090).

21. To Hon CJ Harris Petition for Pardon of James Peacock confined in the National Prison, March 6, 1895, CHN 090.

22. To Hon Samuel Mayes, November 21, 1895, CHN 090.

23. From 1860 to 1900, the president granted 49 percent of the applications for pardon. Kathleen D. Moore, *Pardons: Justice, Mercy, and the Public Interest* (New York: Oxford University Press, 1989), 49–54.

24. Philosophers Immanuel Kant, Jeremy Bentham, and G.W.F. Hegel all opposed the use of an executive pardon, yet also provided exceptions to that position. Writing in the eighteenth century, Kant believed a pardon was unnecessary in a properly functioning democratic system dedicated to liberty and equality for all. He did, however, accept that liberty and equality were not always achieved. He suggested that in order to correct an injustice a ruling body or leader could use a pardon. Bentham, who wrote from the late eighteenth through the early nineteenth century, laid out four conditions that might make a pardon necessary, three of which were predicated on social service concerns, including when punishment would not effectively deter crime (especially when it applied to infants, the insane, the intoxicated, and the incapacitated); when it was groundless, as when the wrong could be repaired or the wrong committed was for a greater good—for instance stealing bandages for someone's wound—and when it was needless. In this instance education and social services could more effectively manage or deter the crime. The fourth condition included issuing pardons for amnesty during war. In this instance punishment potentially created more harm than good. Hegel, Bentham's contemporary, defended his opposition to pardons based on the idea that criminals have a "right" to be punished; "punishing people implicitly acknowledge[d] them to be persons, moral agents making free choices." Moore, *Pardons*, 21–47.

25. John Phillip Reid makes this argument based on Cherokee legal codes of the eighteenth century. However, his work is not concerned with how Cherokees adapted their understandings of those codes within a national context. Reid, *A Law of Blood: The Primitive Law of the Cherokee Nation* (New York: New York University Press, 1970).

26. The Cherokee Nation Papers housed in the Western History Collection at the University of Oklahoma contain in excess of 240 applications. See Kristina L. Southwell, ed., *Cherokee Nation Papers, Inventory and Index* (Norman OK: Associates of the Western History Collections, 1996), 107–15. The high sheriff reported six pardons in 1888 and seven pardons and two commutations in 1894. *Cherokee Advocate*, November 21, 1888, November 13, 1894.

27. It was not uncommon for sheriffs, judges, solicitors, jurors, and clerks to attach their names to these appeals. To Honorable Dennis W. Bushyhead, Novem-

ber 24, 1879; To Honorable Chief of the Cherokee Nation 1881; To Honorable C. J. Harris, October 15, 1892, CHN 090.

28. *Cherokee Advocate*, October 7, 1893.

29. *Cherokee Advocate*, April 6, 1878; Pardon of John Still, Oochalata Charles Thompson Papers, box 021 f. 9, WHC.

30. "An Act Relating to the Judiciary," *Compiled Laws of the Cherokee Nation* (first published 1881; repr., Wilmington: Scholarly Resources Inc., 1973), 96.

31. Pardon of John Still.

32. Letter from the Office of Boudinot, Jackson, and Morgan, August 5, 1882, CHN 090.

33. Petition for the Pardon of William Grapes [n.d.], CHN 090.

34. To Hon. D. W. Bushyhead, January 23, 1880, CHN 090.

35. Ben Marshall, a mixed-descent Creek slaveholder, founded Marshalltown in the Coweta District of the Creek Nation in Indian Territory on the Cherokee Nation's border. He served as the interpreter at the 1843 convention. After the Civil War, Marshalltown remained an African-Creek town. Jeff Marshall listed himself as the former slave of Lafayette Marshall, Ben Marshall's cousin. Tensions between Cherokee cattle herders and African-Creeks increased when Cherokee citizens' cattle wandered across the line and were slaughtered for food. Cherokee Nation vigilantes armed themselves and attacked Creek light horse, killing a number of African-Creeks. David A. Chang, *The Color of the Land: Race, Nation, and the Politics of Landownership in Oklahoma, 1832–1929* (Chapel Hill: University of North Carolina Press, 2010), 29; Jeff Marshall, Creek Freedmen, Creek, Enrollment Cards, compiled 1898–1914, Enrollment Cards of the Five Civilized Tribes, roll 0086, M1186, RG 75, NARA.

36. Gary Zellar, *African Creeks: Estelvste and the Creek Nation* (Norman: University of Oklahoma Press, 2007), 120–40.

37. Zellar, *African Creeks*, 120–40. This exchange was possible as a result of the compact negotiated between the Creek, Osage, and Cherokee in 1843 that subjected Creek and Osage citizens "to the same treatment as if they were a citizen of [the Cherokee] Nation" if they committed serious crimes within the Cherokee Nation. "Compact Between the Several Tribes of Indians," November 2, 1843, *LCN*, 87–89.

38. November 10, 1881, Letters Sent, Received and Other Documents, Cherokee (Tahlequah) Prison and High Sheriff Records, April 16, 1880–March 20, 1909, 007, CHN 95. Sarah Marshall, a woman who shared the same name as Jeff Marshall's mother and who served as a cook at the prison throughout Marshall's sentence, received forty-four dollars for her cooking services the next month. Given the absence of any other Sarah Marshalls in census or the Dawes' records, it is more than likely Sarah Marshall was his mother. There is no record of a Sarah Marshall on the Cherokee, Cherokee Freedmen, Creek, or Creek Freedmen rolls. However, Jeff Marshall's Dawes card lists Sarah Marshall as his mother, though at the time of his enrollment in 1898 Sarah Marshall was no longer living. If she is his mother, it raises a number of interesting questions about her employ at the prison. Was she paid for her silence? Were they both living at the prison in order to keep them pro-

tected from reprisals from Cherokee people? How did prisoners interpret the daily presence of an African-Creek prisoner's mother? What did it mean to the other prisoners and Jeff Marshall that his mother prepared the meals for all of them? December 23, 1881, CHN 95; John Bert Campbell, *Campbell's Abstract of Creek Freedman Census Cards and Index* (Phoenix AZ: Phoenix Job Printing Company, 1915), 56.

39. From the Executive Office of the Cherokee Nation [January 1900?], f 2967, CHN 95.

40. Hudson, *The Southeastern Indians*, 367–70.

Eight

Race, Kinship, and Belonging among the Florida Seminoles

MIKAËLA M. ADAMS

On a winter day in 1895, an American tourist in Florida noticed a black man tending to a Seminole canoe. Assuming that the man was the Indians' slave, the tourist decided to enlighten him on "his true condition" in the post-emancipation United States. At that moment, the black man's Seminole companion, Tustenuggee, returned. After the tourist explained his purpose, Tustenuggee grew furious. He commanded the black man to leave and then turned to the tourist and shouted, "white man's slave free— Injun este lusta (Negro) belong to Injun—now *you* go." The tourist quickly departed.[1]

For white Americans who heard this story, the encounter offered proof that the Seminoles continued to hold black people in bondage long after the Civil War ended. Indeed, southern journalists, perhaps satisfied that the long arm of the federal government had not quite reached the Everglades, reveled in the idea.[2] A closer examination of the relationship between Florida Seminoles and people of African descent in the late nineteenth and early twentieth centuries, however, reveals a more complex story. Fifteen years prior to the tourist's encounter, a census compiled by ethnographer Clay MacCauley showed that Tustenuggee lived in the same camp as Osän-a-ha-tco, a Seminole man married to a black woman named Poq-ti. The black man the tourist saw that day may have been the couple's grandson, Billy Bowlegs III. If this were the case, Tustenuggee's retort to the tourist takes on new meaning. In what ways did the black man "belong" to the Seminoles? How did kinship ties challenge and transform the status of black people who lived among these Florida Indians?[3]

The Seminoles enjoyed a singular relationship with people of African descent that dated back to the eighteenth century. Descended from both Mikasuki-speaking and Muskogee-speaking Creek Indians who migrated into Florida from Georgia and Alabama, the Seminoles developed close ties with escaped African slaves who sought refuge in Spanish Florida. Although they kept some black people as slaves, they also forged alliances with maroon communities and depended on their black allies as translators and diplomats to the Americans. When the Seminoles resisted forced removal in the 1830s and 1840s, the maroons fought alongside them. After the war ended, most of their black allies as well as their slaves joined the Seminoles on the westward trek to Indian Territory. A few people of African descent, however, remained in Florida with those Seminoles who escaped removal. Retreating to the Everglades and the Big Cypress Swamp, they made their life with the Indians.[4]

The incorporation of black people into Seminole society following removal was imperfect. In the racially charged world of the late nineteenth- and early twentieth-century South, Seminole notions of kinship competed with their emerging concepts of race to create a volatile system that permitted neither the full inclusion nor full exclusion of black individuals. At times the Seminoles tried to prevent the integration of people of African descent, in particular by policing interracial marriage. These efforts were hindered by their inability to control human relationships in their isolated camps scattered across southern Florida. Sex and its consequences ultimately forced the Indians to accept the children born of Seminole–black unions as kin, despite their racial backgrounds. The Seminoles eventually resolved the tensions between kinship and race by adopting formal blood quantum criteria for tribal citizenship in the mid-twentieth century.

In the years that followed the end of the Third Seminole War in 1858, the Florida Seminoles struggled to carve out a space for the black people who remained among them. Whereas in the past maroons had lived in autonomous villages and Seminole slaves acted more as vassals than chattel, the black people who stayed with the Indians were too few in number to form their own community. The Seminoles' subsistence-level economic activities, moreover, made slavery a moot point in practice if not always in speech. As MacCauley noted in his report, the supposed slaves lived "apparently on terms of perfect equality" with other Seminoles. No one controlled their movements nor coerced their labor. In the ethnographer's opinion, the tribe had simply "offered a place of refuge for fugitive bondsmen and gradually made them members of their tribe."[5]

At least three black women remained with the Seminoles by the time MacCauley visited the Indians in the 1880s. Captured as young girls before the majority of the tribe departed from Florida, these women initially served the Seminoles as slaves.[6] By the late nineteenth century, however, the Seminoles' conditions in Florida had dramatically changed. Determined to limit their interactions with white Americans as a strategy to avoid renewed removal attempts, the Seminoles had dispersed across the Everglades and Big Cypress Swamp into small, family-centered bands. The black women, who spoke only the Muskogee and Mikasuki languages, went with them. Although the Seminoles may have tried to maintain social distinctions between these women and other tribal citizens, hierarchies proved difficult to preserve.[7] As one white journalist noted, "Their thriftless owners treat them more as companions than slaves, and about the severest work the men are required to perform is hunting, which is a pleasant pastime rather than a labor, while the slight agricultural pursuits are shared about equally between the Indian and the negro women."[8]

Seminole women worked side by side with the black women, and Seminole men engaged in sexual relationships with them. Initially, the Seminoles tried to prevent such unions. Richard Henry Pratt, who visited with them in 1879, reported that "a warrior who had married a negro was outlawed." In 1891, a journalist echoed this report, insisting that the Seminoles had "quite recently banished one to the tribe for marrying a mulatto, the daughter of one of their slaves."[9]

The Seminoles objected to these relationships in part due to their emerging racial beliefs. Their polygenesis origin story, first recorded in 1825, told of three separate racial creations, each endowed with distinctive proclivities and talents. According to this tale, the "Great Spirit" created men from dust. His first attempt was a failure: a white man appeared who looked "pale and weak." His second attempt ended in another disappointment: the man was "black and ugly." Finally, in his third attempt, the Great Spirit got it right—a "red man!" The Seminoles repeated this story well into the twentieth century. In some versions, the Great Spirit (often called Breathmaker) told the men to select from three boxes: the white man chose a box filled with "pens, and ink, and paper, and compasses," the red man chose a box of "tomahawks, knives, war-clubs, traps, and such things as are useful in war and hunting," and the black man was left with a box of "axes and hoes, with buckets to carry water in, and long whips for driving oxen." These choices reflected the Seminoles' understanding of the proper roles of different races and encouraged them to reject intermarriage with racial "others."[10]

Interracial marriage also represented a tangible threat to late nineteenth-century Seminole survival in Florida. As their numbers declined following removal, the Seminoles worried that if they married racial "others" they would lose whatever hold they had left on their separate identity and place in the region. The Indians' survival strategy during this period included a strict avoidance of unions with whites. Allegedly, Seminole women who engaged in such relationships faced execution, although there are no verified reports of such a punishment being carried out. The Indians also killed babies born of white fathers. The Seminoles believed that relationships with white people endangered their position in Florida by creating connections to white Americans that drew unwanted attention to their communities. They perhaps worried that unions with black people further jeopardized their status by calling into question their identity as Indians in the eyes of whites. This fear became especially salient as white Americans in Florida began enforcing Jim Crow legislation and categorizing people as either "white" or "colored."[11]

Seminole resistance to unions with people of African descent, however, could not prevent individual attraction. Although the Seminoles successfully barred relationships with outside whites well into the twentieth century, they found it more difficult to police unions between black people and Indians that took place within Seminole camps. In the case mentioned by Pratt, for example, the "outlawed" man appealed for forgiveness at the Seminoles' next annual Green Corn Ceremony. After Seminole elders deliberated his petition, he was "rehabilitated in the tribe retaining the woman still as his wife." Kinship and cultural considerations outweighed racial fears.[12]

The Seminoles considered relationships with the black people who lived with them more tolerable than those with outside whites in part because these unions involved Seminole *men* and black *women*. Male relationships with "others" threatened the integrity of the tribe less than did female relationships with outsiders because the Seminoles traced kinship matrilineally. They considered the children of Seminole women as Seminole, no matter the identity of the father. In contrast, the children of non-Indian women and Seminole men did not automatically gain tribal citizenship, making these unions less dangerous. Moreover, unlike the potential white partners of Seminole women, the black women that Seminole men slept with were already part of the community. They lived with the Indians, spoke Mikasuki and Muskogee, and acted like Seminoles. The tribal council acknowledged this difference by forgiving transgressing Seminole men and recognizing their unions with black women. According to one report, once a black woman married a Seminole man she formally obtained her freedom. Unable to prevent sexual encounters between Seminole men and black women within their communities, the Seminoles gradually came up with strategies to incorporate the children these unions produced.[13]

By the late nineteenth century, several interracial unions and black–Seminole children existed in the tribe. Molly Pitcher, a former slave, and her son, Charlie Dixie, for example, lived among the Mikasuki-speakers in south Florida. Pitcher also may have had a daughter named Tonagi, although few records of this girl survive. More black Seminoles lived with the Muskogee-speakers north of Lake Okeechobee. These included Poq-ti, also known as Nagey Nancy, her two children and several grandchildren, and another black woman named Si-Si, along with her children,

Han-ne and Me-le. Census takers later reported that another half-black woman, Fikee Jumper, born in 1879, also lived among the Muskogee-speakers. She may have been related to Funke, a black woman who lived with the family of Frank Willie.[14]

Although the Seminoles tolerated the children born of black–Seminole marriages, they did not view them as equals. Despite a late nineteenth-century missionary's assertion that black–Seminole youths were "not regarded or treated as a slave by any one," tribal citizens commonly told whites that children with black ancestry were "no good." Even Han-ne, who lived with the Seminoles for her entire life, met with contempt from her Indian neighbors who, in accordance with their racial creation story, believed "a negro is the lowest of human creatures." In a late nineteenth-century photograph, Han-ne wore only two or three strands of beads, suggesting a lower status than that of other Seminole women who adorned themselves in hundreds of strands of beads, weighing up to thirty pounds.[15]

Seminoles also disliked Si-Si's son, Me-le, although some of this hostility may have stemmed from his proclivity for white culture. The son of a Seminole man, Ho-laq-to-mik-ko, Me-le dressed like a Seminole, including silver ornaments and a turban, but according to MacCauley, he liked "the white man and would live the white man's life if he knew how to break away safely from his tribe." Me-le admired the frame homes in white settlements and the large-scale agricultural efforts of white farmers. Indeed, he tried to bring these elements of white culture to his camp by building a house and planting an orange grove. Perhaps some of his interest in American culture stemmed from feelings of alienation from his own people.[16]

Although children born to black mothers had Seminole fathers, without matrilineal clan ties passed down from Seminole mothers they were not fully Seminole. Clans offered Seminole individuals support and protection. Without a clan, an individual lacked a place in the community. According to MacCauley, the Seminoles resolved the problem of clanless community members by adopting the remaining black women living among them. In this way, the women received clan membership, usually that of their "mistresses," which they in turn passed on to their offspring.

Si-si and Han-ne, who lived with a Seminole man named Talla-hassee, probably became members of his wife's clan, the Deer Clan. Si-si's son Me-le also received this clan membership. Early twentieth-century censuses listed Molly Pitcher's son, Charlie Dixie, as a member of the Bird Clan. Billy Bowlegs III and his half-siblings Lewis Tucker and Lucy Pearce, the grandchildren of Nagey Nancy, belonged to the Snake Clan. Seminole under-standings of race, however, complicated the clan identities of black–Seminole children. According to tribal citizen Betty Mae Tiger Jumper, Seminoles understood the children and grand-children of Nagey Nancy as belonging not to the Snake Clan proper, but to "Little Black Snake Clan." Modification of the Snake Clan name suggested that these black–Seminole children did not belong to Seminole clans in the same way as did racially Indian Seminoles.[17]

Seminole attitudes toward the marriage prospects of Nagey Nancy's children further revealed a racial consciousness. Her daughter, Old Nancy, had children by two different Seminole men, Billy Fewell and Charlie Peacock. These children belonged to their mother's Little Black Snake Clan. The Seminoles denied marriage, on the other hand, to Old Nancy's brother, ostensibly because of his African ancestry. Had he married Big Tommie's daughter as he desired, their children would have belonged to her clan. The Seminoles viewed this relationship as unaccept-able racial mixing because it involved a Seminole woman and a man with black ancestry. Children of black women could belong to "little" clans, but not to the true clans of Seminole mothers. The marriage of black–Seminole men with Seminole women threatened this distinction. The Seminoles' effort to ban men with black ancestry from taking Seminole wives, however, came with consequences.[18]

The most devastating blow to Seminole–black relations occurred on February 15, 1889, when Big Tommie rejected Old Nancy's brother, Jim Jumper, as a suitor for his daughter. In the wake of this refusal, Jumper took a shotgun to the camp of the Snake Clan and murdered at least five Seminoles, including his sister.[19] Apparently drunk or delirious, Jumper attacked men, women, and children indiscriminately, even shooting a pregnant woman. Old Tiger, an important Seminole leader, died in the rampage. Several other Seminoles also lost their lives, including Young Tiger, Martha Tiger, and Jimmy Tiger. Jim Jumper's sister, Old Nancy, rushed forward to stop her brother; her efforts saved the life of another Seminole woman. According to oral tradition, Old Nancy shouted to the other woman, "He's my brother. He can shoot me if he wants. You run." In the ensuing struggle, Jumper killed Old Nancy. The massacre came to an end when Jumper was fatally shot by another Seminole man.[20]

In the months that followed the tragedy, the Seminoles tried to make sense of the killings. Packing up camp, the Snake Clan moved away from the site of the massacre. The survivors buried the victims and threw Jim Jumper's remains into the swamp, symbolically marking their disgust. Why had this man, who had lived among the Seminoles his entire life, committed this atrocity? Some blamed alcohol. Other Seminoles insisted that Jumper had been "crazy," not drunk. Still others, however, saw his actions through a racialized lens. Although he was the son of a black woman, Jumper had wanted a Seminole wife. In response to the massacre, the Seminole tribal council reinvigorated its efforts to prohibit black–Seminole unions.[21]

The effects of the massacre reverberated across the tribe. The camp affected by the killings included both Muskogee and Mikasuki-speaking Seminoles, and Mikasuki-speakers farther south took the tragedy to heart. Compared to the Muskogee-speaking Seminoles, very few people of African descent lived with the Mikasuki-speakers. Molly Pitcher, whom the Seminoles captured as a child, was the only black individual with no Seminole ancestry among them. Initially kept as a slave by John Osceola, she later married a Seminole man named Miami Billie. The relationship did not last, but it produced Charlie Dixie, who was born in 1870. According to oral tradition, when Seminoles in the Big Cypress Swamp learned of Jim Jumper's actions, "they held court . . . to see about killing this 'un [Charlie Dixie] on this side." Fiercely protective of her teenage son, Pitcher vowed that "if they killed Dixie, she'd get up in the night, and she'd take her hatchet, and she'd chop 'em in the head." As a compromise, John Osceola took Dixie into his camp and had the young man wait on him. This arrangement apparently continued until Osceola married, and then he let Dixie go free.[22]

Although the Mikasuki-speakers agreed to spare his life, they forbade Dixie from taking a Seminole wife. Circumstances conspired, however, to subvert this ruling. According to oral tradition, Dixie's father, Miami Billie, had left his mother years before and married a Seminole woman named Aklohpi. The couple had at least two children, Dixie's half-siblings. According to Seminole ideas of kinship, however, these children—a son named Charlie Billie and a daughter named Jim Sling—belonged to their mother's Panther Clan, and thus were not clan kin of Dixie, who belonged to the Bird Clan. When they grew up, the Seminoles uncovered a shocking secret: Charlie Billie had impregnated Jim Sling, a profound violation of clan law. Sex between siblings of the same clan was incest, a crime punishable by death.[23]

To undo the deleterious effects of the union, tribal citizens knew what they had to do. First, they disposed of the infant.[24] Next, the Seminoles dealt with the couple. After deliberations at the annual Green Corn Ceremony in 1893, council members decided to spare Jim Sling, but execute Charlie Billie.[25] They appointed Charlie Dixie to carry out the killing, perhaps because the young man continued serve John Osceola in a state of semi-slavery. When he resisted the task, the councilmen enticed Dixie with a reward: if he executed Billie, he could marry Jim Sling.[26] Finally agreeing to serve as executioner, Dixie met Billie in a clearing. The men cried together before Dixie shot Billie through the chest and throat. As for Jim Sling, the elders forced her to marry Charlie Dixie "to degrade her."[27] Jim Sling accepted her fate and Dixie, although half-black, had a wife.[28]

In the years following the death of Charlie Billie, Charlie Dixie reportedly continued in his role as tribal executioner in the Big Cypress Swamp. As one white man familiar with the Seminoles noted in 1974, "if the tribe sentenced a man to death, why Dixie was the man that shot him—put him to death." Another observer referred to him as the "Black sheriff of the Seminoles." The son of a black woman adopted into the tribe, Dixie held an anomalous place among the Seminoles. Although he inherited the Bird Clan membership bestowed on his mother, this was a recently

invented identity and not one passed down through generations of matrilineal kinship ties. For this reason, the Seminoles
may have seen Dixie as inhabiting a space outside of the clan system. As a partial outsider, he could kill other Seminoles without
bringing the threat of clan vengeance to fellow members of the
Bird Clan. Although Dixie did not relish his task—people who
knew him described him as "a very kindly man"—the role of executioner gave him an important place among the Seminoles.[29]

Although "he lived as an Indian; he lived with the Indians, and
his wife was a pure blood Indian," it took time for the Seminoles
to regard Dixie as one of them. Memories of Jim Sling's check-
ered past, combined with Dixie's racial background, made the
couple a pariah among the Mikasuki-speakers. According to W.
Stanley Hanson Jr., whose father worked with the Indians, other
Seminoles never seemed to interact much with the Dixie family.
Ethel Cutler Freeman, who visited the tribe in the 1940s, reported
that the Seminoles barred Dixie and his family from participating in festivities and games. Over time, these attitudes softened
as Dixie and Jim Sling's children grew up and interacted with
other Seminoles. By the mid-twentieth century "things gradually changed and he was treated more kindly."[30]

The experiences of Billy Bowlegs III, another black Seminole, both contrasted with and reflected those of Charlie Dixie.
Unlike Dixie, Bowlegs spoke Muskogee. Muskogee-speakers in
the Cow Creek settlement north of Lake Okeechobee tended
to accept racial outsiders more readily than did the Mikasuki-
speakers in the Everglades, and these differences manifested
themselves in the Indians' treatment of Bowlegs. Billy Bowlegs
was also more phenotypically Indian than Dixie. One white com-
mentator, who had known Bowlegs prior to his death in 1965,
remarked that he "doesn't look any more Negro than I do."
Indeed, in 1929 Indian Agent Lucien A. Spencer listed both
Bowlegs and his half-sister as "full blood" on an agency census. In contrast, whites remarked that Dixie was "absolutely coal
black." Bowlegs's appearance, combined with the more tolerant
environment of Cow Creek Seminoles, meant that he enjoyed
better treatment than did Charlie Dixie. Like Dixie, however,
Bowlegs continually had to prove his worth as a Seminole, and

the Indians denied him some of the privileges of tribal citizen-ship on account of his ancestry.[31]

Billy Bowlegs III was born in 1862, the son of Old Nancy, the black–Seminole daughter of Osän-a-ha-tco, a Seminole man of the Otter Clan, and Nagey Nancy. Old Nancy later died in the 1889 massacre; Bowlegs was away from home that day. Billy Bow-legs's father, Billie Fewell, was a Mikasuki-speaking trader famil-iar with whites.[32] Fewell, who built the first frame house among the Seminoles, passed down his interest in the outside world to his son.[33] Unlike most Seminoles of his generation, Bowlegs learned to read and write.[34] Although other Indians faced pun-ishment if they adopted white ways, the Seminoles did not cen-sure Bowlegs for these skills, perhaps on account of his black ancestry. Indeed, Seminoles appreciated his knowledge: among other things, he placed orders from Sears, Roebuck, and Mont-gomery Ward catalogs for illiterate tribal citizens. A white couple familiar with the Seminoles described him as "the ambassador to the Indians." His black ancestry made Bowlegs—like Dixie—an anomaly among the Seminoles. He took advantage of this posi-tion to carve out a space for himself in the tribal community.[35]

Although Bowlegs thrived in interactions with outsiders, he also pursued traditional Seminole occupations. Like other Sem-inole men, he hunted a wide range of animals, including deer, otters, and alligators. So skilled was Bowlegs that during one weeklong hunting trip he reportedly killed thirty-eight deer. Leg-ends grew up around Bowlegs's hunting skills. One story asserted that when Al Capone purchased a home in Florida after the St. Valentine's Day Massacre in 1929, he hired Bowlegs "to get him some real Florida wild game" for entertaining guests. Reportedly, Bowlegs brought him a thousand quail, several deer, and a few turkeys. Well paid for his efforts, Bowlegs purchased a second-hand Cadillac, which he planned to drive back to his home near Lake Okeechobee. Unfortunately for Bowlegs, a wooden bridge collapsed under the weight of the car. He survived the accident, but the Cadillac disappeared into the swamp. Bowlegs's hunting skills proved his worth as a Seminole and enhanced his reputa-tion. By honing these talents, Bowlegs projected his identity as Seminole despite his black ancestry.[36]

Billy Bowlegs married a Seminole woman, Pillhooll of the Deer Clan, sometime before the massacre of 1889. That year the couple had a son named Eli Morgan. No evidence suggests that the marriage of Bowlegs and Pillhooll was unusual or opposed. She was sixteen years his senior, but it was common for Seminole men to marry older women due to a shortage of suitable spouses in the small tribal community. There is also no indication why the Seminoles tolerated this marriage, but objected to the proposed marriage of Bowlegs's maternal uncle, Jim Jumper, to a Seminole woman. Perhaps tribal citizens saw Bowlegs as more "Seminole" than Jumper due to his appearance and due to his status as a third-generation community member. In any case, Bowlegs and Pillhooll lived together until her death in 1928. His half-sister, Lucy, also married a Seminole named John Pearce, and the couple had at least four children. As was fitting in the Seminoles' matrilineal clan system, these children developed a close relationship with their maternal uncle, and after the death of Bowlegs's wife, they lived together in the same camp. His niece, Ada Pearce, took care of Bowlegs in his old age.[37]

People who knew Billy Bowlegs asserted that he was universally liked. A white painter who visited the tribe in the 1950s said Bowlegs "was just a grand old man . . . stunning man, just a marvelous man in every way." Seminoles respected him as an ambassador and as a hunter, and whites visited him when they had questions for the tribe.[38] Despite the valuable skills he offered the Seminoles, however, Bowlegs, like Dixie, faced discrimination. One observer described him as "a loner." When a visitor asked why Bowlegs lacked a leadership role despite his talents, a group of Seminoles replied, "Billy Bowlegs [is an] African waterboy." Although Bowlegs made a successful life for himself, he could not escape his ancestry or the racial climate of the Jim Crow South. He made the best of his situation, but remained one step removed from full acceptance.[39]

The children of Charlie Dixie and Billy Bowlegs III, although discriminated against, fared better than their fathers. Charlie Dixie and Jim Sling had at least five children together, three sons and two daughters. Two of the sons and one daughter died young, but Susie Dixie and Walter Huff Dixie grew up to marry

Seminoles and raise children of their own. Like his father, Walter Huff Dixie initially had trouble finding a wife. Although he belonged to the Panther Clan of his Seminole mother, Mikasuki-speakers denigrated him on account of his black ancestry. Finally, the Seminoles handed off Margaret Charlie and her children to Walter to care for after her previous husband abandoned her. She needed a hunter to help support her children, so she agreed to marry Walter despite his racial heritage. Dixie's daughter, Susie, sequentially married two Seminole men, Homespun Billie and Buffalo Jim. Her first marriage produced at least one son, Dodie Dixie. As generations passed and Seminoles with black ancestry married other Indians, the stigma surrounding their African ancestry faded. By the early 1970s a white friend of the Seminoles claimed that the Dixie children "have been accepted into the tribe and treated the same as anybody else in later years, and they have children."[40]

The son of Billy Bowlegs and Pillhooll, Eli Morgan, also married a Seminole woman. Morgan inherited the clan of his mother and became the last surviving member of the Deer Clan at Cow Creek. His clan identity gave him a more secure place among the Muskogee-speakers, allowing him to marry Lena Bowers. The couple had no children together, but Bowers had children from a previous relationship and Morgan acted as a surrogate father. Billy Bowlegs's nieces and nephews also married Seminoles and had children. Over the years their children became more "Indian" in the eyes of white census takers who listed their "blood quantum" on agency records, and in the eyes of Seminoles who regarded them as full community members. By the 1970s a Seminole man explained that, "Today, you will find some Seminoles with Negro blood. Those who would really know have all died by now."[41]

By the mid-twentieth century, the lives of Florida Seminoles had begun to change once again. Missionaries and government officials made inroads among the Indians, and even purchased them official reservation lands. Following the Indian Reorganization Act of 1934, government agents also began pressuring the Seminoles to write a constitution and gain federal recognition. Although some culturally conservative Mikasuki-speakers resisted the effort, the Seminole Tribe of Florida adopted a formal constitution in 1957. In 1962 the Seminoles modified this document to include blood quantum criteria for tribal citizenship. From then on, "any person of one-fourth or more degree of Seminole Indian blood born after the adoption of this amendment both of whose parents are members of the tribe shall be enrolled as a tribal member."[42]

By adopting a blood quantum requirement for tribal citizenship, the Seminoles finally resolved the tensions that had existed between their notions of kinship and their ideas of race. Although not a perfect compromise, the blood quantum requirement allowed tribal citizens to marry whom they chose and raise children of diverse racial backgrounds without forfeiting their tribal citizenship. The requirement also, however, limited the effects of these unions by insisting that tribal citizens never become too distantly related or too racially non-Indian. By the time the requirement came into play, the descendants of the black women who had stayed with the tribe after removal had all so thoroughly intermarried with the Seminoles that no one questioned their rights as tribal citizens. Through sex and kinship, they had achieved the blood quantum level that defined them as full Seminoles.[43]

Notes

1. Minnie Moore-Willson, *The Seminoles of Florida* (Philadelphia PA: American Printing House, 1896), 70.

2. Moore-Willson, *The Seminoles of Florida*, 69–70. An 1889 article published in the *Atlanta Constitution* reported that two white men had "the pleasure of meeting the only genuine slaveholder in the land of the free, namely the Hon. Cypress Tiger, of the Everglade Seminoles." "A Holdover Slaveholder," *Atlanta Constitution*, June 27, 1889, 4. According to another article, Florida cowboys recommended that visitors to the Seminoles bring an African American with them because one could "sell the negro to the Indians for enough to pay all of [one's] expenses." "The Florida Everglades," *New York Times*, March 10, 1889, 10; "The Florida Indians," *Atlanta Constitution*, November 1, 1885, 4; M. M. Folsom, "Among the Seminoles," *Atlanta Constitution*, February 1, 1886, 3.

3. Clay MacCauley, *The Seminole Indians of Florida* (Gainesville: University Press of Florida, 2000), xlvii–xlviii. Originally published in the *U.S. Bureau of American Ethnology, Fifth Annual Report*, 1887. In his survey, MacCauley reported "three negroes and seven persons of mixed breed" among the Seminoles. Acknowledging the rumors that these individuals remained enslaved, MacCauley argued that he "saw

nothing and could not hear of anything to justify this statement." MacCauley, *The Seminole Indians of Florida*, 526.

4. Kevin Mulroy, *Freedom on the Border: The Seminole Maroons in Florida, the Indian Territory, Coahuila, and Texas* (Lubbock: Texas Tech University Press, 1993); Kenneth W. Porter, *The Black Seminoles: History of a Freedom-Seeking People* (Gainesville: University Press of Florida, 1996); Susan A. Miller, *Coacoochee's Bones: A Seminole Saga* (Lawrence: University Press of Kansas, 2003). The migrating bands of Creeks that entered Florida in the eighteenth and early nineteenth centuries brought with them different languages. Although Muskogee (Creek) was the dominant language used by the Creeks, many lower Creek towns internally spoke Hitchiti, a related but mutually unintelligible tongue. Hitchiti-speakers named one of their earliest towns in Florida "Mikasuki." Over the years, the language these Seminoles spoke became known by the name of the town. By the time of the Second Seminole War, the Seminoles spoke two distinct languages: Muskogee and Mikasuki. See Harry A. Kersey Jr., "Private Societies and the Maintenance of Seminole Tribal Integrity, 1899–1957," *The Florida Historical Quarterly* 56 (January 1978): 298.

5. MacCauley, *The Seminole Indians of Florida*, 526.

6. MacCauley, *The Seminole Indians of Florida*, 526; Betty Mae Jumper and Patsy West, *A Seminole Legend: The Life of Betty Mae Tiger Jumper* (Gainesville: University Press of Florida, 2001), 12.

7. Mary Frances Johns, a Seminole tribal citizen, commented on the efforts of the Seminoles to maintain social distinctions between Indians and blacks in a 1970s oral interview. She claimed that in her grandmother's day, black people who lived with the Indians "weren't even allowed to sit at the same table and eat with 'em." Interview with Mary Frances Johns by Tom King, January 5, 1973, Samuel Proctor Oral History Program, Oral History Collections, George A. Smathers Libraries, University of Florida Digital Collections, Gainesville, Florida (hereafter cited as Samuel Proctor Oral History Program).

8. I M'Queen Auld, "The Seminole Indians," *Atlanta Constitution*, February 27, 1885, 5. The men Auld refers to were the black–Seminole sons of the black women who lived with the tribe.

9. Richard Henry Pratt to E. A. Hayt, Commissioner of Indian Affairs, August 20, 1879, reprinted in "R. H. Pratt's Report on the Seminole in 1879," presented and annotated by William C. Sturtevant, *The Florida Anthropologist* 9 (March 1956): 12; "Florida Happenings," *Atlanta Constitution*, July 26, 1891, 7.

10. Thomas L. McKenney and James Hall, *The Indian Tribes of North America, With Biographical Sketches and Anecdotes of the Principal Chiefs* (Edinburgh: John Grant, 1934), 2:267; William G. McLoughlin, "Red Indians, Black Slavery, and White Racism: America's Slaveholding Indians," *American Quarterly* 26 (October 1974): 384.

11. Jumper and West, *A Seminole Legend*, 39; Interview with James Billie by Tom King, February 1972, and interview with Seminole Housewife (E.F.), Bird Clan, 1970s, Samuel Proctor Oral History Program.

12. Pratt to Hayt, August 20, 1879, 12.

13. I M'Queen Auld, "The Seminole Indians," 5.

14. Reconstructed Florida Seminole Census of 1914, Records of the Statistics Division, Census Rolls and Supplements, 1885–1940, box 846, PI-163, Entry 964, Record Group 75 (hereafter cited as RG 75), National Archives and Records Administration, Washington DC (hereafter cited as NARA); Seminole Clan and Kinship Data, 1942, Ethel Cutler Freeman file, Seminole Indians, Notes: Florida Seminoles, 1942, vol. II, Kinship, Ethel Cutler Freeman Papers, box 38, Smithsonian Institution, National Anthropological Archives, Washington DC; MacCauley, *The Seminole Indians of Florida*, xlvii–xlviii; Census of Seminoles, Indians of Miami Agency, Florida, taken by Lucien A. Spencer, Special Commissioner, July 1915, National Archives Microfilm Publications, microcopy no. 595, Indian Census Rolls, 1885–1940, roll 486, Seminole (Florida), 1913–29, NARA.

15. Dr. Brecht's letter to Charles H. Coe in *Red Patriots: The Story of the Seminoles* (Gainesville: University Presses of Florida, 1974), 240; Jumper and West, *A Seminole Legend*, 12. Moore-Willson, *The Seminoles of Florida*, 90, 107, 108–9; Henry Windsor Villiers Stuart, *Adventures Amidst the Equatorial Forests and Rivers of South America; Also in the West Indies and the Wilds of Florida, To Which is Added "Jamaica Revisited"* (London: John Murray, Albemarle Street, 1891), 111.

16. MacCauley, *The Seminole Indians of Florida*, 490.

17. MacCauley, *The Seminole Indians of Florida* , xlvii, li; Jumper and West, *A Seminole Legend*, 13; Reconstructed Florida Seminole Census of 1914. In a 1973 oral interview, John Belmont asserted that "the clans can be broken down in sort of sub-clans where the relationship between the people is considered to be of a different order." The Little Black Snake Clan may have been one of these sub-clans. See interview with John Belmont by Tom King, April 1973, Samuel Proctor Oral History Program.

18. Jumper and West, *A Seminole Legend*, 13, 15; Interview with John Belmont.

19. Jumper and West, *A Seminole Legend*, 13–15. It is unclear from the available documents whether Big Tommie was a member of the Snake Clan, or if he was married to a Snake Clan woman. If his wife was from the Snake Clan, then his children would also have been Snake Clan members, according to matrilineal rules of descent. If this were the case, then the opposition to Jim Jumper's marriage proposal could have stemmed as much from rules against incest as from ideas about race. As a member of the "Little Black Snake" Clan, which seems to have been a subdivision of the Snake Clan for black–Seminole individuals, Jim Jumper would not have been permitted to marry a woman from the Snake Clan, regardless of race. If the object of his affection was from another clan, however, then the objection to the union may well have been racially motivated.

20. "Victims of an Insane Indian," *New York Times*, March 3, 1889, 5; Jumper and West, *A Seminole Legend*, 13–14; Interview with Lawrence E. Will by Tom King, November 29, 1972, Samuel Proctor Oral History Program.

21. Moore-Willson, *The Seminoles of Florida*, 85–87; Jumper and West, *A Seminole Legend*, 14–16; U.S. Congress, Senate, *A Survey of the Seminole Indians of Florida*, report by Roy Nash (71st Cong., 3rd Sess., 1931, doc. 314.), 26.

22. Interview with Milton D. Thompson by John Mahon, June 25, 1975, Samuel Proctor Oral History Program; February 24, 1942, Ethel Cutler Freeman, Seminole

Indians, Notes Florida Seminoles, 1939, vol. 2, Ethel Cutler Freeman Papers, box 35; Reconstructed Florida Seminole Census of 1914; Seminole Clan and Kinship Data, 1942, Ethel Cutler Freeman file, Seminole Indians, Notes: Florida Seminoles, 1942, vol. 2, Kinship, Ethel Cutler Freeman Papers, box 38; Interview with Rose Kennon by Harry Kersey, September 24, 1971, Samuel Proctor Oral History Program.

23. Interview with Bob Mitchell by Harry Kersey, July 15, 1971, Samuel Proctor Oral History Program.

24. Jim Sling's mother supposedly strangled the child. February 24, 1942, Ethel Cutler Freeman file. According to another version of the story, Molly Pitcher executed the child by leaving it exposed near an alligator hole. See interview with Rose Kennon.

25. According to information collected by Freeman in the 1940s, there may have been a scarcity of Indian women of marriageable age in the tribe at the time, which helps to explain the incestuous relationship and also why the council spared Jim Sling. Deaconess Bedell, 1939, Ethel Cutler Freeman file, Seminole Indians, Negro Relations with Seminoles, Ethel Cutler Freeman Papers, box 32; "Death Decrees, Informant—Miss Conrad, Ind. Off, Nurse, March 1940," Ethel Cutler Freeman file, Seminole Indians, Seminole Killing, Ethel Cutler Freeman Papers, box 31.

26. E. C. Freeman, 1940, Ethel Cutler Freeman file, Seminole Indians, vol. 1, 1940s, Misc. Notes, Florida Seminole (1942–43), Ethel Cutler Freeman Papers, box 35. According to another white observer, "to the half-breed the maid represented a reward for a bitter task because the full blooded Seminoles had previously denied him a wife." See Hanson "R" Liddle, August 8, 1936, Ethel Cutler Freeman file, Seminole Indians, Notes Florida Seminoles, 1940, vol. 1, Ethel Cutler Freeman Papers, box 36.

27. "Death Decrees, Informant."

28. According to another version of the tale, Jim Sling was the unfaithful wife of a Seminole man. Her husband punished her for her infidelity by cropping her nose and her ears, but she continued the extramarital relationship. The Seminole man finally decided that she was no longer worth anything to him, so he made a bargain with Charlie Dixie, who, according to the story, was held as a slave by the tribe. He promised Dixie he could take Jim Sling as his wife if Dixie killed her lover. Dixie performed the execution, married Jim Sling, and thereafter became a citizen of the tribe. This version of the story was supposedly recounted by tribal citizen Howard Osceola to white journalist Jane Wood Reno in 1955 or 1960. See Interview with Jane Wood Reno by Marcia Kanner, October 21, 1971, Samuel Proctor Oral History Program.

29. "Death Decrees, Informant"; Interview with Marshall O. Watkins by John Mahon, November 15, 1974, Samuel Proctor Oral History Program; Interview with Jane Wood Reno. Interview with Bob Mitchell.

30. Interview with W. Stanley Hanson Jr. by John Mahon, June 25, 1975, Samuel Proctor Oral History Program; E. C. Freeman, 1940; Interview with Bob Mitchell.

31. Interview with Robert D. Mitchell by John K. Mahon, March 26, 1975, Samuel Proctor Oral History Program; Census of the Seminole Indians of Florida Agency,

taken by Lucien A. Spencer, Special Commissioner, on June 30th, 1929, National Archives Microfilm Publications, microcopy no. 595, Indian Census Rolls, 1885–1940, roll 486, Seminole (Florida), 1913–29, NARA; Interview with Jane Wood Reno.

32. MacCauley, *The Seminole Indians of Florida,* xlvii–xlviii; Jumper and West, *A Seminole Legend,* 14–15; Reconstructed Florida Seminole Census of 1914.

33. Interview with Albert DeVane and Jessie Bell DeVane by Foster L. Barnes and Thelma Boltin, 1960, Samuel Proctor Oral History Program. According to Clay MacCauley, this home consisted of "a cypress board house . . . furnished with doors and windows, partitions, floors, and ceiling." The construction included a wooden stairway to the home's upper floor. MacCauley, *The Seminole Indians of Florida,* 501.

34. Billy Bowlegs may have learned this skill from his paternal uncle, Ko-nip-hat-cho, who had received a Euro-American education at Fort Myers. Moore-Willson, *The Seminoles of Florida,* 169.

35. Interview with Albert DeVane and Jessie Bell DeVane.

36. Interview with Albert DeVane and Jessie Bell DeVane; Interview with August Burghard by Tom King, December 19, 1973, Samuel Proctor Oral History Program.

37. Reconstructed Florida Seminole Census of 1914; Interview with Albert DeVane and Jessie Bell DeVane.

38. Interview with James Hutchinson by John Mahon and Tom King, August 1973, Samuel Proctor Oral History Program. During one such visit, a white man asked Bowlegs how the weather was going to be that day, expecting a sage response. Bowlegs jokingly replied that he could not tell them because "the picture tube had blown out on his TV." Evidently, he enjoyed playing with white assumptions of what it meant to be "Indian." See Interview with Bessie DuBois by Tom King, December 14, 1973, Samuel Proctor Oral History Program.

39. Interview with James Hutchinson; Interview with Sister St. Anthony by R. T. King, August 28, 1976, Samuel Proctor Oral History Program; Interview with John Durham by John K. Mahon, November 3, 1975, Samuel Proctor Oral History Program.

40. Reconstructed Florida Seminole Census of 1914; Ethel Cutler Freeman file, Seminoles Indians, Notes Florida Seminoles, 1939, vol. 2, Ethel Cutler Freeman Papers, box 35; Seminoles in Florida Census, taken by F. J. Scott on January 1, 1937, National Archives Microfilm Publications, microcopy no. 595, Indian Census Rolls, 1885–1940, roll 487, Seminole (Florida) 1930–40, NARA; Interview with Bob Mitchell.

41. Interview with Albert DeVane and Jessie Bell DeVane; Seminoles in Florida Census; Interview with Mr. Osceola by Jean Chaudhuri, 1970s, Samuel Proctor Oral History Program.

42. Harry A. Kersey Jr., *An Assumption of Sovereignty: Social and Political Transformation among the Florida Seminoles, 1953–1979* (Lincoln: University of Nebraska Press, 1996), 88–89.

43. Certainly, "blood quantum" is a problematic concept, given the fictitious nature of race. Yet, the Seminoles had been race-making for more than a century by then, and it was a difficult concept to drop. In essence, they used blood quantum as a proxy for kinship and as a way to preserve the racially "Indian" identity of their tribal citizens.

Nine

Witnessing the West

Barbara Longknife and the California Gold Rush

ROSE STREMLAU

> I would like very much to see all my old friends in the nation. California is not what it was represented to be, if I was back again, I would let California be the last place that I would go to.

When she wrote these lines, Barbara Longknife was a young wife and mother working in a gold rush settlement.[1] In June 1854 she sent a letter home to the Cherokee Nation. She did so again in October 1857. These seven pieces of paper are part of the larger documentary record of the gold rush.[2] While Longknife was one of hundreds of thousands of migrants who came from all over the world to California to experience this epic event, nearly all of her fellow fortune seekers were men. Historian Susan Lee Johnson called the gold rush "among the most demographically male events in human history."[3] Out of the thousands of chroniclers of the period, most of whom were white, middle-class American men from the Northeast, her voice was distinctive.

Longknife's reflections on the gold rush share some common themes with those of demographically normative writers. They described social instability, the comings and goings of men, the luck of those who struck a good claim, and the hard work of those who did not. Unlike the male commentators, however, she never succumbed to the "contagion of optimism and ambition," as J. S. Holliday, a historian who wrote about the gold rush from the majority perspective, put it.[4] Overall, Longknife's opinions of California were decidedly negative ones, and by 1854 she wasted no ink sharing her happiness. She had no good news to share.

California proved a difficult place for a Cherokee woman, and her letters demonstrate that *who* she was very much shaped *how* she experienced the gold rush.

Longknife's unique perspective on the California gold rush is important for several reasons. First, her experiences as a working-class woman whose prospects declined the longer she remained in California provide a counterpoint to those who benefited from increased opportunities and gained wealth and power during the settlement of the state. Second, although her productive labor had value to male miners, she was a wife and a mother whose days also were shaped by the reproductive work and domestic obligations that she performed alone. Third, unlike most other Cherokee women of her generation, she lacked the companionship and support of other Cherokee women. Longknife left behind nearly all of her kin in Indian Territory, and her letters reveal the strain and loss resulting from such separation.

Longknife crossed cultural and geographic boundaries, and her letters enable us to compare and contrast her experience with those of other participants, particularly Anglo-Americans whose stories of the overland trails and diggings (as mining camps were called) have received the most attention from historians of the West and retained their hold on the popular imagination. Supported by other sources of evidence including county, state, and tribal records; newspapers; and contemporary personal correspondence and journals, Longknife's letters enrich the master narrative. At the same time, Longknife's story is also a cautionary one. We should be careful to avoid simplistic assumptions underlying revisionist narratives that identify indigenous people and women primarily as victims of the rush. Longknife willingly participated in the colonization of California, which meant that she was one more outsider occupying land and using resources claimed by other indigenous people. Her choices defy neatly packaged conclusions about gender and ethnic or racial solidarity. Above all, Longknife's letters provide an opportunity to explain a major event in world history from the perspective of a southeastern Indian woman. Her story suggests a counter narrative of the gold rush that is no less true and, in fact, richer for its complexity. Longknife's letters, emphasizing work, motherhood, and kinship, reveal the durability of traditional Cherokee understandings of appropriate gendered behavior and the adaptability of an average woman, living through an exceptional moment in time, in a place far away from the kin she loved and missed.

In January 1848 the discovery of gold at John Sutter's mill initiated a flood of migration into the area that had been home to diverse, distinct indigenous societies for thousands of years. After centuries of contact with both the Spanish and Russians, Native civilizations in California were already very much changed when Americans began moving into the region in the 1830s, and American settlers had little positive to say about either indigenous Californians or Mexicans, who, in return, resented the newcomers. The United States formally claimed California in 1846. By the end of that year, over 100,000 Americans had relocated to California. In addition to miners from Europe, Asia, and Latin America, the rapid intrusion of young, white American men transformed the area, and in 1850 California was admitted to the Union as a state with a growing population and a prosperous economy based on resource extraction.[5]

The first historical studies of the California gold rush, written in the latter decades of the nineteenth century while participants, including some who were then prominent citizens, were still alive, were triumphalist and emphasized the atypical experiences of the relative few who acquired enormous fortunes. This traditional history of California lauds the exploitation of natural resources, the extension of American sovereignty through military occupation, and the expansion of capitalist markets while it forgives the brutality of the period as an unfortunate consequence of the rise of Anglo-American civilization.[6]

Beginning in the late twentieth century, historical studies began to include white women and African American, indigenous, and Hispanic peoples, too. These works have emphasized that political oppression and economic exploitation was a central component of the colonization of the region by the United States. The inclusion of women and non-white racial and ethnic groups did not replace the celebratory narrative with one more pessimistic but equally simplistic. After all, just like the white men who were the numerical majority, their presence threatened the survival of indigenous Californians, too, and many Natives also participated in mining and its related industries.[7] Despite several decades of attention to this diverse gold rush, however, stories of American Indians from the East have received little scholarly attention.[8]

The first published Cherokee writings about the gold rush were critical, although fictional. In 1854 John Rollin Ridge, a friend of Longknife, wrote *The Life and Adventures of Joaquin Murieta: The Celebrated California Bandit*, a dime novel inspired by the Robin Hood-esque tale of an honorable young Mexican man who defied the Anglo-American power structure and paid with his life (and his head).[9] Ridge's romanticized account was published less than a year after the real Murieta came to his violent end. Ridge downplayed actual events and emphasized the importance of protecting the freedom of individual men against bigotry and repression. That spin was a particularly fitting one for Ridge, whose own Cherokee people had been robbed of their homeland by the state of Georgia and the Jackson administration through the Indian Removal Act and whose father, grandfather, and uncles were seen by many Cherokee people as complicit with that theft. The Ridges, also known as the Treaty Party because they negotiated and signed the treaty providing for the removal of the Cherokee Nation to Indian Territory, also paid with their lives. Ridge, however, was not calling for a challenge to the white supremacy that threatened tribal sovereignty. Rather, he hoped to succeed as a writer after failing as a miner.

The earliest historical account of Cherokees who migrated to California celebrated their participation. These Cherokees were called "Argonauts" and "cavaliers" by historian Edward Everett Dale, a non-Indian who implied that Cherokees' involvement in the gold rush testified to their ability to assimilate into Anglo-American civilization. Decades before the emergence of women's history, Dale described these Cherokees in the heroic language of male domination that has been used to describe the American colonization of California in general. In fact, although aware of Longknife's participation, he refers to Cherokee participants in the gold rush as men.[10] Likewise, the uncritical use of the term

"Argonaut" is telling.[11] The term, of course, refers to the Greek epic recounting the journey of Jason and his men in their search for the Golden Fleece. The story of the Argonauts is one of a journey away from the familiar and known, of violence and suffering, and ultimately, of domination and conquest.

Longknife's journey was no less epic than that of Jason. The story begins with her ancestors, who shared a survival strategy in common with the women of Lemnos. Longknife was born into a family shaped *both* by epic travel and intermarriage. Her paternal grandfather John was the grandson of emigrants from Germany. His ancestors immigrated to Pennsylvania in 1732. Part of the family moved to North Carolina in the 1760s. Two decades later, John joined them. He married and had a family.[12] About twenty years later, John left his first wife and took his five children into the Cherokee Nation. He had been hired by the U.S. government to build a gristmill according to the terms of an 1806 treaty. John remarried a Cherokee woman named Susannah Womancatcher.[13] A Cherokee woman named Diana Graves took a liking to John's son George, and they, too, married. In fact, all of John's children by his first wife married Cherokee spouses and made their homes in the Cherokee Nation. They had chosen to relocate among Cherokees, and Cherokee women and men had welcomed them into their families. George and Diana had ten children. Barbara, born in 1828, was the eighth.[14] The extended family resided in in the Valley Towns region, which is now part of the state of Tennessee.[15]

Throughout the colonial era, Cherokees responded to the loss of homelands, crushing debt incurred through trade deficits, chronic warfare, and epidemic disease by adapting new technologies and practices to bolster their economy and sustain their independence. As populations declined, land bases diminished, ecosystems evolved, and political instability disrupted traditional patterns of life, Cherokees made a living by retaining some old ways and experimenting with new ones. The latter was supported by the United States. Reflecting the federal government's commitment to "civilizing" American Indian people living within the boundaries of existing states, treaties signed in the Early Republic included enticements to adapt to Anglo-American culture. Many Cherokees saw the material resources provided under civilization policy, including spinning wheels, plows, livestock, and mills, as valuable tools enabling their self-sufficiency and prosperity.[16] For example, Barbara's parents practiced a diverse subsistence strategy reflecting innovation and tradition. George worked as a mechanic while three members of the family farmed. Two were weavers. Three were spinners. Although it was not clear who was farming, it is almost certain the spinners and weavers were women. The family was also bilingual, as a group. Seven members of the family read English while two read Cherokee.[17]

The extended family prospered as well. George's father John Hildebrand and his wife Susannah operated the mill that served as a hub of economic and social activity in the region. They also housed travelers and traded provisions. George's older brothers lived nearby. The family of Michael Hildebrand, the eldest by four years, owned five slaves. In addition to farming, his family operated two mills and a ferryboat. The family of Peter Hildebrand, who was two years older than George, owned eight slaves and also ran a mill and a ferry. The extended family lived in a region that embodied the diversity of relationships and economic strategies in the Cherokee Nation. Those Cherokee families who had intermarried with whites lived among those who had not. Peter Hildebrand's neighbors also included a free family of African descent.[18]

Presumably, Hildebrand familial networks included Cherokee kin, as well, but the fact that most of the intermarried Hildebrands were males and the use of paternal surnames in the pre-removal census created by the U.S. government makes documenting this difficult. This emphasis on male heads of households reflected the bias of non-Indians, and it obscures the property ownership of Cherokee women, in this case, the Hildebrand men's wives. Cherokee women owned slaves and improvements made to their property during this period, and they retained ownership upon their marriage.[19] Likewise, according to the customs of kinship common among Cherokees during this period, the intermarried Hildebrands would have been expected to treat their in-laws with generosity. Their successful integration into Cherokee society suggests that they did conform to cultural norms.

The policy of Indian removal had a dire impact on the family. The intermarried Hildebrands removed with their Cherokee spouses and children. Barbara was ten when her uncle Peter Hildebrand led their detachment to the West.[20] Cherokees experienced removal as the loss of loved ones, homeland, and prosperity. According to historian Grant Foreman, Hildebrand's detachment included 1,776 people when it left Tennessee. Eighty-eight wagons and 881 horses, stretching for several miles, carried the youngest and oldest. Most walked. On March 25, 1839, 1,312 human beings reached their destination.[21] Eventually the family settled in Delaware District, one of the eight civic subdivisions of the Cherokee Nation in Indian Territory.

As the extended family reestablished their households, they continued to work and trade with kin and neighbors. The Hildebrands reestablished the family's milling business.[22] The ancient customs of reciprocity associated with the Cherokees' kinship system continued to regulate commercial activity, and Cherokees continued to marry across social divisions. Although historians emphasize the divisive factionalism between those Cherokees aligned with the Treaty Party and those who supported Principal Chief John Ross, relationships among Cherokees during the 1840s suggests that boundaries were fluid and at least some Cherokees were forgiving. The Hildebrands made their new homes among neighbors who included members of the Treaty Party, and Barbara married one of them, William Longknife.[23]

While most Cherokee people worked to reestablish their livelihoods in the Cherokee Nation, some looked beyond its boundaries for opportunities. The majority of Cherokees continued to make their living as subsistence farmers, but most of the Cherokees who participated in the gold rush were from families associated with increasing engagement in the market economy beyond the Cherokee Nation both before and after removal. The lists of Cherokee migrants to California included surnames of families who had prospered in the Old Nation, who had lost improved property during removal, and who struggled to rebuild in Indian Territory. Accounts in the *Cherokee Advocate* echo a common theme: Cherokee men who wrote back to their local newspaper sought fortunes. Those same letters also emphasize that these young men planned to come home.[24] In this sense, Cherokee men who participated in the gold rush behaved quite traditionally. Before the nineteenth century, young men had spent months away from home trading, making war, and hunting with the goal of coming home with honor, good stories, and items valued by their communities. If the editors of and writers to the *Cherokee Advocate* were representative, Cherokees both welcomed an infusion of wealth into their economy and looked forward to the return of their young men.[25]

The investment was needed. Some Cherokees had been compensated for losses incurred during removal, but others had not. Throughout the 1840s, Ross lobbied the U.S. government for redress, and partial payment was eventually received in 1852.[26] Cherokees trying to rebuild farms could not eat promises until then, however. Longknife's decision to go to California might have been part of a larger familial economic strategy and further evidence of Cherokee peoples' continued adaptability to changing economic circumstances. As anthropologists Alice Littlefield and Martha Knack have emphasized, "Native American wage labor participation . . . was largely self-motivated. Native peoples did not wait for government agents to direct them to wage opportunities; rather, they perceived those openings and sought them out."[27] The same can be said of Native speculators in precious metals.

And so Longknife was part of the "considerable number" who went to California, in Dale's words, "in search of fortune." Although her gender differentiated her from most other Cherokee migrants, she, too, had at one point dreamed of her own "good claim."[28] The group that traveled west included her husband and her brother Jack.[29] They left on April 27, 1850, from Stand Watie's home along Honey Creek. Watie, the surviving leader of the Treaty Party, supplied many of the migrants, who included his brother Charles, and accompanied the group to a meeting point along the Verdigris River. At some point, they were joined by a group from Missouri that included John Rollin Ridge.[30] Longknife, then twenty-two years old, was pregnant. On route in Utah, she gave birth to a daughter, Mary Jane. The party reached El Dorado County, California, the epicenter of the gold rush in October 1850.[31]

In both the Cherokee Nation and California, Longknife was a working woman, but in the diggings, the experience of her labor changed and her status declined. The Longknife family stopped in Placerville and then spent several years in nearby Coloma, which was located in the Sierra Nevada foothills drained by the lower Sacramento River.[32] This region was called the Northern Mines (as opposed to the Southern Mines region drained by the San Joaquin River). The community was located along the South Fork of the American River. There she worked as a laundress. She charged per piece to wash the clothes of other men besides her husband. Johnson emphasized that some women prospered by performing feminized work, such as preparing meals and having sexual intercourse, for relatively high prices. Longknife, however, performed low-skill work in a trade in which she faced competition from Chinese and African American men who, having been forced from the mines by exclusionary, racist laws, sought to make money by filling the demand for clean clothes in a region where there were few women to do this traditionally female work. They kept prices low, and Longknife could not charge more than her male competitors just because she was a woman doing what male miners thought was rightfully women's work. Instead, she "worked as hard as the next one in the Country and all I have is a living."[33]

Longknife's entrance into the service sector was not unusual for indigenous women in frontier settlements. Native women had long served as partners to European (and, eventually, Euro-American and Euro-Canadian) traders and merchants and, in doing so, provided important services, such as translation, and the social capital of kinship in return for access to material goods and new economic opportunities. Women in her family had made such decisions when partnering with American men, after all, and Longknife may have noticed the California Native women who formed long-term relationships with men at Sutter's Fort. Unlike Native women whose spouses increased the resources available to them and who remained in their own communities or near kin who continued to share labor and its fruits among them, however, Longknife's decision to travel to California isolated her and limited her access to resources.[34]

Gender informs cultural constructions of work and shapes the economic system through which work is rewarded. In the Cherokee Nation, Longknife contributed to an extended-family economy, and barring unusual misfortune, such as removal, she would not have gone hungry. The customs of reciprocity among extended family members remained vital well into the twentieth century (and arguably persist in some communities even today). In California women worked at the intersection of multiple distinct labor economies that were differentiated from and subordinated to those of men. Without kin and access to communal land, Longknife had lost control of food production, a primary source of women's power in Cherokee society, and she was instead dependent on others who were neither kin nor bound to her through the customs of reciprocity for income and a fair price on commodities. Moreover, Longknife seemed to have been the lone adult female laborer in her household. In her letters she never mentioned any other women, Native or non-Native. She also explained that the family moved frequently, a characteristic of life in the diggings.[35] Although a lucky few made fortunes in California, the rapid transition to a nuclear family unit impoverished her.

Longknife surely observed California Native women, both Miwok and Nisenans, working under different conditions. Despite dramatic and traumatic change, traditional gendered labor practices persisted. California Native women controlled their labor and owned what they produced. In the surface mines of the San Joaquin River valley, for example, Miwok women panned for gold alongside immigrant men, and, like them, they kept or sold their findings. They also continued to do subsistence work, such as gathering and processing acorns into flour for food, a task that would have been familiar to Longknife. Cherokee women, although their methods varied slightly, had processed acorns into meal for centuries. Sexual violence against women was prevalent in the diggings, and so perhaps Longknife could not have gathered safely on her own, but even if she had, she also might not have been able, as one woman, to do the work typically shared by a group. Compared to California Native women, Longknife's impoverishment, in other words, was social as well as economic.[36]

Longknife struggled in a regional economy characterized by a surplus of cheap labor, a scarcity of staple goods, high demand for these products that drove commodity prices up, and by land use and labor conflict that discouraged subsistence practices. Simply put, California has long been an expensive place to live, and even then it was difficult to do so on the earnings of a common laborer. Longknife came from a nation of farmers who, despite upheaval and removal, had remained remarkably self-sufficient. In one passage, Longknife drove home how Cherokees' diets had adapted since contact and the sharp contrast between the economies of the Cherokee Nation and California. Longknife listed the high prices of bacon, pork, mutton, flour, cornmeal, rice, potatoes, eggs, and chicken.[37] The amounts surely were intended to shock the readers of her letter, but they also indicated that Longknife, unlike nearly all Cherokee women in her nation, had transitioned from a producer to a consumer of food. At home, her family had the ability to produce most of these items themselves.[38]

Longknife was not alone in struggling just to survive. Charles Watie, her friend, had told Longknife that the hard work of a day laborer had aged him. He earned three dollars a day, which was not a living wage.[39] After an initial economic boom, wages had fallen, as Longknife explained: "The times is gon [*sic*] when Labor was from 5 to 8 a day."[40] Most people did not earn enough to pay for their room and board let alone save for a return trip. Longknife lamented that she did not have the money to come home. Chronic poverty trapped the family.

Longknife's letters also convey the challenges of being a mother in the diggings. Although informed by common biological processes, motherhood is socially constructed and varies across cultures. In the mining communities of California, maternal behavior was structured differently than it was in the Cherokee Nation. Among Cherokees, relations with kin, particularly siblings and cousins of one's age cohort, were as important as with spouses. The work of parenting, in particular, was shared by women in an extended family. Female kin provided stability and support, particularly to young mothers and in times of crisis. For Longknife, her daughter Mary Jane's ongoing sickness was that life-changing event.

Cherokees were experienced survivors of the diseases associated with colonization. By the end of the eighteenth century, disease had taken a catastrophic toll on indigenous societies. Although particular microbes impacted individual bodies, disease was experienced socially. Kin cared for their sick because the traditional Cherokee understanding of wellness was not individual but collective. The persistence of that outlook was evident in the *Cherokee Advocate*'s coverage of the global cholera pandemic. In 1849 cholera affected passenger ships and merchant vessels and crept closer to Arkansas and, ultimately, to Tahlequah, the capital of the Cherokee Nation. The tone of the reporting was serious. Cholera was not an unknown killer. It was a familiar enemy Cherokees had faced before, mostly recently during removal.[41] This time, the entry point was the one most familiar to Cherokees and that which had introduced sickness into their towns during the colonial era—trade. Cherokees could not stop the flow of people or diseases through their territory, and their understanding of the risks posed by disease informed behaviors, including decisions to travel or not.[42] The approaching cholera epidemic may have influenced Longknife's decision to go west.

Longknife's experiences with sickness during the gold rush were devastating. Disease stalked the overland trails. Reflecting both the lack of sanitation and health care and the influx of people from all over the world, the diggings were also unhealthy places. Outbreaks of infectious diseases were chronic. Members of Longknife's party, including her brother Jack, died en route and after arriving in California.[43] The family's struggles with ill health were ongoing. In 1854 Longknife wrote that "we have had a great deal of sickness in our family since we came to this County [*sic*] and our doctor bills has cost us a great many dollars together with expenses connected with Dr bills." She did not specify who, among herself, William, and Mary Jane, needed medical treatment, but in 1857 Longknife recounted a terrifying ordeal with Mary Jane in her letter to Stand Watie. Mary Jane had contracted "the billious fever," a term then used by doctors for typhoid. It left her blind. Longknife provided her with medical care, an expense that drained the family's resources, and yet there had been no improvement. Longknife's despair was obvious from the context she provided. She wrote about how bright Mary Jane had been in school. Although only six years old, Mary Jane was already able to work through the "third reader." Her daughter, who had been a gifted student only a few months earlier, remained physically weak and, if she survived, faced an uncertain future.[44]

Longknife shared the details of her daughter's sickness in detail not to evoke pity. Rather, she sought something else: advice. Cherokees had experienced typhoid in the mid-1830s and on several occasions thereafter.[45] Had Mary Jane taken sick in the Cherokee Nation, relatives would have pooled their knowledge and resources to provide treatment options. In Coloma she had seen the "best doctor" with no result. Back home, Longknife's kin also would have helped care for Mary Jane. Longknife seems to have done so alone. It is unclear whether William helped. Longknife barely mentioned him.[46]

Isolated from those kin who would have been her primary support, Longknife depended on her husband, but their marriage deteriorated in California. Before social instability and changes in gender roles resulting from colonization began to alter marriage among Cherokees, domestic abuse was rare among them. In extended matrilineal households, an unhappy husband did not dare abuse his wife, and a women displeased with her husband simply threw him out. When she migrated to California, however, Longknife found herself surrounded by those who believed that a woman's identity was subsumed to that of her husband, who believed marriage to be a sacred, permanent bond, and who believed domestic violence to be normal. As early as 1857, Longknife and William were at odds. She wrote to Stand Watie that she had given William an ultimatum: "I will not put up with it if I can help it I am willing to help all I can but I am tyeard [sic] of this Country."[47] Longknife's complaints in a letter addressed to a man were a striking deviation from the submission expected from Anglo-American wives. Longknife did not leave William in 1857, nor did she leave him in 1859 when their daughter Anna Diane was born. By 1863, however, he had become physically violent.[48] William threatened to kill her, and she took him to court. Her use of the judicial system in defense of her bodily integrity and in defiance of her husband was remarkable. The judge's response, however, was predictable. He released William on the promise that he would "behave himself properly."[49] William did not. In August 1865, as the Cherokee Nation lay in ruins, burned over by factional violence among Cherokees during the Civil War, Longknife left William. With her two daughters, she sailed from San Francisco to Honolulu.[50]

Since she left in 1850, Longknife had remained in communication with family back in the Cherokee Nation. Because Cherokee people had embraced literacy in the 1820s, letter writing served as a primary means through which Cherokees communicated with one another. In this way, Longknife was like other Cherokee participants in the gold rush in using the written word to maintain relationships and convey her ongoing sense of belonging.[51] Cherokee letter writers updated loved ones back home about all those they knew in California, and they also testified to the durability of connections among Cherokees within California. Visiting other Cherokees was an important component of life in California. For example, four people—Barbara and William Longknife, John Rollin Ridge, and Charles Watie—were listed together in a census taken in Placerville, California, in 1850, and continued to mention one another in letters. They clearly remained in contact. In 1856 Charles Watie wrote his brother about a visit with John Rollin Ridge, and referred to an upcoming planned visit with "Bill Longknife and his wife."[52] In her letters to Watie, of course, she also mentions them. The letters hint at a nascent Cherokee diaspora community emerging in California during the gold rush and provide evidence of what scholars of twentieth-century urban Indian life now suggest to be true: that urban indigenous communities should be defined not by the disintegration of distinct markers distinguishing cultural boundaries and the presumed eventual assimilation into Anglo-American society but by the persistence of relationship-based networks, providing resilient connections among one another and to home communities.[53]

When she wrote home, Longknife was exhausted in the ways that hard work and, more so, the drudgery of loneliness wears down human beings. Beyond bone tired, there is heart and soul tired.[54] Longknife's experiences in California were not happy ones, but her letters were not hopeless. They are tangibly loving. It is her want "to enjoy the pleasure of sitting and talking with you all one more time" that prompted her to write to her kin, and, after she sent it, to keep working to one day return to them.[55] Longknife eventually traveled even farther away from the Cherokee Nation and those she longed to see. She spent the last forty years of her life in the Sandwich Islands (now known as Hawaii), where she died on January 31, 1905.

It is important to interpret American history through indigenous understandings and experiences if we are to appreciate American Indians as fully human and write about them as such. These seven precious pieces of paper provide a glimpse into one southeastern Indian woman's thoughts about a watershed historical event. Beyond that, they provide a brief glimpse into the emotional life of a working-class Cherokee mother at a turning point in her life. Historians risk being called foolish when they read feelings into the historical record, and yet if we accept the challenge of understanding those who lived in the past, we cannot dismiss the depth of emotion with which they experienced their lives. Although they may have understood their longings differently than we do now, the people of the past ached no less in their time for their loved ones, security, and comfort. The emotional well of the human past is not a shallow one, and through the skillful use of the documentary record, we can refresh our staid, sanitized national myths with the water of our shared human ability to relate across time, place, and culture. In other words, we can take the master narrative to water, to use a Cherokee cultural reference, by purifying it of assumptions that dehumanize Native people and restoring balance through the inclusion of their perspectives. We should want to understand not just the political and economic factors that made Longknife's migrations possible, but seek to answer why she, as a Cherokee human being, made them and how she experienced her epic journey.

Notes

Thanks to Glen Winterbottom, a descendant of Barbara's, and Andrew J. White, a Hildebrand descendant, for their generosity in sharing their research on her and the extended family.

1. The epigraph is from a letter from Barbara Longknife to Stand Watie, June 8, 1854, Cherokee Nation Papers microfilm edition, roll 39, folder 4094, Western History Collections, University of Oklahoma Libraries, Norman, Oklahoma (hereafter cited as Longknife letter, 1854). Throughout her life, Longknife changed surnames at least twice. In addition, her spelling and that of others in reference to her varied. This lack of consistency is common across nineteenth-century sources. In this chapter I refer to her as Barbara Longknife. In the larger project from which this is drawn, I discuss the range of names and reasons for the changes.

2. Longknife's California letters inspired this project, and I believe they were written by her own hand. In *Cherokee Cavaliers*, Edward Everett Dale and Gaston Litton concluded that she dictated the contents to someone else. I disagree. The handwriting is fairly consistent, and her family was a literate one. Her writing, like anyone's, changed over time, and we also should take the kind of work she did into consideration. Her letter dating from 1854 is written in a noticeably sloppier script. Longknife stated in this text, however, that she was working very hard as a laundress. Could someone performing manually intensive labor all day have sat down to write a letter with tired, fatigued hands, and could that have resulted in a messier letter? Yes, I think so. Dale and Litton, *Cherokee Cavaliers: Forty Years of Cherokee History as Told in the Correspondence of the Ridge-Watie-Boudinot Family* (Norman: University of Oklahoma Press, 1939), 78n44.

3. Susan Lee Johnson, *Roaring Camp: The Social World of the California Gold Rush* (New York: W.W. Norton Company, 2000), 12.

4. J. S. Holliday, *The World Rushed In: The California Gold Rush Experience* (first published 1981; repr., Norman: University of Oklahoma Press, 2002), 50.

5. Many historians have written comprehensive histories of the California gold rush. Two, in particular, have helped me understand the world that Longknife encountered: H. W. Brands, *The Age of Gold: The California Gold Rush and the New American Dream* (New York: Doubleday, 2002) and Albert L. Hurtado, *John Sutter: A Life on the North American Frontier* (Norman: University of Oklahoma Press, 2006). Demographic data from John E. Pomfret, ed. and introduction, *California Gold Rush Voyages, 1848–1849: Three Original Narratives* (Westport CT: Greenwood Press, 1974), 3–8.

6. Johnson, *Roaring Camp*, 11.

7. The scholarship on woman and non-white participants in the gold rush is too abundant to note comprehensively here, but important studies influencing my

work include the following: Virginia M. Bouvier, *Women and the Conquest of California, 1542–1840: Codes of Silence* (Tucson: University of Arizona Press, 2004); Maria Raquel Casas, *Married to a Daughter of the Land: Spanish-Mexican Women And Interethnic Marriage in California, 1820–80* (Reno: University of Nevada Press, 2009); Albert L. Hurtado, *Indian Survival on the California Frontier* (New Haven CT: Yale University Press, 1990); Hurtado, *Intimate Frontiers: Sex, Gender, and Culture in Old California* (Albuquerque: University of New Mexico Press, 1999); Rudolph Lapp, *Blacks in Gold Rush California* (New Haven CT: Yale University Press, 1995); Louise Pubuls, *The Father of All: The de la Guerra Family, Power, and Patriarchy in Mexican California* (Berkeley: Huntington Library and University of California Press, 2010); Kevin Starr and Richard J. Orsi, eds., *Rooted in Barbarous Soil: People, Culture, and Community in Gold Rush California* (Berkeley: University of California Press, 2000).

8. James W. Parins's book on John Rollin Ridge is the only book-length study of eastern American Indians in California during this period. *John Rollin Ridge: His Life and Works* (Lincoln: University of Nebraska Press, 2004).

9. Yellow Bird (John Rollin Ridge), *The Life and Adventures of Joaquin Murieta: The Celebrated California Bandit* (first published 1854; repr., Norman: University of Oklahoma Press, 1977).

10. Dale collaborated with archivist Gaston Litton, but I believe the introductions to the chapters were written by Dale, the historian. Dale and Litton, *Cherokee Cavaliers*, 56–97.

11. For example, see Emmett Starr, *History of the Cherokee Indians and their Legends and Folklore* (first published 1921; repr., Baltimore MD: Genealogical Pub. Co., 2003), 665.

12. Andrew J. White, "Descendants of Conrad Hildebrand of Earl Township, Lancaster County, Pennsylvania," *Pennsylvania Mennonite Heritage* 15, no. 4 (1992): 30–37.

13. George Morrison Bell Sr., *Genealogy of Old and New Cherokee Indian Families* (first published 1972; repr., Bartlesville OK: Watie Bell Press, 2006), 219. Barbara's daughter Anna called her maternal grandmother Diana, and so I used this name. Nineteenth-century Cherokees used these names interchangeably. Anna Carden, Eastern Cherokee Application #11510.

14. Bell, *Genealogy of Old and New Cherokee Indian Families*, 218.

15. Carden, Eastern Cherokee Application.

16. Historians have emphasized Cherokee resilience during the Early Republic. See Theda Perdue, *Cherokee Women: Gender and Culture Change, 1700–1835* (Lincoln: University of Nebraska Press, 1998); and William G. McLoughlin, *Cherokee Renascence in the New Republic* (Princeton NJ: Princeton University Press, 1992).

17. James W. Tyner, *Those Who Cried: The 16,000* (first published 1974; repr., Muskogee OK: Thomason Printing Co., 1992), 185. This reflects the combination of the listings of George and Moses Hildebrand. Moses was George's oldest son, and considering his age, it is unlikely that he had established a separate household. This discrepancy reflects a difference between Cherokee and American definitions of a "household."

18. Tyner, *Those Who Cried*, 184, 188.

19. Perdue, *Cherokee Women*, 44–45 and 151–53.

20. Carden, Eastern Cherokee Application.

21. The rest, 464, included those who died and, according to Foreman, those who diverted to other areas before reaching Tahlequah. Grant Foreman, *Indian Removal* (first published 1932; repr., Norman: University of Oklahoma Press, 1972), 311–12.

22. Dale and Litton, *Cherokee Cavaliers*, 96.

23. I say "seems to" in regards to William being associated with the Ridges because of the familiarity implied in Charles Watie's reference to "Bill and his wife" in his 1856 letter to his brother. Letter reprinted in Dale and Litton, *Cherokee Cavaliers*, 90.

24. Extensive coverage of the gold rush began in spring 1848. The *Cherokee Advocate* began promoting migration in the September 18, 1848, issue. From that point, nearly every issue had a story about California, and the newspaper printed regular announcements about groups organizing to go west.

25. Albert L. Wahrhaftig, "Making Due with Dark Meat: A Report on Cherokee Indians in Oklahoma," in *American Indian Economic Development*, ed. Sam Stanley (The Hague: Mouton, 1978), 409–510.

26. This payout resulted in the Drennan roll, which is the first official list of Cherokees who moved to Indian Territory as a result of the Treaty of New Echota.

27. Alice Littlefield and Martha C. Knack, *Native Americans and Wage Labor: Ethnohistorical Perspectives* (Norman: University of Oklahoma Press, 1996), 14.

28. Barbara Longknife, Petition for Citizenship, March 2, 1894, book B, no. 2963, Cherokee Nation Records, Oklahoma Historical Society, Oklahoma City (hereafter cited as Longknife petition).

29. Jack's given name was John. In a letter included in Longknife's petition, George Hildebrand, Barbara and Jack's father, identified him as John and added that he was commonly called Jack.

30. Longknife petition. Parins, *John Rollin Ridge*, 61–71.

31. Longknife petition.

32. 1850 California census, Placerville and vicinity. Longknife letter, 1854.

33. Letter of Barbara Longknife to Stand Watie, October 11, 1857, Cherokee Nation Papers microfilm edition, roll no. 39, folder 4104, Western History Collections (hereafter cited as Longknife letter, 1857).

34. Hurtado, *John Sutter*, 114–19.

35. She is listed as such in the 1850 California census. William Longknife is listed in San Francisco city directories between 1860 and 1865, but the listings do not include married women. Longknife letter, 1854. Longknife letter, 1857. Longknife petition.

36. Johnson, *Roaring Camp*, 11–12.

37. Longknife letter, 1857.

38. Longknife letter, 1857.

39. Longknife letter, 1857.

40. Longknife letter, 1857.

41. Russell Thornton, *The Cherokees: A Population History* (Lincoln: University of Nebraska Press, 1992), 50–51, 71, 75; Paul Kelton, *Epidemics and Enslavement: Biolog-*

ical Catastrophe in the Native Southeast, 1491–1715 (Lincoln: University of Nebraska Press, 2007), 153–53, 158.

42. In 1834 some Cherokees refused to migrate west because of the reported presence of cholera there. Thornton, *The Cherokees*, 50.

43. Longknife letter, 1854; Longknife petition.

44. Longknife letter, 1857.

45. Thornton, *The Cherokees*, 75–76.

46. Longknife letter, 1857.

47. Longknife letter, 1857.

48. Longknife petition.

49. "The Longknives at War Again," *Daily Alta Californian*, October 5, 1864, 1.

50. Longknife petition.

51. Longknife letter, 1857.

52. Dale and Litton, *Cherokee Cavaliers*, 90.

53. For an example of this scholarship that explains the role of women in diaspora communities, see Susan Lobo, "Urban Clan Mothers: Key Households in Cities," *American Indian Quarterly* 27, no. 3 (2003): 505–22.

54. Longknife letter, 1857.

55. Longknife letter, 1857.

Ten

Cherokee Women and the Woman's Christian Temperance Union

IZUMI ISHII

In the late nineteenth century, the United States adopted a policy of allotting the tribally held lands of Native nations to individuals, assimilating Indian people as individuals into American society, and dissolving tribal governments by making the citizens of sovereign tribes subject to state law. In most cases, the Native victims of allotment became economically impoverished and politically marginalized by the white majority. Among the peoples who experienced allotment were the Five Tribes in the Indian Territory, including the Cherokee Nation. Traditionally scholars have focused almost exclusively on the economic and political impact of allotment. More recently, Rose Stremlau has examined the social bonds that enabled the survival of Cherokee families, communities, culture, and tribal identity. Whatever the focus, the consensus of scholars is that allotment was incredibly destructive to Indian peoples. One of the casualties of allotment in the Cherokee Nation was the involvement of Cherokee women in the broader temperance movement.[1]

Temperance in the Cherokee Nation had been a male-dominated movement that often served political purposes.[2] In the 1880s, however, the emphasis of the movement shifted from the sovereign right of tribes to regulate alcohol to the morality of drinking. Just like American women, Cherokee women had been excluded from institutionalized politics, but once temperance became a moral issue, they assumed a leadership role. The involvement of Cherokee women in temperance efforts coincided with the rise of the Woman's Christian Temperance Union (WCTU) in the United States. Part of a broader late nineteenth-century social reform movement, the WCTU was founded in Ohio in 1874. Just as the founders of the WCTU did, some Cherokee women found temperance to be an issue on which they could assert influence in the public arena.

Alcohol abuse was widespread in nineteenth-century America, but in the Cherokee Nation, it tended to present problems primarily in times of stress, especially those times, such as removal, when the Cherokee government lost the ability to govern effectively. In the late nineteenth century, the Cherokee Nation once again faced serious challenges as non-Indians flooded into Indian Territory. These intruders were not subject to Cherokee laws regulating alcohol, and they flouted applicable federal laws. The destruction and violence that alcohol precipitated upset Cherokees as did the images that such mayhem presented, those of the drunken Indian and the inept tribal government. Non-Indian temperance reformers took note of the alcohol-fueled chaos and brought their crusade to Indian Territory.[3]

In 1879 an International Temperance Convention met in Tahlequah, capital of the Cherokee Nation, and organized a committee to ask the Commissioner of Indian Affairs to enforce more stringently the federal liquor laws in the territory. The site of the convention was the Cherokee Nation, but the convention organizers were not Indians. Nevertheless, many Indians attended, which impressed the organizers. One of the American women in attendance expressed her wish for more effective enforcement of the federal intercourse acts that prohibited the sale of alcohol to Indians, but she also applauded the Cherokees for their decision to enact their own prohibitory laws, under which their citizens would be "doubly protected." Her discovery of Native involvement in the cause of temperance "modified previous impressions" of Indian drunkenness, but she still found room for improvement. In conjunction with the convention, WCTU president Frances Willard sent a letter advocating temperance legislation and a copy of one of her addresses to the Cherokee National Council. Local Indian newspapers, the *Cherokee Advocate* and the *Indian Journal*, published the address with Cherokee and Creek translations.[4]

President Willard included the Indian Territory on her 1881

speaking tour. Her fame preceded her, and the Cherokee chief, Dennis W. Bushyhead, asked Jane Stapler, together with several other women and clergymen, to form a committee to welcome Willard to the capital of the Nation and to make her visit "pleasant and agreeable to herself, and profitable to our people." Much to her surprise, perhaps, Willard encountered "not a wigwam nor blanket nor warwhoop" during her visit to Indian Territory. Instead, she found a prosperous people engaged in farming, ranching, and commerce, which she attributed "to the absence of the drinking customs." Jane Stapler, niece of former chief John Ross and wife of a Tahlequah merchant who was Ross's brother-in-law, soon emerged as a leading temperance reformer in the Indian Territory.[5]

With Stapler at the helm, the cause of temperance gained ground among Cherokee citizens. The men's Tahlequah Christian Temperance Union already held mass meetings and temperance lectures regularly, and the women soon organized a chapter of the wctu. Residents of Tahlequah collected 112 signatures to a memorial asking Chief Bushyhead to protect children more thoroughly from the vice of alcohol. The National Council granted a town lot in the capital to the business committee of the Tahlequah Christian Temperance Union to build a reading room and library in order to generate public support for temperance. The *Cherokee Advocate* proclaimed: "The outlook now for a grand temperance boom is most auspicious."[6]

In November 1883 reformers invited the temperance lecturer Emma Molloy to Tahlequah. Molloy mesmerized her Cherokee listeners. According to one witness, "For two hours she held the attention of the audience, so completely that the falling of a pin to the floor could have been heard all over the house." At the close of her address, many signed the pledge of total abstinence, and she did not leave the lecture hall until eleven o'clock. After this great success, Molloy became a regular visitor to the Cherokee Nation, and her audiences remained large, but the number who pledged abstinence declined. A Cherokee woman named Elizabeth Ross explained the disparity: "Women speakers were seldom seen and heard, and for the purpose of listening to a woman a number of persons, who otherwise probably would have remained at home, were present." In particular, the temperance message had little effect on Americans who squatted illegally on Indian land and used their anomalous legal position to engage in unscrupulous and even criminal behavior, including the importation, consumption, and sale of alcohol.[7]

Nevertheless, Molloy invigorated the Tahlequah Woman's Christian Temperance Union and linked Cherokee women to the movement in the United States. In February 1884 the *Union Signal*, an official organ of the WCTU, reported on the Tahlequah chapter's success: "God has wonderfully blessed us within the past three months. . . . The whole country is stirred on the subjects of temperance and religion. Many drunkards have been reclaimed." Just as WCTU chapters in the United States did, the Tahlequah WCTU focused in particular on the responsibility of mothers to raise children who would not be tempted by whiskey, and it encouraged participation in the Band of Hope, a temperance organization for children, by inviting them to official gatherings.[8] Temperance, however, would not remain simply a domestic or moral issue; legal and political dimensions could not be ignored.

When Ada Archer of the Cherokee Female Seminary became the first Cherokee woman to lecture in public on temperance in 1884, she condemned Cherokee citizens for their unwillingness to observe U.S. laws designed to prevent liquor sales by American citizens to Indians. The refusal of Cherokees to obey federal alcohol regulations exacerbated the liquor traffic among her people. What was worse, she charged, fear of private revenge prevented Cherokees from reporting cases "either to our own courts or to the U.S. Court," and "public virtue carries a blind eye" to the illicit liquor trade. Standing before the Tahlequah Christian Temperance Union, whose membership included the most powerful politicians in the Cherokee Nation, Archer accused the Cherokees of failing to cope with the problem: "Let us clearly understand the fact . . . that we cannot enforce our own law for want of public sentiment, and moral courage among our citizens." She believed that the Cherokees needed "live moral force" to reinvigorate "the force of law."[9] Gradually, the Tahlequah WCTU moved into the political realm.

In 1886 Martha G. Tunstall, the wife of a missionary, became the WCTU organizer in the Cherokee Nation. She encouraged Cherokees to sign the total abstinence pledge and urged the Tahlequah WCTU to pursue legislative solutions for intemperance. The Cherokee National Council was receptive and invited the Tahlequah chapter to present whatever propositions it had in mind. Members prepared a memorial beseeching the Cherokee council to enact a tribal law to punish drunkenness. Ten WCTU members met with the council, and their spokeswoman presented a petition for legislative action. The lower house of the Cherokee Nation passed the bill, but opposition from the president of the Cherokee Senate prevented the Nation from branding drunkenness a misdemeanor.[10]

This failure encouraged doubt among the American women who led the national WCTU that the Cherokee Nation had the will to enforce temperance. Correspondence in the *Union Signal* complained that the Indian Territory was "a very discouraging field more so, because the leaders in every good work must come from among the missionaries, and they have so many cares connected with their church work." Cherokee women tried to counter this dismissive attitude toward Indians by pointing out the long history of Cherokee temperance and the Nation's "admirably enforced" prohibitory laws, which contrasted with the failure of "our national, paternal government" to enact meaningful alcohol regulations.[11]

The Tahlequah WCTU also had become a major force for social reform in Indian Territory. Members visited the national prison regularly to teach Cherokee convicts the importance of a temperate life. They introduced "scientific" temperance instruction in Indian schools. They encouraged the high sheriff to stamp out the illicit liquor trade, and they rewarded him with a cake and a bouquet of flowers for his efforts. Nevertheless, some Cherokees remained cynical. The *Tahlequah Telephone* commented that "if we had kept a list of all the organizations that have been formed in Tahlequah, for temperance purposes and for good intentions, it would fill up the Telephone; and yet what has become of them all?"[12]

On July 18, 1888, women temperance reformers in Indian

Territory held a two-day, territory-wide Woman's Christian Temperance Union convention in Muskogee and formed an Indian Territory WCTU. They elected Jane Stapler president and Tennessee M. Fuller corresponding secretary. The delegates included African American women, who sought to organize a chapter, and the territorial WCTU resolved to appoint "a colored superintendent for work among that race." Sarah M. Perkins, a national organizer, monitored the convention. Having campaigned for temperance in the Creek and Choctaw nations as well as among the Cherokees, Perkins expressed her satisfaction: "I was astonished that the women, unaccustomed to public speaking, could express themselves so well in little impromptu speeches." The following year, the Indian Territory WCTU met in Tahlequah, and with national WCTU president Frances Willard present, Stapler addressed the convention. The corresponding secretary announced in her report that "the W.C.T.U. has come to stay. The golden seed has been sown and the good women from all parts of our fair Territory are here to tell us that it is springing up to bring forth an abundant harvest for the future."[13]

While the WCTU was having a major impact on the Cherokee Nation and its citizens, the growth of the temperance movement in Indian Territory seemed to change the image of Native people among temperance reformers. After visiting Indian Territory, WCTU organizer Barbara O'Brian concluded that "the expression 'as dirty as an Indian,' could not have had its birth among the Cherokees, for the full-blooded women could easily give lessons in neatness to many women in Kansas, Missouri and Texas; in fact, to women all over the United States." Consequently, the WCTU leadership welcomed Cherokee women to its national convention and in 1890 invited Jane Stapler to address the annual meeting in Atlanta.[14]

In her address Stapler challenged stereotypes about Indians. Although Indians, perhaps, had felt the woes of alcohol more keenly than others, "it does not necessarily imply that they have been the hardest drinkers." She recounted how unscrupulous Americans in the territory helped perpetuate this "drunken Indian" stereotype. They distributed alcohol among Indians, became intoxicated with them, and soon began fighting with them. When friends of both parties joined in the fray, "a rush to the frontier post with an alarm that 'The Indians are on the War-path' has caused a hasty parade of troops which has been met by an ambitious chief with his warriors," and a more deadly battle ensued. Although these alarming conditions led Congress to ban the sale and use of intoxicating liquors in Indian Country, the federal liquor laws never entirely suppressed the traffic. With enforcement, however, "the war-whoop, white and red, [would] become a thing for historical allusion only."[15]

Stapler's hopes for the future were dashed a year later when a federal judge in Texas ruled that the sale of malt liquor, a beer with high alcohol content, did not violate federal law. Temperance women had criticized the shipment of malt liquors by railroad and express companies into Indian Territory. When the territorial WCTU petitioned the Missouri, Kansas, and Texas Railway for cooperation in the prevention of the liquor traffic, that company assured President Stapler that it also would make every effort to stop the flow. But the ruling in 1891, according to the Cherokees' agent Leo E. Bennett, immediately "opened up [to] the breweries the most profitable field they have ever delighted in debauching." Agent Bennett lamented: "Year by year the Territory seems to become a more inviting field to the avaricious venders of the various kinds of intoxicating beverages." The secretary of the interior authorized Bennett to seize beer shipped into the territory and hand it over to the U.S. marshal. The *Cherokee Advocate* applauded the secretary's decision as "eminently proper" and added that "with the toleration of this beer or hop tea or by what other name it may be called, will come other and more pernicious stuff and the result will be, blood shed and riotous conduct followed by sorrow, shame and grief in many house holds." When Agent Bennett seized a carload of beer, however, the U.S. marshal refused to hold it for him. What was worse, the U.S. attorney general concurred with the court decision and declined to "take any steps which might render the marshal responsible on his bond."[16]

The corresponding secretary of the territorial WCTU reported to the national headquarters in 1892: "The special work of our Unions this year has been against beer." The members petitioned local authorities to prevent its sale, and they circulated for signatures a memorial addressed to President Benjamin Harrison appealing for a ban on the sale of malt liquors among Indians. Meanwhile, President Stapler asked a lawyer in Washington to lobby for a prohibition bill in Congress. When Judge Isaac C. Parker of the U.S. District Court in Fort Smith finally called a halt to the beer business in Indian Territory, "the beer venders were brought to realize that perhaps, after all, they were not to be allowed to violate the laws with impunity." On July 23, 1892, Congress provided that "no ardent spirits, ale, beer, wine, or intoxicating liquor or liquors of whatever kind shall be introduced, under any pretense, into the Indian country." The women of the Tahlequah WCTU rang all the church bells in the town in celebration.[17]

The struggle to ban beer coincided with an equally intense effort to eliminate the sale of alcohol in Indian Territory for medicinal purposes. Cherokee law licensed physicians to prescribe alcohol. Charlatans rushed to open drugstores and distributed alcoholic patent medicines freely within the Nation. In the fall of 1892, Chief C. J. Harris attempted to expel from the Nation "quack" doctors who practiced medicine without a Cherokee license and endangered "the lives of innocent and often ignorant people" with the prescriptions for alcohol. It was, however, extremely difficult to ferret out these self-styled professionals because customers, knowing that they themselves would be charged with the possession of intoxicants, protected them. President Stapler solicited state WCTUs for contributions to a one-hundred-dollar reward fund for individuals who informed on those who were distributing Jamaica ginger, which was 90 percent alcohol, and other alcoholic medicines among Cherokees. As a result, the Tahlequah WCTU succeeded in forcing a number of druggists in the Nation to desist from selling patent medicines that produced intoxication.[18]

Just when the Tahlequah WCTU was winning significant victories, political issues began to undermine its relationship with the national organization. The same reform impulse that had given rise to temperance in the late nineteenth century sparked calls for the reform of U.S. Indian policy. Independent Indian nations seemed to many Americans to be anachronistic obstacles to national economic development and progress. Furthermore, the tribal ownership of land contradicted the late nineteenth-century veneration of the individual. Rhetoric criticized the inability of Indian nations to stem the flow of alcohol, and the reported persistence of alcohol abuse suggested that the collective nature of tribes contributed to individual moral failure. The reform of Indian policy focused on the allotment of Indian lands to individuals and the dissolution of tribal governments. As a result, the national WCTU gradually backed away from its positive views of Indians and its confidence in tribal legislative action. American reformers increasingly saw Cherokee sovereignty as an impediment to moral uplift, and an Indian presence in the U.S. temperance movement waned. Jane Stapler's address to the 1890 WCTU convention marked the apex of Indian inclusion in the movement.

The national WCTU began to undermine tribal sovereignty by publicizing incidents of alcohol-related lawlessness in Indian Territory and concluding that blame lay with Native people because "it was difficult to control their thirst for fire-water." Reformers found the stereotype of "drunken Indians" to be a powerful weapon to promote their own cause because it illustrated the depravity that resulted from intemperance. It also served the cause of allotment and statehood. The image of the drunken Indian dominated the descriptions of Native people in the *Union Signal*: "A sober Indian may be made into a good citizen, but drunk, his savage instincts and passions convert him into a demon."[19]

In 1893 Congress created the Commission to the Five Civilized Tribes, commonly called the Dawes Commission, and charged it with negotiating agreements with the tribes to allot tribal land to individuals and dissolve tribal governments in preparation for the admission of a new state to the Union and the assimilation of Indian people into American society as individuals. In 1898 Congress enacted the Curtis Act, which provided for the allotment of Cherokee land upon completion of tribal rolls and the abolition of the judicial functions of the Cherokee Nation. Congress allowed the state of Arkansas to extend its jurisdiction over the Indian Territory and gave it the power to enforce all state laws except the one legalizing the liquor traffic within the state boundaries. With no alternative except to acquiesce to an imposed agreement, in 1902 the Cherokees consented to a somewhat more favorable plan for the dissolution of tribal government and the merging of the Indian and Oklahoma territories into a new state. Many Indians, however, insisted that they should have a state of their own, independent of Oklahoma.[20]

Prohibition became an issue in the debates over Oklahoma statehood. At the 1901 national WCTU annual convention, a longtime Baptist missionary among the Choctaws asserted that "the WCTU need not concern itself with the question of single or double statehood for Indian Territory and Oklahoma, but that it could not afford to lose one inch of prohibition territory." The national WCTU promptly telegraphed President Theodore Roosevelt to urge him to retain prohibition among the Indians "because it is well known that the Indian race has a peculiar and most powerful appetite for intoxicating liquors," which, it feared, would "very speedily" destroy the entire Native population if the federal government legalized drinking among the Indian tribes. For American temperance reformers, securing prohibition in the new state was the top priority; whether or not Indians retained self-government in a state separate from Oklahoma was inconsequential. In a half-hearted attempt to take the Native peoples' sentiments into consideration, on March 9, 1904, the national WCTU presented to Congress a memorial "remonstrating against . . . the union and admission of Indian Territory and Oklahoma Territory as one state unless the sale of intoxicants therein is prohibited." Still, the national WCTU thought that the Native people would eventually agree to unite with citizens of Oklahoma for joint statehood if they could obtain prohibition in the new state.[21]

Indians, however, objected to joint statehood because "it means the extension over Indian Territory of laws admitting intoxicants, which will be peculiarly disastrous and ruinous to the Indian people." For WCTU members in Indian Territory, a separate state for Indians, one that could enact and enforce prohibition, was essential. They reported to the national WCTU convention in 1902: "We have been working to hold our Prohibitory Law by not being annexed to Oklahoma." Most problems with alcohol in Indian Territory, after all, could be traced to American citizens. The Indian Territory WCTU repeatedly petitioned the president of the United States and Congress to preserve prohibition laws among Indians and to oppose the annexation of Indian Territory to an Oklahoma rife with saloons. The temperance movement became a voice for the sovereignty of Indian Territory and an advocate for Indian control of their political, as well as their moral, status. The Indian Territory WCTU's position, however, ultimately sundered its relationship with the national organization.[22]

To many citizens of the Indian Territory, the loss of sovereignty after the dissolution of their tribal governments was of prime importance, and their leaders worked vigorously to retain their peoples' right to control their own lives. Leaders advocated prohibition because they thought that insistence on prohibition would help them secure separate statehood, which they believed permitted a vestige of tribal sovereignty. When he received a letter from a WCTU member in March 1903, therefore, Choctaw chief Green McCurtain recognized her temperance organization as "of much assistance to our plan of separate statehood." The letter writer cited the importance of pursuing prohibition along with separate statehood because "there is very little hope of a continuance of the Indian race unless intoxicating liquors is kept from them." McCurtain thought that Native people should advocate prohibition "for the preservation of the Indian race together with his vast estate" and urged the leaders of other Indian tribes, including Cherokee chief T. M. Buffington, to assure his correspondent that they supported prohibition. The delegates of the Five Tribes confirmed this position once again in a convention held in Eufaula two months later by resolving that their councils send memorials to various temperance and religious organizations in an effort to obtain their assistance in securing a state government separate from that of Oklahoma.[23]

The Campaign Committee of the Constitutional Convention for independent statehood for Indian Territory convened in Muskogee on August 21, 1905, and proposed a separate state of Sequoyah. Delegates proclaimed that "all people naturally desire self government." The integration of Indian Territory

into Oklahoma against its will, they warned, would also "offend
... the feelings of the people of Oklahoma." The code of laws
Oklahoma had enacted were not "agreeable or suitable to the
people of Indian Territory in a vast number of particulars." The
most objectionable provision permitted saloons in Oklahoma.
An American sympathizer in Philadelphia charged: "Oklahoma
boldly proclaims that she will not have prohibition. By this very
disregard of the wishes and rights of her proposed mate she shows
herself unfit for Statehood." Except for "medicinal, mechanical,
and scientific purposes," the proposed constitution for the state
of Sequoyah declared the use of alcohol unlawful and empow-
ered the governor to appoint three "enforcement commissioners" to implement prohibition.[24]

The temperance movement in Indian Territory initially was
divided over the issue of statehood. In her 1904 annual address,
the territorial WCTU president declared that "we are in favor of
prohibition statehood regardless of boundaries," but her constituents in the organization did not unanimously agree on this
statement. The president asked the national organization for
help in achieving prohibition over "the state formed from Oklahoma and Indian Territory," a slap in the face to those who had
worked for the right of Indian people to retain their prohibition
laws and the government that enforced them. The corresponding secretary, on the other hand, reported that "the W.C.T.U.
have advocated separate statehood with prohibition." The president apparently had failed to convince her members. The terms
by which Oklahoma entered the Union pleased neither side. In
1906 Congress prohibited the sale of alcohol in the Indian Territory part of the new state for twenty-one years after statehood
but gave the Oklahoma side the right to decide what it would
do about the liquor trade.[25]

After Indian Territory lost the battle for separate statehood,
the Oklahoma Territory WCTU began fighting to secure "a uniform constitution for the whole state." At the 1906 national convention, the WCTU announced that "we have good reason to
believe that forty thousand square miles will be added to the
prohibition territory when in a few months the people of Oklahoma declare in the Constitutional Convention, or by the votes

of their people, that their state shall be free from the legalized saloon." The ratification of the new state's constitution was scheduled for September 17, 1907. The Indian Territory WCTU president rallied her troops: "Do your best to get temperance men from Indian Territory elected to the constitutional convention so a prohibition clause may be inserted in the state constitution." Indeed, the Oklahoma state constitution prohibited alcohol.[26]

Following a suggestion by the national and territorial WCTU presidents, in 1906 the Indian Territory WCTU Executive Committee presented a proposal to "call new WCTU work Sequoyah" when the Indian Territory and Oklahoma amalgamated. In the territorial annual convention of that year, however, the delegates concluded that they would remain a separate union and, after Oklahoma statehood in 1907, would change their name to the Eastern Oklahoma Woman's Christian Temperance Union. When the president of the Oklahoma WCTU attended the Indian Territory WCTU's annual meeting the following year and invited the group to unite with the Oklahoma union, the territorial union declined her offer and elected its own officers. She was not entirely discouraged: "The white women were unanimously in favor of it, but some of the Indian women felt that the time had not yet come for Union. I am sure the two organizations will be united in their efforts to eradicate the saloon and all its evils."[27]

In November 1907 the national WCTU Executive Committee passed the following resolution:

> Inasmuch as former Indian Territory is now a part of the State of Oklahoma, and as the National W.C.T.U. can recognize but one State Union (except in states having colored organizations, or where geographical conditions make it necessary) your Committee recom[m]end that plans be made by the Presidents of Indian Territory and Oklahoma looking toward the union of the two organizations, said plans to be submitted to the General Officers of the National Woman[']s Christian Temperance Union who shall have power to ratify, amend or reject the same. We further recommend that one year be given to make all needed changes.[28]

The reform organization that had linked Indian women to the temperance movement in the United States was about to come to an end. Allotment and statehood had blunted the assimilative effects of this social reform movement, and the national organization had marginalized its own Indian members.

On September 11, 1908, members of the former Indian Territory WCTU gathered for its last annual convention. President Lilah D. Lindsey declared: "The Indian Territory Woman[']s Christian Temperance Union has reached its majority as does a voting citizen of the United States at the age of twenty one. . . . How little our pioneers realized at that time what their efforts would bring forth with that small membership." On this memorable day, Lindsey announced to her colleagues that the national union had asked the organization to merge with the one in Oklahoma to work together for the cause of temperance. Four days later, President Lindsey and other Indian Territory delegates left for Oklahoma City, where on September 18, 1908, the Indian Territory and Oklahoma WCTUs formally dissolved, and their members formed the Greater Oklahoma State Woman's Christian Temperance Union.[29]

The temperance movement that American women led had welcomed Indian women to join them in the struggle. For Indian and non-Indian women, temperance was a moral issue that initially took precedence over political affairs in which they had no voice. When allotment and statehood threatened tribal sovereignty, however, Native women struggled to understand what it meant for their cause. Those who had long advocated for temperance found themselves increasingly disheartened by their American colleagues who resurrected the stereotype of the drunken Indian. Unwilling to support tribal sovereignty or a separate state of Sequoyah, the WCTU placed universal prohibition above the hope of Cherokee and other Indian WCTU members to save their own people from an evil introduced by Americans. In the process, the WCTU eliminated from its own organization a significant voice for reform.

Notes

1. Rose Stremlau, *Sustaining the Cherokee Family: Kinship and the Allotment of an Indigenous Nation* (Chapel Hill: University of North Carolina Press, 2011). For allotment and its influence on Indian tribes, see Arrell Morgan Gibson, "The Centen-

nial Legacy of the General Allotment Act," *Chronicles of Oklahoma* 65 (1987): 228–51; William T. Hagan, *Taking Indian Lands: The Cherokee (Jerome) Commission, 1889–1893* (Norman: University of Oklahoma Press, 2003); and Wilcomb E. Washburn, *The Assault on Indian Tribalism: The General Allotment Law (Dawes Act) of 1887* (Philadelphia PA: Lippincott, 1975).

2. Izumi Ishii, "Alcohol and Politics in the Cherokee Nation before Removal," *Ethnohistory* 50 (Fall 2003): 671–95.

3. Izumi Ishii, *Bad Fruits of the Civilized Tree: Alcohol and the Sovereignty of the Cherokee Nation* (Lincoln: University of Nebraska Press, 2008). The standard work on the Woman's Christian Temperance Union is Ruth Bordin, *Woman and Temperance: The Quest for Power and Liberty, 1873–1900* (Philadelphia PA: Temple University Press, 1981).

4. "Report of the Corresponding Secretary, Indian Territory," *Minutes of the Woman's National Christian Temperance Union, at the Seventh Annual Meeting, in Boston, October 27th to 30th, 1880 with Reports and Constitution* (New York: The National Temperance Society and Publication House, 1880), 92; Woman's Christian Temperance Union National Headquarters Historical Files, joint Ohio Historical Society–Michigan Historical Collections–Woman's Christian Temperance Union microfilm edition, Woman's Christian Temperance Union series, roll 1 (hereafter cited as WCTU Historical Files with roll and folder numbers, when available); Sarah P. Morrison, "Report of Committee on Work among the Indians, Chinese, and Colored People," *Minutes of the Woman's National Christian Temperance Union Annual Meeting, 1880*, 61–62.

5. D. W. Bushyhead to L. J. Stapler, May 18, 1881, WCTU Historical Files, roll 12, folder 12; Frances E. Willard Journal, May 19, 1881, typescript, Frances E. Willard Memorial Library, Evanston, Illinois; Cherokee National Records, J. Ellen Foster to D. W. Bushyhead, February 18, 1882, CHN 115, Cherokee (Tahlequah)-*Whiskey Traffic & Gambling Suppression*, microcopy, Archives and Manuscripts Division, Oklahoma Historical Society, Oklahoma City, Oklahoma (hereafter cited as CHN with roll number). For Jane Stapler's biographical sketch, see Works Progress Administration, Project S-149, Indian–Pioneer History Collection, Mrs. Roy Bradshaw, vol. 104, 132–44, typescript, Archives and Manuscripts Division, Oklahoma Historical Society, Oklahoma City, Oklahoma (hereafter cited as IPH, OHS, with interviewee's name and volume and page numbers).

6. *Cherokee Advocate*, September 21, 1883; *Minutes of the Woman's National Christian Temperance Union Annual Meeting, 1880*, 132; John S. Adair, Allen Ross, Wm. Johnston, and others to D. W. Bushyhead, n.d., CHN 115, Cherokee (Tahlequah)-*Whiskey Traffic & Gambling Suppression*; *Laws and Joint Resolutions of the Cherokee Nation, Enacted during the Regular and Special Sessions of the Years 1881–2–3. Published by Authority of an Act of the National Council* (first published Tahlequah, Cherokee Nation, 1884; repr., Wilmington DE: Scholarly Resources Inc., 1975), 153–54 (page references are to reprint edition).

7. "A Great Rally for Temperance, Morality and Christianity at the Cherokee Capital," *Cherokee Advocate*, November 30, 1883; "Return of Mrs. Molloy," *Cherokee Advocate*, January 11, 1884; "Mrs. Molloy at Ft. Gibson," *Cherokee Advocate*, February 1, 1884; Emma Hicks to Ann Eliza Worcester Robertson, January 31, 1884,

Alice Mary Robertson Papers, series II, box 12, folder 3, McFarlin Library, Department of Special Collections, University of Tulsa, Tulsa, Oklahoma; IPH, OHS, Elizabeth Ross, vol. 43, 28. The *Cherokee Advocate* consistently called her "Emily" Molloy although her real name was Emma Molloy. For Molloy's biographical sketch, see Phebe A. Hanaford, *Daughters of America; or, Women of the Century* (Boston MA: B. B. Russell, 1883), 673–76.

8. Katie Ellett, "News from the Field, Indian Territory," *Union Signal*, February 21, 1884, 11; "Cherokee," "To the Members of the Woman's Christian Temperance Union," *Cherokee Advocate*, March 28, 1884; "Drops of Water," *Cherokee Advocate*, June 6, 1884.

9. "Temperance Lecture," *Cherokee Advocate*, January 25, 1884; *Cherokee Advocate*, May 2, 1884.

10. "Indian Territory, A New Union and Its Work," *Union Signal*, December 23, 1886, 11; "Report of the Corresponding Secretary, Indian Territory," *Minutes of the National Woman's Christian Temperance Union, at the Fourteenth Annual Meeting in Nashville, Tenn., November 16 to 21, 1887. With Addresses, Reports and Constitutions* (Chicago IL: Woman's Temperance Publication Association, 1888), 116, WCTU Historical Files, roll 2; Martha G. Tunstall, "Legislation, Indian Territory," *Minutes of the National W.C.T.U. Annual Meeting, 1887*, ccxxiii.

11. Mrs. J. A. Rogers, "Indian Territory, Interesting Notes," *Union Signal*, March 17, 1887, 10; Mary E. Griffith to the *Union Signal*, June 13, 1888, "Prohibition in Indian Territory," *Union Signal*, June 21, 1888, 5.

12. Mrs. Helen R. Duncan to the *Union Signal*, "Scientific Temperance Instruction in Indian Territory," *Union Signal*, April 11, 1889, 5; "Letter from Helen R. Duncan," *Cherokee Advocate*, August 1, 1888; *Union Signal*, September 20, 1888, 12; *Cherokee Advocate*, November 14, 1888; T. M. Fuller and N. K. Fite, *Cherokee Advocate*, June 6, 1888.

13. Sarah M. Perkins and others, "Indian Territory, Call for Convention," *Cherokee Advocate*, July 11, 1888; Alice M. Robertson, *Cherokee Advocate*, July 11, 1888; "W.C.T.U.," *Muskogee Phoenix*, July 12, 1888; Annual Convention Program for 1889 with press cutting tipped in, Lilah D. Lindsey Collection, series III, box 2, folder 20, McFarlin Library Department of Special Collections, University of Tulsa, Tulsa, Oklahoma (hereafter cited as Lindsey Collection); Sarah M. Perkins, "Indian Territory," *Union Signal*, August 2, 1888, 10; Mrs. S. M. Perkins, "Reports of National Organizers," *Minutes of the National Woman's Christian Temperance Union, at the Fifteenth Annual Meeting in New York City, October 19 to 23, 1888. With Addresses, Reports and Constitutions* (Chicago IL: Woman's Christian Temperance Publication Association, 1888), 281–84, WCTU Historical Files, roll 2; *Minutes of the Indian Territory Woman's Christian Temperance Union. Held at Tahlequah, Indian Territory, June [sic] 4, 1889* (Muskogee IT: Our Brother in Red Pub. Co., n.d.), 1–11, Lindsey Collection, series III, box 2, folder 20.

14. Barbara O'Brian, "Indian Territory, News and Notes," *Union Signal*, December 26, 1889, 11; *Minutes of the Indian Territory W.C.T.U., 1889*, 10.

15. Mrs. L. Jane Stapler, "Address of President of Indian Territory to National Convention," *Minutes of the National Woman's Christian Temperance Union, at the Seventeenth Annual Meeting in Atlanta, Georgia, November 14th to 18th, 1890. With Addresses, Reports*

and *Constitutions* (Chicago IL: Woman's Temperance Publication Association, 1890), 390–92, WCTU Historical Files, roll 3. According to the *Cherokee Advocate*, these U.S. soldiers were ready customers of alcohol, and such disorderly conditions pleased many whiskey peddlers. "When times became too quiet on the frontier to need the presence of soldiers," in fact, these criminal traders attempted to "draw custom" by hiring gunmen who would commit crimes for them and produce "a general disturbance sufficient to cause the Indian agent to dispatch to Washington—'Indians on the war path—send soldiers immediately.'" *Cherokee Advocate*, June 17, 1899.

16. "Sale of Liquor to Indians," *Report of the Commissioner of Indian Affairs*, October 1, 1891, *Executive Documents*, 52nd Cong., 1st sess., serial 2934, 74–75; T. M. Fuller, "W.C.T.U. Notes," *Cherokee Advocate*, October 15, 1890; "Intoxicating Liquors," in Leo E. Bennett to the Commissioner of Indian Affairs [Thomas Jefferson Morgan], September 26, 1892, *House Executive Documents*, 52nd Cong., 2nd sess., serial 3088, 259; "Intoxicating Liquors," in Leo E. Bennett to the Commissioner of Indian Affairs [Thomas Jefferson Morgan], September 7, 1891, *Executive Documents*, 52nd Cong., 1st sess., serial 2934, 248; *Cherokee Advocate*, August 28, 1891; "Sale of Liquor to Indians," *Report of the Commissioner of Indian Affairs*, August 27, 1892, *House Executive Documents*, 52nd Cong., 2nd sess., serial 3088, 103–4.

17. Tennie M. Fuller, "Indian Territory," *Minutes of the National Woman's Christian Temperance Union at the Nineteenth Annual Meeting, Denver, Col., October 28th to November 2d, 1892 with Addresses, Reports and Constitution* (Chicago IL: Woman's Temperance Publishing Association, 1892), 222, WCTU Historical Files, roll 3; "Intoxicating Liquors," in Leo E. Bennett to the Commissioner of Indian Affairs [Thomas Jefferson Morgan], September 26, 1892, *House Executive Documents*, 52nd Cong., 2nd sess., serial 3088, 259; *U.S. Statutes at Large*, 27:260–61; *Union Signal*, August 11, 1892, 12.

18. *Compiled Laws of the Cherokee Nation Published by Authority of the National Council* (Tahlequah IT: National Advocate Print, 1881), 162; *Purcell Register*, September 30, 1892, C. Johnson Harris Collection, box H-55, folder 8, Western History Collections, University of Oklahoma Libraries, Norman, Oklahoma; Leo Bennett, Bootlegging, Grant Foreman Collection 83.229, box 4, folder 6, Archives and Manuscripts Division, Oklahoma Historical Society, Oklahoma City, Oklahoma; *Union Signal*, December 15, 1892, 12; Sarah Ford Crosby, "Indian Territory," *Union Signal*, January 12, 1893, 11; T. M. Fuller, "Indian Territory," *Minutes of the National Woman's Christian Temperance Union at the Twentieth Annual Meeting Held in Memorial Art Palace Chicago, Illinois, October 18–21, 1893* (Chicago IL: Woman's Temperance Publishing Association, 1893), 169, WCTU Historical Files, roll 4.

19. "Prohibition for the Indian," *Union Signal*, June 1, 1899, 8; Dorothy J. Cleveland, "Work among Indians," *Union Signal*, August 28, 1902, 11.

20. Francis Paul Prucha, *The Great Father: The United States Government and the American Indians* (Lincoln: University of Nebraska Press, 1984), 2:659–86, 746–55; *U.S. Statutes at Large*, 30:495–519; "Whiskey Selling Still a Crime in Territory," *Cherokee Advocate*, April 22, 1905; *U.S. Statutes at Large*, 32, pt. 1:716–27; "An Act Approved by W. C. Rogers," *Collinsville News*, November 24, 1904, William Charles Rogers Collection, box R-35, folder 97, Western History Collections, University of Oklahoma Libraries, Norman, Oklahoma.

21. "National Convention 1901," November 19, 1901, *Union Signal,* November 23, 1901, 15; "Convention," *Report of the National Woman's Christian Temperance Union Twenty-eighth Annual Meeting Held in the First Baptist Church, Fort Worth, Texas. November 15th to 20th, 1901,* 66–67, WCTU Historical Files, roll 6; L.M.N.S., "Shall the Government Keep Faith with the Indians," *Union Signal,* April 7, 1904, 8; United States Congressional Serial Set, U.S. Senate, *Sale of Intoxicants in Indian and Oklahoma Territories, Etc.,* 58th Cong., 2nd sess., 1904, S. Doc. 194, serial 4591.

22. L.M.N.S., "Shall the Government Keep Faith with the Indians," *Union Signal,* April 7, 1904, 8; Lillian M. N. Stevens, "Address of the President," *Report of the National Woman's Christian Temperance Union Twenty-ninth Annual Meeting Held in the Jefferson, Portland, Maine October 17th to 22d, 1902,* 118, WCTU Historical Files, roll 6; Mrs. J. M. Escoe, "Indian Territory (Amanda Richey)," *Report of the National W.C.T.U. Annual Meeting, 1902,* 158; "Petition President and Congress," *Muskogee Evening Times,* April 25, 1902; Mrs. Belle Brendel, "Indian Territory, Mid Year Conference," *Union Signal,* June 12, 1902, 11; *Union Signal,* January 14, 1904, 11.

23. University of Oklahoma Libraries, Western History Collections, Cherokee Nation Papers microfilm edition, roll 24, folder 2620, Correspondence from Choctaw principal chief Green McCurtain to Principal Chief T. M. Buffington regarding the transmittal of the following, March 27, 1903; and from Mrs. J. S. Morrow [*sic*] to Green McCurtain regarding liquor, March 26, 1903; "For Single Statehood," *Cherokee Advocate,* May 30, 1903.

24. *An Address to the People of Indian Territory on the Question of Independent Statehood for Indian Territory, by the Campaign Committee of the Constitutional Convention. Authorized and Assembled, August 21, 1905* (Muskogee IT: Phoenix Printing Co., 1905), Thomas Gilcrease Institute of American History and Art, Tulsa, Oklahoma; S.N. to the editor of *Public Ledger,* January 16, 1906, quoted from *Public Ledger* in "Indians and Prohibition," *Cherokee Advocate,* February 10, 1906; "Constitution of the State of Sequoyah," in United States Congressional Serial Set, U.S. Senate, *Proposed State of Sequoyah,* 59th Cong., 1st sess., 1906, S. Doc. 143, serial 4912, 81–82.

25. Lucy Belle Davis, "Indian Territory Holds Successful Convention," *Union Signal,* September 29, 1904, 13; *Report of the National Woman's Christian Temperance Union Thirty-second Annual Meeting Held in First Congregational Church, Los Angeles, Cal. October 27–November 1, 1905,* 61, WCTU Historical Files, roll 6; Mrs. Lucy Belle Davis, "Corresponding Secretary's Report, Indian Territory," *Report of the National W.C.T.U. Annual Meeting, 1905,* 154; U.S. Statutes at Large 34, pt. 1:269–70.

26. "The Battle Royal Is on in Oklahoma," *Union Signal,* August 29, 1907, 2. See also Petition for Statewide Prohibition Signed by Several Individuals, Lindsey Collection, series III, box 3, folder 6; Lillian M. N. Stevens, "Oklahoma and Prohibition," *Report of the National Woman's Christian Temperance Union Thirty-third Annual Convention Held in Parson's Theater, Hartford, Connecticut, October 26–31, 1906,* 99, WCTU Historical Files, roll 7; Mabel R. Sutherland, *Champion,* August 1906, 4, Lindsey Collection. For the Oklahoma statewide prohibition campaign and the birth of the prohibition state of Oklahoma, see Jimmie Lewis Franklin, *Born Sober: Prohibi-*

tion in Oklahoma, 1907–1959, with a foreword by J. Howard Edmondson (Norman: University of Oklahoma Press, 1971).

27. Mary T. Cranston, "Minutes of the Executive Meeting of the Indian Territory W.C.T.U., Held at Tulsa, I.T., April 26 and 27, 1906," *Official Proceedings of the 19th and 20th Annual Meetings of the Women's [sic] Christian Temperance Union of Indian Territory Held at Afton, October 26–30, 1906, Tulsa, October 16–20, 1907*, 11, Archives and Manuscripts Division, Oklahoma Historical Society, Oklahoma City, Oklahoma; Mrs. Lila J. Ross, "Indian Territory," *Report of the National W.C.T.U. Annual Convention, 1906*, 149; Clara Hopson, "Indian Territory's Twentieth Convention," *Union Signal*, November 14, 1907, 13; "W.C.T.U. Will Not Merge," *Muskogee Times-Democrat*, October 21, 1907; Abbie B. Hillerman, "President's Letter," *Oklahoma Messenger*, November 1907, 3, Lindsey Collection.

28. Lilah D. Lindsey, President's Address [1908], Lindsey Collection, series III, box 2, folder 19.

29. Lilah D. Lindsey, President's Address [1908]; "State W.C.T.U. to Meet Here," *Muskogee Times-Democrat*, September 5, 1908; "Oklahoma and Indian Territory Unions Are United," *Union Signal*, October 8, 1908, 12; Mrs. Harriet D. Heberling, "Oklahoma," *Report of the National Woman's Christian Temperance Union Thirty-fifth Annual Convention Held in the Auditorium, Denver, Colorado October 23–28, 1908*, 166–67, WCTU Historical Files, roll 7; "Mrs. M'Kellop Is Honored," *Muskogee Times-Democrat*, September 19, 1908.

Eleven

Kinship and Capitalism in the Choctaw and Chickasaw Nations

MALINDA MAYNOR LOWERY

Before the Civil War in Indian Territory, the Choctaw and Chickasaw nations established specific arrangements to accommodate their overlapping families, residences, and business concerns. The Treaty of 1855 was negotiated to consolidate annuity payments from previous treaties and settle the payments due for lands ceded in Mississippi in 1830. In exchange, the Choctaw government granted the first right of way to a railroad entering Indian Territory. This treaty further provided for Choctaw and Chickasaw shared territory, while stipulating that each nation governed itself and controlled its own finances. According to the fifth article of the treaty, Choctaw citizens were given all the rights of Chickasaw citizens, and vice versa. Those rights, however, were not completely reciprocal. The article added that "no member of either tribe shall be entitled to participate in the funds belonging to the other tribe." These funds, of course, were derived from sales of territory to the United States and from economic activities and natural resources exploited by tribal citizens. In a unique arrangement, each southeastern tribe that removed to Indian Territory held a collective, fee-simple title to its land. Individual citizens could profit from the use of the land, but not from buying or selling it. The treaty not only defined formal categories of citizenship in the two nations, but it also prescribed the access those citizens had to the national treasury and to the economic resources the land provided.[1]

To some degree, the Treaty of 1855 codified a different view of land, not as a subsistence or spiritual resource but as a commodity whose profits would provide services for Choctaw and Chickasaw citizens. The evolving definitions of "citizen" in the two nations, moreover, incorporated traditional ideas about gender and marriage, as well as ideas about allegiance to a nation-state with a specific territory and economic resources. At first, kinship was key to the Choctaws' development of natural resources, especially their vast coal deposits, but eventually the obligations of kinship clashed with the free license inherent in capitalism. In this chapter, I will consider how Choctaws and Chickasaws reconciled the reciprocal rules of kinship with the freedoms of capitalism, both for themselves and their nations.[2]

In doing so, I want to tell the story of two Chickasaw women, Rebecca Burney and Annie Guy, who lived in the Choctaw Nation. Both stories begin with family, of course, and the rapid changes Chickasaw kinship systems underwent before, during, and after their removal from the South. While matrilineal family identities remained strong in the Chickasaw Nation through the early nineteenth century, patriarchal ideas brought on by engagement with American economic and religious institutions competed with them and elevated the visibility of fathers in Chickasaw families. Historians, therefore, know the most about the fathers, and especially those fathers who were political or military leaders. But the mothers were important as well, as under Chickasaw kinship obligations, husbands remained members of their mothers' clans but moved into the houses of their wife's mother, their *haloka*. (*Haloka* was the term used for mother-in-law, daughter-in-law, and son-in-law, and translates to "sacred" or "beloved.") Rebecca Burney and Annie Guy developed their identities as Chickasaw women within the context of these changing ideas about nationhood and kinship. At the same time, outsiders' ideas about patriarchy, and the privilege accorded to a man's social and economic prosperity, encouraged both women to become facilitators of capitalist development.[3]

Annie's family's story, particularly that of her female relatives, represents the dynamic shifts in authority, and the autonomy of women, in the Chickasaw Nation. Annie belonged to the storied Colbert lineage of Chickasaw chiefs; she was the great-great-great-granddaughter of James Logan Colbert and his Chickasaw wife. Colbert's son Billy (Annie's great-great-grandfather), and his wife, along with all of their descendants, belonged to the *Chok-ka'Falaha* division (*Chokka'Falaha* translates to "Long House" and was synonymous with the group of "red" or war villages in Mississippi, the division responsible for protecting the Nation against outside threats). This duty had always created conflicts of loyalty in Chickasaw leadership, and the Colbert family reign was not new in this regard. Colberts—both men and women—dealt with diplomatic questions through both trade and war, making their political signals seem murky. Billy Colbert himself was a controversial war leader who, following obligations negotiated in the Treaty of Hopewell (1786), allied with the United States against Red Stick Creeks and other Indians in the Ohio Valley after the American Revolution. After Billy fought alongside Andrew Jackson against the Red Sticks, Billy's brother George negotiated against Jackson to secure the highest possible price for Chickasaw lands, mightily offending Jackson's notions of Indians' gullibility in the process.[4]

The Colberts were both warriors and shrewd business people. By the time of the removal of the Chickasaws, Billy Colbert's descendants had established wealth in cattle and slaves; combined with their influence over tribal leaders and the U.S. government, they possessed formidable weapons of state. For example, it seems that many of Billy's female descendants married men (some Indian, some white) who served as interpreters for the Chickasaws in the eighteenth and nineteenth centuries. These men followed Chickasaw tradition and became part of their *haloka's* houses. Colbert women's wealth and high status reinforced these connections to Chickasaw and American political power. Billy's daughter Molly (Annie's great-grandmother) is one woman who seems to have prioritized her own autonomy above social convention. Molly raised her children, including Betty (Annie's grandmother), in a house that sat atop a mound near Pontotac, Mississippi, an ancient center of the Chickasaw Nation and the town where the Presbyterians built their long-running mission. Molly's first husband, Betty's father, was a Cherokee who served the Chickasaw leadership as interpreter; after he died, she married a wealthy British loyalist. Later, the Presbyterians excommunicated her for impenitence (though the record does not say for which sins she refused to beg forgiveness). Betty's daughter Jane (Annie's mother) married William Richard Guy, who was a commissary and conductor on the Chickasaws' trail of tears in 1837 and 1838. William was white, born in Tennessee. Jane had followed a long tradition in her maternal line, marrying a man with considerable influence both inside and outside the Chickasaw Nation.[5]

Annie was most likely born in the Old Boggy Depot settlement of Indian Territory around 1852 (her father became the postmaster there in 1849). Located near the boundary between the Chickasaw and Choctaw Nations, and in territory rich with coal, Boggy Depot remained a place of business and cultural exchange for over two decades. Presbyterian missionaries built a church there that included members from an older congregation in Mississippi. The church building also served as a boarding school, where a Presbyterian Chickasaw woman oversaw the care of the children. The school at Boggy Depot was part of the Choctaw national school system, which operated under contract with the American Board of Commissioners for Foreign Missions. After Cyrus Byington created a written system for the Choctaw language, American Board missionaries published scripture and religious tracts, as well as a dictionary, spelling books, arithmetic books, and an almanac, in Choctaw. Teachers used English, however, in the schools. By 1860 nine hundred Choctaw children were enrolled in various schools across the nation. During the Civil War, the Presbyterian church became a hospital for Indian and non-Indian soldiers. Annie was thus born into a nest of business, education, and governance institutions conducted primarily by Chickasaws and Choctaws.[6]

Annie and Rebecca Burney had similar affiliations within the Chickasaw kinship system. Rebecca's parents, Lucy James and David Burney, were both Chickasaw citizens. Lucy's mother was Lotty Colbert, a daughter of military and political leader Levi Colbert, and his Chickasaw wife. Rebecca's father David also had a Colbert maternal grandmother, Levi's half-sister, which placed both David and his wife into the *Chokka'Falaha* division. Lucy James and David Burney removed to Indian Territory in 1844, eight years later than Annie Guy's parents and most of the

Chickasaws. In fact, they may have been hoping to avoid removal by taking advantage of reserved land that was granted to David's mother, Margaret Allen, in the Treaty of 1834. Furthermore, David's father Simon may have been ill—he died in 1842—and his considerable property, including thirty-four slaves, doubtless encouraged David Burney to wait and see what, if anything, he could do to avoid removal.[7]

But in 1844 they decided to move, apparently along with David's *haloka*, his mother-in-law. Unlike Jane and William Guy, who removed under the direction of the U.S. Army, Lotty Colbert, her daughter Lucy, and her *haloka*, David, moved themselves and their slaves.[8] But their greater resources did not mean an easy journey. On the riverboat, Lucy gave birth to a baby boy, and they named him Benjamin Crooks Burney, after the boat's captain. And, unlike the majority of Chickasaw slaveholders—and Annie Guy's family—who settled in the Choctaw Nation, the James–Burneys ventured further out, to the region of the Nation beyond Fort Washita, into territory controlled by the Kiowas and Comanches. Perhaps ill from childbirth and the hardship of removal, Lucy James died in 1845, leaving behind her husband, the baby Benjamin, and four older girls, including three-year-old Rebecca. But David remarried quickly to another Chickasaw, retaining his kinship with the *Chokka'Falaha* division. In the meantime, he held onto his slaves and farmed. As the area around him became more densely settled, he became an attorney and judge in the Chickasaw courts and a deacon in the Cumberland Presbyterian Church. By the 1850s, for the Guys and the Burneys, belonging to the Chickasaw warrior division perhaps meant protecting personal and national economic interests, more than it did going to war.[9]

But what did it mean for Rebecca and Annie? Each woman took a different path to navigate the ways removal had disrupted kinship systems, but both involved education. In 1852 the Nation established Bloomfield Academy, a girls' school about seventy-five miles from Rebecca's home in Burneyville. Despite the distance and her age—she was only twelve—Rebecca became one of the school's first students. According to historian Amanda Cobb, Bloomfield represented a continuation of the value Chickasaws placed on literacy. Literacy, in Cobb's words, was "a way to control their own transformation" as a society, and helped create a sense of citizenship that went beyond family and to the Nation as a whole. Rebecca's courage may have inspired her father to found another school, the Burney Institute, about thirty miles from his home. The Chickasaw National Council appropriated $3,000 per year for the school. This school, too, was for girls and opened in 1859.[10]

In Rebecca's days, girls at Bloomfield were educated to read and write at the primary level and taught needlework, sewing, drawing, and housework. With missionaries as teachers, Christian religious training also received heavy emphasis. Teachers instructed students in English and banned the Chickasaw language. Amanda Cobb portrays the curriculum as heavily influenced by contemporaneous American ideals of republican motherhood. She argues that the training prepared girls for citizenship in the Chickasaw Nation and, at the same time, to be able to interact with the white community. Suffering a loss of maternal kin, Rebecca found another kind of kinship at Bloomfield and developed a Chickasaw national identity. While matrilineality persisted in the Nation, patriarchy was on the rise, and men wielded more economic power than ever before. Rather than disempowering her, however, Rebecca's education at Bloomfield prepared her to meet this challenge.[11]

Annie encountered the politics of Chickasaw nationhood at a much younger age than Rebecca. Annie's mother died when Annie was five, in 1857, and her father died two years later. Her mother's brother, Cyrus Harris, may have taken her in along with her siblings (according to one historian, Annie's oldest brother William lived with Harris); a farmer and cattleman, he was the Chickasaw Nation's first principal chief, a position he assumed a year before his sister's death. By that point Annie had probably left Boggy Depot and moved with Harris to Tishomingo, the Chickasaw capital. Under Harris's leadership the Chickasaw Nation was the first among Indian Territory nations to ally with the Confederacy. When the Civil War erupted, eight-year-old Annie and her younger brother moved to central Massachusetts, apparently alone. They lived with a white family whose father was a prosperous shoemaker, and they probably attended the public schools. Cyrus Harris was undoubtedly entrenched in the wartime affairs of the Nation, and the survival of the Chickasaws' educational system may also have been in doubt. Bloomfield Academy, a logical place for Annie to go, closed its doors as a school and reopened them as an army hospital.[12]

After the war, the Chickasaw Nation recommitted itself to education. Rebecca's baby brother, Benjamin, who would later become chief, supervised Bloomfield after the Civil War. He later told the Chickasaw legislature, "Education is the lever by which our people are to be raised to a mental level with our surroundings and I desire to impress seriously upon you how important it is that you use your influence in getting our people to see to the education of the young." The educations of Rebecca and Annie were different, but both of their families were committed to their literacy, in the broadest possible sense, and saw it as a conduit for their citizenship in the Chickasaw Nation.[13]

Annie must have moved back to Boggy Depot, Indian Territory, soon after the war ended, where, by age twenty, she had married Robert Ream and given birth to a son. Ream was an American from Wisconsin who had moved to Arkansas before the war and then enlisted in the Confederate army. In Arkansas he became acquainted with noted Cherokee entrepreneur Elias Cornelius Boudinot, and after the war Robert must have relocated to Indian Territory. Boudinot's ties with the Ream family were so close that in 1871 he established a town on the Missouri, Kansas, and Texas Railway (MKT) in the Cherokee Nation, and named it Vinita, after Robert's sister, the sculptor Vinnie Ream. Robert and Annie had three children—Robert, Boudinot, and Vinnie, and Robert was born near Boggy Depot. But Boggy Depot quickly became obsolete when the MKT built its track twelve miles east of the town in 1872. Annie and her family then relocated even closer to the coal deposits of the Choctaw Nation and the MKT railroad.[14]

Choctaws were probably using coal in the 1840s, soon after their arrival in Indian Territory. The Commissioner of Indian Affairs noted large deposits in 1837. In 1853 a railroad surveyor commented on an "inexhaustible supply" of coal and mentioned that it was already being mined. Choctaw blacksmiths also used coal in their forges and loaded it up in wagons to sell at Fort Sill and Fort Arbuckle. As early as 1851, coal claims were bought and sold among Choctaw citizens.[15] According to the Choctaw constitution, "any person" discovering coal had the right to claim that coal for a mile in every direction from the place of discovery.[16] The claimant also had the right to lease the coal; Choctaws understood this claim to mean mineral and subsurface rights only— the claimant had no right to the surface of the soil, "except so far as it was necessary for development and operation."[17]

Annie and Robert's move represented how economic forces were shifting in the Choctaw and Chickasaw nations after the Civil War. Just as education became an important factor in Chickasaw citizenship, so did economic development and the nation building that it fostered. The Treaty of 1855 guaranteed the Chickasaws control over their own finances, but it also gave them a share in the economic development of the Choctaw Nation. The treaty also ensured that a citizen of one nation acquired certain privileges of citizenship in the other.

Yet the Civil War so vastly disrupted the economies and institutions of both nations that the war's end required a reset in relations with the United States. At the end of the war, Rebecca's father David signed a preliminary peace treaty with the U.S. government on behalf of the Chickasaw Nation that conceded their defeat but emphasized their autonomy. The treaty stated that the Chickasaws did not recognize U.S. authority over "local affairs or national organizations" and that rather than believing them to be conquered allies of the Confederates, the United States should recognize that they fought the war for their own reasons, namely "as a means of preserving our independence and national unity."[18]

Indeed, even the Civil War's destruction had not dismantled Chickasaw and Choctaw nationalism. The governments of both nations were eager to maintain their autonomy and increase their self-sufficiency by creating conditions under which their economies could thrive. The goal of tribal government was to regulate commerce so that individuals could profit and to protect the Nation's fundamental source of wealth—their land—

from alienation. In a sense, this had always been the goal of the Chickasaw and Choctaw governments, but after the Civil War the economic activity to profit from was coal mining and cattle ranching, not hunting, trading, or farming.

During the Gilded Age, both Native and non-Native societies wrestled with how wealth should be distributed. Issues such as citizenship and immigration rose to the forefront as governments and corporations restricted access to capital. Capitalism, a system that transfers wealth to private individuals who are motivated by profit, easily influenced political decisions about which individuals could belong to American society, as well as which individuals could be Choctaw or Chickasaw. There was a political economy of Indian identity, a capitalist marketplace in which Choctaw identity was used as a kind of currency to buy and sell the right to exploit coal. During this era, issues of identity, economy, and nation converged.

Rebecca Burney's education at Bloomfield had prepared her for citizenship in this society, and she embraced it. Her brother Benjamin was becoming increasingly politically active. For instance, he joined the Chickasaws' Pullback Party, which was known for opposing schemes that would privatize economic resources. Around this time Rebecca met a white trader, James Jackson McAlester. They may have met in Tishomingo, where McAlester worked at a general store. In 1870 McAlester relocated to the Choctaw Nation settlement of Bucklucksey, where he opened his own store. There he formed a partnership with Joshua Pusley, a Choctaw, and Daniel Morris Hailey, a railroad physician. Both of these men had purchased and speculated on coal claims in the area around Bucklucksey; McAlester entered into an agreement with Pusley and Hailey to strip mine coal, and they worked out a deal with the MKT to transport it to Kansas.[19]

In June of 1872 Joshua Pusley signed a lease with the Osage Coal and Mining Company, which allowed his partnership to mine the coal, provided they pay the company a royalty. Since McAlester was not a Choctaw citizen, he would have to pay Pusley to acquire an interest in the mine, which he apparently did. But if he married a Choctaw or a Chickasaw, McAlester could profit directly from coal claims himself, without having to pay for the right to exploit coal. Two months after Pusley signed his lease with Osage Coal, McAlester and Rebecca Burney married.[20]

Of course, from Rebecca's perspective, this was not unusual— Chickasaw and Choctaw women had a long tradition of incorporating outsiders to serve their economic and political interests. But in the 1840s, both nations established formal citizenship for those outsiders who married Indian women. They passed laws regulating marriage with non-citizens that granted intermarried men the rights and privileges of citizenship, while preventing a man from disposing of his wife's property and stripping him of citizenship if he left her. These laws may have been an effort to control and regulate the growing numbers of white men entering both nations with the railroad and as traders. According to the 1855 treaty, the Choctaws and Chickasaws had no jurisdiction over these people and could not regulate their behavior unless they became citizens. Clearly, it was to each nation's advantage to naturalize intermarried whites. In 1872 the Choctaw Nation also passed a law requiring white men to pay $1.50 to marry a Choctaw. When Rebecca Burney married McAlester, he acquired citizenship in both the Chickasaw and Choctaw Nations, according to both the terms of the 1855 treaty and Choctaw and Chickasaw law.[21]

McAlester profited too, and handsomely. He surely recognized the Burney family's standing in the Chickasaw and Choctaw Nations, their wealth, and Rebecca's own adventurous qualities. Rebecca may have seen James as someone who would protect the wealth and property of her Chickasaw and Choctaw Nations. Soon after the marriage, McAlester acquired a controlling interest in Osage Coal, sank a new mine shaft, and then convinced New York financier Jay Gould to fund the opening of mines around the town of Bucklucksey, which by then had been renamed McAlester.[22]

By this time, Rebecca McAlester and Annie Ream had probably come to know each other well—their husbands were business partners, and Annie herself was engaged in coal development. Pusley and McAlester entered into partnership with Robert Ream and another Choctaw citizen, Tandy Walker, a former principal chief. Together they expanded their coal interests and combined them with railroad investments, even signing a lease with the MKT to build a spur to one of their mines.[23]

But for Choctaw principal chief Coleman Cole, this deal took the freedoms of capitalism too far. Railroad lines could only be approved by treaty between the Choctaw Nation and the United States. Chief Cole believed that the McAlester and Ream lease constituted an illegal sale of land, which was punishable by death. Cole believed that the coal lands should be held in common and not individualized, and he wanted the royalties to support Choctaw education. A year earlier, in 1875, Chief Cole had declared that "all the mines of coal, lead and other materials, and all the timber belongs to the Choctaw and Chickasaw Nations and not to individual Indians who may occupy the soil."[24]

However, who actually owned the coal and whether coal could be a type of "land" subject to the law was a matter of debate. Chief Cole had his opinion and seized the opportunity to use McAlester's and Ream's questionable actions to demonstrate it. In 1876 he ordered the Choctaw police force, known as the Lighthorsemen, to arrest them. The Lighthorsemen surrounded McAlester's store and informed the men that they had been sentenced to death for selling Choctaw land. They also had a warrant for the arrest of Tandy Walker, who was involved in the scheme. The Lighthorsemen informed the prisoners of their crime and their execution date, and then released them while they went to apprehend Walker. This was not unusual. Choctaw men did not typically avoid a death sentence; and the Lighthorsemen had a long tradition of releasing condemned prisoners, who typically showed up for their execution. But McAlester, Pusley, and Ream did not fulfill this principle of Choctaw citizenship. They left the scene and hid until dark; then they stole a railroad handcar and escaped, pumping themselves fifty miles into the Creek Nation.[25]

We can only imagine what Rebecca thought when she heard her husband had fled the town he built as a fugitive from the law. It may have occurred to her that she had made the wrong choice: that here was a man who had little understanding or respect for the obligations of kinship, whether familial or national. Her brother Benjamin subscribed to the same general principles as Coleman Cole—economic resources were not to be individualized but should remain national property to be used for the benefit of all citizens. On the other hand, she may have felt that Coleman Cole's actions were unjustified, and that a compromise could be worked out. Apparently, other Choctaws felt the same way. One month after McAlester, Ream, and their partners fled the Choctaw Nation, they returned with an armed posse of fifty men to physically threaten Chief Cole. Following this confrontation, the chief compromised. He agreed that McAlester could split royalties from coal mining with the Nation.[26]

In fact, this agreement settled very little concerning coal mining in the Choctaw Nation, partly because Annie Ream was herself actively disrupting the Choctaws' ability to recover coal royalties. Around 1875, Annie took the lead on a scheme to use Osage Coal funds to build a house on land that included a coal mine owned by D. M. Hailey; she then argued that her dwelling gave her ownership over the mine. Hailey did not dispute her (he almost certainly profited in some way from this arrangement), and she sold the mine to the Texas Central Railroad, which then sold it to McAlester's company, Osage Coal. According to historian Clara Sue Kidwell, the scheme was likely a way to consolidate Osage Coal's various mines. It set a precedent to alienate the coal resource from the Choctaws and transform it into private property owned by non-citizen–run corporations. Even though Choctaw law prevented individuals from selling land, and the Nation had to profit from coal that was extracted from the land, the mines themselves were private property, and could be bought and sold. Annie and others were among the willing group of Choctaw Nation citizens who turned their property over to a corporation operating within the borders of the Nation. McAlester, in fact, received letters from Choctaws wishing to sell him their coal claims, which he bought for prices ranging from $50 to $500; at least one transaction was used to pay a debt to McAlester's store.[27]

These acts had a seismic effect on Choctaw nation building. Kidwell observes, "[Annie] Ream's coal claims were the entering wedge in a process by which the federal government worked to impose its jurisdiction in Indian Territory. The chief means of achieving this goal was corporations controlled by non-Indians that attempted to do business with and assert their rights with respect to Choctaws who controlled resources." These corporate relationships seemed to be a way of circumventing treaty provisions that allowed Choctaws to regulate corporate activity on their land. For example, the relationship between the MKT and Osage Coal was suspect—the two companies shared directors; and while the MKT had a treaty right to operate in the Nation, its supplier, Osage Coal, did not. Congress held hearings on the relationship in 1877 and deposed Jay Gould, but the hearings did not find a conflict of interest between the MKT and Osage Coal.[28]

In 1880 the consolidation of Osage Coal's operations that Annie Ream facilitated resulted in a complex legal case that ultimately gave the U. S. secretary of the interior jurisdiction over Choctaw citizens, jurisdiction that had previously belonged solely to the Choctaw courts. Annie herself got the secretary involved because the Choctaw Supreme Court overturned a lower court ruling that had affirmed her claim. According to the Supreme Court, the land thus reverted to the Choctaw Nation, and Ream was dispossessed. The secretary argued that the treaty provisions giving the Choctaw court jurisdiction did not apply in this case because the Choctaw defendants had a contract with a private non-Indian–run corporation. The U.S. attorney general acknowledged that the secretary had the right to intervene, effectively ruling that United States law, not Choctaw law, applied to contracts with non-Indian–run corporations. The secretary also doubted the proper functioning of the Choctaw courts, because the circuit court judge was related to Annie and the court had not officially filed the decision. According to Kidwell, this case "breached the wall of treaty rights the Choctaw government had actively maintained around itself" and set further precedent for giving the United States jurisdiction over non-citizens in the Choctaw Nation and Choctaws as well.[29]

Perhaps alarmed by Annie Ream's success with the Interior Department, the Choctaw General Council acted in 1880 to establish a procedure to collect a royalty on coal mining that accounted for the Chickasaws' interests. Rebecca's brother Benjamin may have helped broker the conflict, as he had spent the previous two years as Chickasaw principal chief. As a result, coal royalties were an immediate boon to the Choctaw and Chickasaw treasuries; in 1885–1886 the Nation received over $39,000 in royalties. By 1890 coal royalties amounted to almost $58,000, nearly a third of the Nation's total income.[30]

These funds went to support Choctaw and Chickasaw schools. By 1877 there were fifty-four day schools, one boarding school, and one vocational school in the Choctaw Nation. Expenses for the schools amounted to $29,022.50 in 1876, of which only $1,522.50 came from coal royalties. But after 1880, the royalties grew rapidly, and all of those funds were under the direct control of the Choctaw Nation; schools, therefore, were controlled directly by the Choctaws. The same was true with Chickasaw royalties and Chickasaw schools. Complete royalty figures have not been compiled, but in 1905, the Chickasaws alone used over $17,500 from coal to fund their schools.[31]

Even as allotment unfolded in Indian Territory, with citizens of each nation taking various sides on the issue, everyone agreed that Indian control of Indian schools was paramount. The Atoka Agreement of 1897, which provided for the allotment-in-severalty of Chickasaw and Choctaw territory and clarified the distribution of coal and asphalt lands, provided that royalties would go exclusively to support education in the two nations, and that the U.S. government could not put them to other uses. Despite the agreement, the United States engineered to seize authority over the royalties, which were to be paid into the U.S. treasury and withdrawn only on order of the secretary of the interior. Consequently, control over the funding of Chickasaw schools was subject to the oversight of the Interior Department. When some Chickasaws saw how the Bureau of Indian Affairs mishandled Choctaw education, they resisted the government's efforts to take over their schools, and the bureau dropped the matter. But Interior officials would not allow coal royalties to be spent for education. In 1901 the Chickasaws made a small concession, giving Interior one seat on a board of examiners that they created to oversee teacher certification. Interior agreed to release the funds, if the Chickasaw board of examiners provided it with information on the schools, whenever requested. This was an example of how Chickasaws continued to hold on to their coal wealth as a means of exerting control over a relationship with the federal government, in which they could otherwise exercise little leverage.[32]

Annie Ream sent her children away from Indian Territory to school, as she had been educated. But at least one of them, Robert Ream Jr., returned and became a Chickasaw national agent (akin to a tax collector), and through the early twentieth century he continued to accrue power in Chickasaw and Choctaw politics. Robert Jr. became so influential with the U.S. government because he backed the election of D. H. Johnston, the last Chickasaw Nation principal chief before Congress abolished Indian Territory and integrated it into the new state of Oklahoma. Johnston had brokered the deal with Interior over the Atoka Agreement and Chickasaw schools.[33]

Eventually, Annie herself became involved in education at Bloomfield Academy, where Rebecca Burney had begun her schooling. Johnston appointed Annie superintendent at Bloomfield, where she served from 1907 until the buildings burned in 1914 and the Nation relocated the school. Appointing Annie was one of Johnston's last acts of patronage, and one that acknowledged the political value of Annie and her son.[34]

Kinship, economic development, and education all contributed to an increasingly national sense of citizenship for Indian people during the Gilded Age. Rebecca Burney's education, both in the familial and the national kinship systems, prepared her well for prosperous times, both for her personally and for the Chickasaw and Choctaw Nations. Rebecca's skills, her status as a Chickasaw woman, and the cultural value placed on kinship became the key to coal development in the Choctaw Nation. Annie Guy Ream, on the other hand, epitomized an entrepreneurial drive to separate one's wealth from the responsibilities of Chickasaw and Choctaw kinship. Her own initiatives and her relationship with Robert Ream, unfortunately, resulted in her nation losing control of its national resources. At the same time, she and her family continued to support the formal education of Chickasaw children to prepare them, by the early twentieth century, for citizenship in both the United States and the Chickasaw Nation. We do not know if Rebecca and Annie thought of themselves as

Chickasaw nationalists or as Chickasaw capitalists, but their stories demonstrate that the two are not mutually exclusive and are deeply intertwined.

Notes

1. Clara Sue Kidwell, *The Choctaws in Oklahoma: From Tribe to Nation, 1855–1970* (Norman: University of Oklahoma Press, 2007), 15–16, 19, 28; "Treaty with the Choctaw and Chickasaw, 1855," in *Indian Affairs: Laws and Treaties, Treaties*, comp. Charles J. Kappler (Washington DC: Government Printing Office, 1904), 2:707–8.

2. Kidwell, *The Choctaws in Oklahoma*, 24–25.

3. John Reed Swanton, *Chickasaw Society and Religion* (Lincoln: University of Nebraska Press, 2006), 12.

4. Arrell M. Gibson, *The History of Oklahoma* (Norman: University of Oklahoma Press, 1984), 65, 73, 75–76, 100, 150. For information on Chickasaw moieties, see Ronald Eugene Craig, "The Colberts in Chickasaw History, 1783–1818: A Study of Internal Tribal Dynamics" (PhD diss., University of New Mexico, 1998), 53–54, 64–67; and Swanton, *Chickasaw Society and Religion*, 22–23.

5. John Bartlett Meserve, "Governor Cyrus Harris," *Chronicles of Oklahoma* 15, no. 4, 373–86; John Bartlett Meserve, "Governor William Malcolm Guy," *Chronicles of Oklahoma* 19, no. 1, 10–13.

6. Mrs. S. J. Carr, "Bloomfield Academy and Its Founder," *Chronicles of Oklahoma* 2, no. 4, 379; Caroline Davis, "Education of the Chickasaws," *Chronicles of Oklahoma* 15, no. 4, 415–48; Muriel H. Wright, "Old Boggy Depot," *Chronicles of Oklahoma* 5, no. 1, 4–17.

7. Much of the genealogical research for this chapter was drawn from a website maintained by Chickasaw historian Kerry M. Armstrong, who, in 2010, was seriously injured in a car accident and no longer able to maintain his website. Some of the information has been reposted on other sites, however, and here I have used the original URLs, which can now only be accessed through the Internet Archive; I have also added website URLs where the information can currently be found. I have found some discrepancies in genealogical research that require further investigation; the lineage relationships I describe here are verified by multiple online sources but require further research to be definitive. For more on Mr. Armstrong, see Richard Green, "Chickasaw Historian, Researcher Battling Back from Auto Crash," *Chickasaw Times*, February 2010, 9, 22; https://www.chickasaw.net/Our-Nation/History/Historical-Articles/News/Serious-Accident-Sidelines-Family-Historian.aspx, accessed September 8, 2014; Kerry M Armstrong, "Descendants of James Logan Colbert—Second Generation," http://web.archive.org/web/20110504181400/http://www.chickasawhistory.com/colbert/i0000916.htm#i916, accessed September 12, 2009; http://web.archive.org/web/20080517061651/http://www.chickasawhistory.com/colbert/i0000981.htm#s2, accessed September 9, 2014; see also Linda Jean Giles, "Descendants of James Logan Colbert—Second Generation," http://familytreemaker.genealogy.com/users/g/i/l/Linda-J-Giles/gene5

–0002.html, accessed September 8, 2014; Jennifer Barnes Mieires, "Descendants of Benjamin James I," http://jenniferhsrn2.homestead.com/jamesfamily.html, accessed September 9, 2014; Albion K. Parris to Wm L. Marcy, July 1, 1845, in Kerry M. Armstrong, "Chickasaw Letters—1845," http://web.archive.org/web/20111025065510 /http://www.chickasawhistory.com/CHICl_45.htm, accessed September 16, 2009; http://web.archive.org/web/20080512011917/http://www.chickasawhistory.com /chicl_45.htm, accessed September 9, 2014; John Bartlett Meserve, "Governor Benjamin Franklin Overton and Governor Benjamin Crooks Burney," *Chronicles of Oklahoma* 16, no. 2, 226; "Article 10, Treaty with the Chickasaw, 1834," in Kappler, *Indian Affairs: Laws and Treaties*, 2:421; Armstrong, "Descendants of James Logan Colbert—Third Generation," http://web.archive.org/web/20090901151459/http ://www.chickasawhistory.com/colbert/i0000917.htm#i835, accessed September 19, 2009; http://web.archive.org/web/20080516093225/http://www.chickasawhistory .com/colbert/i0000917.htm#i835, accessed September 9, 2014; see also Linda Jean Giles, "Descendants of James Logan Colbert—Third Generation," http://family treemaker.genealogy.com/users/g/i/l/Linda-J-Giles/gene5–0005.html#child45, accessed September 8, 2014; Trena M. Gleason, "Susan Colbert (d. 1848)," http ://familytreemaker.genealogy.com/users/g/l/e/Trena-M-Gleason/website-0001 /uhp-0147.html, accessed September 9, 2014; Gleason, "Margaret Allen (b. 1800, d. 29 Apr 1857)," http://familytreemaker.genealogy.com/users/g/l/e/Trena-M-Gleason /website-0001/uhp-0279.html, accessed September 9, 2014.

8. Armstrong, "Descendants of James Logan Colbert—Second Generation," http://web.archive.org/web/20100905151149/http://www.chickasawhistory.com /colbert/i0001073.htm#i1073, accessed September 16, 2009; http://web.archive .org/web/20080517061651/http://www.chickasawhistory.com/colbert/i0000981 .htm#s2, accessed September 9, 2014. For Lucy James's removal with her mother, see Albion K. Parris to Wm L. Marcy, July 1, 1845, which is a list of amounts paid to individual Chickasaws to cover their own removal expenses. On March 17, 1845, Lotty (Colbert) James was paid $480.00 "for emigrating self and family," which presumably means her daughter Lucy James and her son-in-law David Burney, along with their children. "D. James," presumably Lotty's husband, was also reimbursed, on March 5, 1845. I could not find a separate amount for David Burney. See Armstrong, "Chickasaw Letters—1845," http://web.archive.org/web/20111025065510 /http://www.chickasawhistory.com/CHICl_45.htm, accessed September 16, 2009; http://web.archive.org/web/20080512011917/http://www.chickasawhistory.com /chicl_45.htm, accessed September 9, 2014.

9. Meserve, "Governor Overton and Governor Burney," 226; Michael D. Green, "Removal of the Chickasaws," in *Historical Atlas of Oklahoma*, 4th ed., ed. Charles Robert Goins and Danney Goble (Norman: University of Oklahoma Press, 2006), 70–71; James P. Pate, "Chickasaw," *Encyclopedia of Oklahoma History and Culture*, http://www.okhistory.org/publications/enc/entry.php?entry=CH033, accessed September 12, 2009. David's status as a slaveholder is indicated in the OIA removal records cited at Estelusti Foundation, "Enslaver—Burney," http://www.estelusti

.com/burney.htm, accessed September 12, 2009; now found at http://web.archive
.org/web/20081122141615/http://www.estelusti.com/burney.htm, accessed September 9, 2014. David is referred to as "Judge" throughout the Chickasaw genealogy records I have seen. See also D. C. Gideon, *Indian Territory: Descriptive, Biographical, and Genealogical* (New York: Lewis Publishing Co., 1901), 589, https://archive.org /details/indianterritoryd02gide, accessed October 10, 2016. His position as deacon is cited in Carr, "Bloomfield Academy," 373.

10. Carr, "Bloomfield Academy," 373; Arrell M. Gibson, *The Chickasaws* (Norman: University of Oklahoma Press, 1972), 236. These details are also confirmed by a highway marker, a picture of which is at Vicki Bell-Reynolds, "The Burney Academy," http://www.rootsweb.ancestry.com/~okbits/burneyacad.html, accessed September 14, 2009.

11. Amanda Cobb, *Listening to Our Grandmothers' Stories: The Bloomfield Academy for Chickasaw Females, 1852–1949* (Lincoln: University of Nebraska Press, 2000), 46–51.

12. Meserve, "Governor William Malcolm Guy," 10–13; Meserve, "Governor Cyrus Harris," 373–86; Record of Annie A. Guy and James H. Guy, U.S. Census of 1860, National Archives and Records Administration (NARA) microfilm publication M653, roll 533, Hubbardston, Worcester, Massachusetts, page 311, family 620, household of Joab C. Wright, accessed at Ancestry.com September 17, 2013; Joseph B. Thoburn, *A Standard History of Oklahoma* (Chicago IL: The American Historical Society, 1916), 3:1082; Cobb, *Listening to Our Grandmothers' Stories*, 52–53.

13. Cobb, *Listening to Our Grandmothers' Stories*, 56; Meserve, "Governor Overton and Governor Burney," 227.

14. Kidwell, *The Choctaws in Oklahoma*, 104; Thoburn, *A Standard History of Oklahoma*, 3:1082; James W. Parins, *Elias Cornelius Boudinot: A Life on the Cherokee Border* (Lincoln: University of Nebraska Press, 2008), 156–59; "Vinita," Oklahoma Historical Society, *Encyclopedia of Oklahoma History and Culture*, http://www.okhistory.org /publications/enc/entry.php?entry=VI009, accessed February 13, 2014; Muriel H. Wright, "Old Boggy Depot," *Chronicles of Oklahoma* 5, no. 1: 4–17. Robert L. Ream Jr. was born in 1871 or 1872, and records show that Annie Guy and Bob Ream were married by 1875; Records of the Bureau of Indian Affairs, Record Group 75, NARA, *Applications for Enrollment of the Commission to the Five Civilized Tribes, 1898–1914,* microfilm publication M1301, roll 441. Annie may have lived in Boggy Depot after she lived in Pittsburg County; according to one source by James B. Thoburn, their oldest son was born in Pittsburg County at Ream's Switch but the second son was born in Boggy Depot. According to another of Thoburn's writings, Boggy Depot was later renamed Ream's Switch. It's possible that all her children were born in the same place, or that the same place had two different names, but given the Reams' interest in profiting from the MKT (discussed below), it seems equally likely that they first lived in Boggy Depot and then relocated to a home closer to the railroad. Joseph B. Thoburn and Muriel H. Wright, *Oklahoma, A History of the State and Its People* (New York: Lewis Historical Publishing Company, 1929), 3:1082, 1239; 4:768.

15. Gene Aldrich, "A History of the Coal Industry in Oklahoma to 1907" (PhD diss., University of Oklahoma, 1952), 4, 6, 10; Michael J. Hightower, "Cattle, Coal, and Indian Land: A Tradition of Mining in Southeastern Oklahoma," *The Chronicles of Oklahoma* 62, no. 1, 4; I. C. Gunning, *When Coal Was King: Coal Mining in the Choctaw Nation* (N.p.: Eastern Oklahoma Historical Society, 1975), 6; Thoburn and Wright, *Oklahoma*, 1:469.

16. According to Aldrich—I assume this means any Choctaw citizen, as per Gerald L. Sparks, "James Jesse McAlester, The Choctaw Nation's Omnipresent Entrepreneur, 1871–1894" (MA thesis, University of Oklahoma, 1997), 6; Gunning, *When Coal Was King*, 7.

17. Aldrich, "A History of the Coal Industry in Oklahoma," 11.

18. Gibson, *The Chickasaws*, 273–75.

19. Meserve, "Governor Overton and Governor Burney," 223; Sparks, "James Jesse McAlester," 2–3, 6–8; Kidwell, *The Choctaws in Oklahoma*, 103; Linda C. English, "Inside the Store, Inside the Past: A Cultural Analysis of McAlester's General Store," *The Chronicles of Oklahoma* 81, no. 1, 41.

20. Aldrich, "A History of the Coal Industry in Oklahoma," 135; Sparks, "James Jesse McAlester," 8, 11; Kidwell, *The Choctaws in Oklahoma*, 103; Aldrich, "A History of the Coal Industry in Oklahoma," 40.

21. Kidwell, *The Choctaws in Oklahoma*, 246n2; Sparks, "James Jesse McAlester," 8.

22. Gunning, *When Coal Was King*, 47.

23. Gunning, *When Coal Was King*, 10; Sparks, "James Jesse McAlester," 10–12; Aldrich, "A History of the Coal Industry in Oklahoma," 41–42.

24. Aldrich, "A History of the Coal Industry in Oklahoma," 151; Kidwell, *The Choctaws in Oklahoma*, 109–10. Quote in Sandra Faiman-Silva, *Choctaws at the Crossroads: The Political Economy of Class and Culture in the Oklahoma Timber Region* (Lincoln: University of Nebraska Press, 1997), 67; also referenced in Kidwell, *The Choctaws in Oklahoma*, 111.

25. Gunning, *When Coal Was King*, 10; Sparks, "James Jesse McAlester," 10–12; Aldrich, "A History of the Coal Industry in Oklahoma," 41–42; Hightower, "Cattle, Coal, and Indian Land," 9; Thoburn and Wright, *Oklahoma*, 3:879.

26. Gunning, *When Coal Was King*, 10; Aldrich, "A History of the Coal Industry in Oklahoma," 42; Sparks, "James Jesse McAlester," 12; Hightower, "Cattle, Coal, and Indian Land," 9; Angie Debo, *The Rise and Fall of the Choctaw Republic* (Norman: University of Oklahoma Press, 1975), 128.

27. Sparks, "James Jesse McAlester," 13.

28. Kidwell, *The Choctaws in Oklahoma*, 104; H. Craig Miner, *The Corporation and the Indian* (Norman: University of Oklahoma Press, 1989), 69–70.

29. Kidwell, *The Choctaws in Oklahoma*, 111–13.

30. Aldrich, "A History of the Coal Industry in Oklahoma," 152–54; Sparks, "James Jesse McAlester," 9, 25. In addition to paying royalties, companies had to pay for permits for each of their laborers, ranging in price from twenty to twenty-five cents per person per month. Aldrich, "A History of the Coal Industry in Oklahoma," 156.

31. Aldrich, "A History of the Coal Industry in Oklahoma," 208–9; United States, Office of Indian Affairs, *Annual Report of the Commissioner of Indian Affairs, for the year 1905*, Part I (Washington DC: Government Printing Office, 1905), 210.

32. Davis, "Education of the Chickasaws," 437–41.

33. Thoburn, *A Standard History of Oklahoma*, 3:1238–39; Davis, "Education of the Chickasaws," 440.

34. Carr, "Bloomfield Academy," 379.

Twelve

"Engaged in the Struggle for Liberation as They See It"

Indigenous Southern Women and
International Women's Year

MEG DEVLIN O'SULLIVAN

On the second day of the 1977 Oklahoma Women's Conference, during a heated plenary session, a group of Native American women "walked out of the ballroom in protest." They objected to a conservative umbrella organization's dissemination of leaflets that instructed participants to select specific delegates to the national conference for International Women's Year (IWY) in Houston that fall. Ultimately, these women and others (many of whom hailed from the conference's minority caucus) would form a dissenting group that upheld the spirit of International Women's Year and challenged the right-wing anti-Equal Rights Amendment supporters who had overrun the Oklahoma gathering.[1] In their roles as conference planners, participants, delegates, members of the continuing committee, and even dissenters, Native southern women were integral to this national women's initiative.

The historiography of Native women's political activism suggests that during the 1960s and 1970s indigenous women could identify with two main movements—one rooted in a struggle against colonialism and the other waged against sexism. And when pushed to choose, Native American women activists—like other women of color—frequently selected movements of nationalism or civil rights.[2] Southern indigenous IWY contributors, however, do not conform to this interpretation. From the earliest stages of planning state gatherings to post-conference networking, their analyses and concerns influenced the national conference of 1977 and its respective report, which Congress submitted to the president of the United States. Their efforts highlighted issues specific to Native American populations and helped frame the national planks that came out of Houston. They neither stood outside of this established women's initiative, nor did they relinquish their political goals as indigenous people to better serve the objectives of the mainstream feminist movement. Rather, as IWY rhetoric promised, they helped "form a more perfect union."[3] Alongside other activists, southern Native women created a blueprint for policy making and a trajectory for the women's movement for the coming decade. In part, this agenda asked the United States to grapple with the legacies and present realities of its colonial history. Largely excluded from a historiographically whitewashed feminist movement and physically far removed from the iconic sites of Red Power resistance in the Northern Plains and the West Coast, southern indigenous women have not fit neatly into the various rights movements that defined the sixties and seventies. Yet, as their involvement in the IWY makes clear, examining the contributions of indigenous southern women provides for a far richer understanding of Red Power consciousness and second-wave era activism.[4]

This is not to suggest that Native women's experiences and politics fit seamlessly into larger feminist narratives. The women's liberation movement asked women to develop their personal authority, but Native women overwhelmingly garnered power from their tribes. Indigenous women activists frequently worked for political change for Native people generally, not women specifically, and focused on the experience of the collective rather than on themselves as liberated leaders. Thus trying to fit Native American women into a paradigm of white women's leadership or as individuals acting outside of the context of their tribe, nation, or Native people generally is a mistake. As one Native woman argued: "Most Native American women see no need for involvement in the women's movement, [but] some of the young women are very ardently engaged in the struggle for liberation as they see it."[5] Choctaw historian Devon Mihesuah maintains that "if feminists want to learn about themselves and others . . . they should approach indigenous women only with a genuine, but respectful curiosity about another way of life." This assertion implies that not only will indigenous feminisms vary from white feminists' models but also from one indigenous woman to the next. For example, Joy Harjo, a Creek writer, defined "tribal feminism" as a "multi-sphered concept with the family as the center, surrounded by clan identification, and then tribe and tribal relations." Wilma Mankiller, former principal chief of the Cherokee Nation, employed the term to describe using female power to assist her tribe.[6] IWY conferences in the United States provided precisely this type of exchange: they afforded non-Native feminists opportunities to observe and learn from alternative perspectives and granted Native women a way to represent their political goals and those of their nations and communities.

International Women's Year Southern State Conferences

The United Nations named 1975 "International Women's Year" in an effort to improve the condition of women worldwide. President Gerald Ford issued Executive Order 11832 creating a national commission on its observance. He appointed thirty-five women and men, including La Donna Harris (Comanche), to investigate issues affecting women and charged the commission with producing a formal report on how to achieve gender equality. After a year of surveys, interviews, and studies, the committee completed *To Form a More Perfect Union: Justice for American Women.* The report included 115 suggestions that resulted in 26 general positions. Starting in January 1977, every state and territory in the United States held meetings to discuss the planks and add their concerns to the agenda in preparation for the national conference. Local committees selected by the national commission met for weeks in advance of these state conventions to organize and plan them. The state conferences welcomed the entire population of each state and permitted any resident over sixteen years of age to vote on the platform. The planks addressed numerous issues including the Equal Rights Amendment, violence against women, reproductive rights, education, and economic realities, among others.[7] Participants also nominated delegates to represent their state in November at the national conference in Houston. All told, more than 150,000 people came to the IWY state meetings.[8]

The success of the Texas state conference rested heavily on the work of Choctaw organizer Owanah Anderson. The self-described homemaker and businesswoman of Wichita Falls served as the permanent chair of a nine-person IWY executive committee (which included one other Native woman). Anderson, like her counterparts on the coordinating committee, was chosen "from a large pool of names" generated by women's groups across the state in order to implement the 1976 Congressional mandate in honor of International Women's Year. Ultimately, thirty-nine Texas women served on the coordinating committee, and from this larger group came the steering committee of nine, with Anderson as its elected executive.[9]

The planning committee and its executive subgroup worked hard to balance the needs, input, and presence of Texas women, who were ethnically diverse. According to some who were present during the planning stages of the conference, Owanah Anderson's "acceptable ethnic neutrality" and "earth mother personality . . . made the Lone Star State hang together." While this assessment of Anderson conflates individual personality traits with stereotypes of indigeneity, it also suggests that Anderson deftly and effectively advanced issues significant to Native Americans and other women. For example, Anderson also sat on the Financial Assistance Committee, which awarded most of its aid to Latina, African American, and indigenous women; roughly two out of every three assistance awards went to women of color. For many of these women, participation at the days-long conference rested on such economic support. The committee granted this aid consciously with an eye to "ethnic balance." Such economic assistance not only helped recipients, it ultimately benefited all attendees. In addition to educational and professional expertise, grant recipients brought with them perspectives, skills, and analyses acquired by virtue of their respective sociopolitical environments. Translating organic knowledge into political change demanded the presence of individuals who possessed myriad identities and experiences. IWY, like most feminist projects, predicated itself on this type of experiential comprehension and thrived when it could access it.[10]

Ultimately, the roughly 3,000 people registered for the state conference considered 212 nominees, elected 58 delegates, and ratified 27 amendments. The Texas convention sent twenty-seven "Caucasians," seventeen "Chicanas," eleven "Blacks," and three "American Indians" to represent them at the national conference several months later. Owanah Anderson was among those elected, earning more votes than over half of the other delegates. She also received accolades for the superior job she did in organizing and overseeing the event (including officiating at the opening ceremony and managing the voting on resolutions). The Texas conference resolved that: "Her calm spirit and her dedication to the common problems and . . . goals shared by all the women of Texas" compelled them to offer "deep thanks and heartfelt appreciation to Owanah Anderson."[11]

Anderson's central role, both in her state's convention and later at the national meeting, belies an interpretation scholars perhaps unconsciously repeat: that Native American women existed outside of, or at the fringes of, feminist causes during the 1970s. Although Owanah Anderson's leadership was extraordinary, it was not exceptional; and it exemplifies how Native women were at the center of this national effort to improve the status of women.

Similarly, Ruth Dial Woods (Lumbee) played a central role in North Carolina's state IWY conference. Reflecting on her larger participation in the women's movement, Woods noted that she and other activists "didn't get bogged down into ethnicity" but rather focused on the "problems and issues that affect women" while honoring "cultural diversity." Woods participated in the North Carolina Women's Political Caucus, the ERA United, the North Carolina Business and Professional Women's Organization, the North Carolina Women's Forum, and the Native American Women's Caucus of the United Methodist Church. In her work on behalf of women's rights, Woods identified an alternative to the separatism that would, in part, come to define the civil rights movement, of which she was also a part. In Woods's estimation, activists for women's issues identified "a common goal" and let this focus guide their work, despite cultural or racial differences. "We were Black and white and red and brown and Asian," she said. Woods's recollections provide a nuanced take on women's activism and the complications of identity politics; namely, that for some participants in these movements the sisterhood metaphor was neither completely correct nor completely fallacious.[12]

As a result of her feminist activity, Woods participated in the North Carolina IWY Coordinating Committee that helped to plan the state meeting. In June, Woods along with 827 other North Carolinians gathered in Winston-Salem for their state's IWY conference. The meeting's official report boasted "geographic representation [from] all sections of the state" including "women from small communities from the west and mountain areas." Those assembled elected thirty-three delegates and four alternates to represent their concerns in Houston. Five of the designees (four delegates, including Woods, and one alternate) were Native American.[13]

Woods flew to Texas—eight months pregnant, and despite discouragement from doing so—to serve in Houston. "I wouldn't have missed the IWY for anything in the world," she said, "We had met and caucused and we knew exactly what we were going to vote for. We were going to be pro-state on the whole platform." Yet this focus on being universally pro-state—that is, having delegates vote in unison for all of the planks advanced by their state— posed a problem for Woods around the issues of abortion and "sexual orientation." Her state's platform supported both abortion and lesbians but at this historic moment her Southern Baptist "mentality" gave her pause. Yet, rather than compromise her state's unity or her religious instruction, Woods absented herself from the floor to avoid having to cast a vote on these issues. She later remarked that her pregnancy allowed her to "get away with it," as few people would question a woman's need to excuse herself while eight months pregnant. Woods wrestled with some of the high-profile and contentious issues in feminist circles: reproductive justice and the role of lesbians in the movement. While her upbringing put her at odds with her state's delegates and likely some of her contemporaries, this did not prevent her from active participation. Woods was able to negotiate this tension in a way that maintained her personal worldview without sabotaging the goals of the collective.[14]

Woods not only had to balance a southern religious upbringing with national feminist agendas; she also had been raised in a culture that maintained that "women are supposed to let the man walk first and the man's supposed to make the decisions." While Woods did not follow this expectation, she did not learn to challenge it by participating in a white feminist movement. In her own words, she became "a feminist before I knew what a feminist was."[15]

Relatedly, prevalent issues among feminist groups in other parts of the country, such as coercive sterilization in New York City, were not on the agendas of most southern white feminists, but they were of great concern to indigenous women and other women of color. The Louisiana conference, for instance, put forward recommendations calling for an end to "coerced sterilization, hysterectomy, and other experimental practices on the bodies of women, especially poor, minority, and Third World women," while the health panel of the state conference "condemned" the "use of minority and poor women as experimental guinea pigs and the racism inherent in the forced sterilization of minority women." These recommendations likely came from indigenous women and other women of color for whom sterilization abuse had been a pressing concern for years.[16]

When the Louisiana Workshop on Racial and Ethnic Minorities—comprised, predominantly, of African-American women, along with "one white lady, two black men, and one Indian"—addressed the subjects of "social, political and economic implications of the woman's movement" on men "as well as the Black and Third World family," they reconceptualized precepts fundamental to branches of the mainstream feminist movement that had privileged the experiences of women over men, defined men as the root of their oppression, and at times constructed the family as an obstacle to liberation. The same panel demanded attention to the experiences of incarcerated women, voter registration, health care, housing standards, and community control of schools. They also called for greater availability of government jobs and for "extra attention" to "the employment needs of minority women, especially blacks, Hispanics, Asian Americans, and Native Americans." This resolution accorded with decisions coming out of the Texas "Sexism, Classism, Racism" workshop that argued for assistance to help minority women develop grant-writing skills to make them more competitive for federal grants; for state institutions of higher education to recruit minority women; and for general funding streams for minority programs because of the legacy of sexism and racism in education, employment, and credit. Indigenous southern women and other women of color infused these state meetings with issues of specific interest to them, but their proposals had the potential to advance economic, educational, and employment justice for all women, children, and families.[17]

Thus, when Carmen Votaw, the president of the National Conference of Puerto Rican Women, commented on the relative absence of "Cuban, Mexican, American Indian and disabled" women in her speech delivered at Florida's closing plenary session, she reminded conference attendees that "our cultural heritage is an asset, not a liability." While Florida's coordinating committee had advanced the names of two Native Americans, JoAnn Jones and Lori Wilson, to serve as delegates to Houston, neither was chosen. Wilson hailed from Waynesville, North Carolina, identified as one-sixteenth Cherokee, and served as an independent Florida state senator. Despite her political career—or perhaps because of it—Wilson was not among the forty women elected as delegates to Houston. The conference also did not select Jones. This decision was not lost on conference goers. At the closing plenary session they declared: "Any policies promulgated by this conference cannot speak for the American Indian women because the Indian representation at this conference is significantly small." They also requested that "the International Women's Year Conference in Houston not attempt to speak for Indian Women unless American Indian Women are adequately represented." It is hard to document why Native American participation was so low (only 17 of 2,916 participants identified as American Indian). Perhaps it was because culturally conservative indigenous women in Florida had no interest in the initiative. Or maybe it was because those who planned the conference saw meaningful Native participation in having Miss Indian America lead the pledge of allegiance before a plenary session. However explained, by the conference's end, those gathered had identified the absence of Native American women as a problem and acknowledged this shortcoming directly.[18]

Lack of Native women's participation did not compromise the Oklahoma state meeting, but participants struggled mightily with other challenges. Fourteen hundred Oklahomans attended the conference, of which more than one thousand had assembled by the second day with the near-express purpose of defeating the Equal Rights Amendment plank. Prior to the conference, the nominating committee advanced a slate of twenty-two potential delegates that combined with forty-two nominations from the floor. Ultimately, the total list of delegates, which the coordinating committee identified as having "19 Anglos, 1 Black, and 2 American Indians" were all anti-ERA and in direct conflict with the spirit of International Women's Year.[19]

The Eagle Forum and NO ERA group members co-opted the meeting by busing in like-minded supporters (including men and children) who collectively identified themselves as the "IWY Citizens Review Committee" to vote with them during the elections. Led by "red-gloved hands," largely belonging to male church leaders, these conservative participants and their supporters worked hard to shut down not only the ERA (which was only one of the thirty-two issues under consideration) but also minority initiatives during the plenary session. According to the conference's final report, "the Eagle Forum followers voted down most of the minority and ethnic related resolutions with little or no consideration for the needs and concerns of these Oklahoma women." As one anonymous attendee commented: "I have never before been in the same room with 1,000 bigots." In the Focus on Minority Women workshop, eleven of the seventeen resolutions under consideration were defeated, all of which centered on economic improvement, gender parity, and government assistance to achieve these goals; one was postponed indefinitely; and the five that passed in no way threatened traditional gender norms or supported national programs. The proposals they passed included support for "Indian representatives on all policy making boards" in education, health, welfare, programs for the elderly, and criminal justice; an affirmation of the "God-given right" of Native Americans to "reproductive freedom" and thus a cessation of "involuntary sterilization practices"; and laws that bolstered Native American foster and adoptive families for Native children.[20]

Although the five proposals that came out of the workshop benefited Native women and families, the reality of the conference's conservative control overwhelmed such advances. Some participants went home discouraged and angry. Two hundred others separated from the larger gathering and formed their own caucus. This collection of "minority women, feminists and others who believed in the Conference's purposes" created the Representative International Women's Year Caucus. They elected a four-member steering committee, which included a Native woman, Carole Butler, a minority recruiter and counselor out of Tulsa. They also elected their own slate of delegates, who they believed to be in concert with the meeting's original purpose. These nominees included Butler as well as three other Native women: Iola Hayden of Norman, Joyce Ryan of Shawnee, and Ruby Haynie of Broken Arrow.[21]

The breakaway Representative International Women's Year Caucus declared that all delegates and decisions coming out of the Oklahoma conference were null and void because the "main" conference lacked "an equitable number of minority women, Blacks, Indians, and Hispanics." The conference, they said, violated Public Law 94–167, which had required the appropriate representation of minority women. The Representative IWY Caucus, on the other hand, maintained that it was "in compliance with the mandate and spirit of Public Law 94–167, Robert's Rules of Order, and the human decency that respect for ourselves and our sisters requires." The breakaway group then approved all of the resolutions coming from the American Indian Women's Caucus. Despite this resistance, the conservative interlopers had five times the number of supporters; and as a result, they declared that all of the "resolutions presented were anti-IWY recommendations." As one participant noted: the "intent of this conference was totally lost."[22]

Oklahoma indigenous women served the conference from its earliest planning stages (eight Native women were on the coordinating committee) through its dramatic and divisive conclusion. In between they led panels on the needs of rural and urban Indian women, on the "double discrimination" of being a woman and an Indian, and on employment and housing. Darleen Parkinson of the Creek Nation of Oklahoma spoke on the interactions between Oklahoman women and women transnationally. (Parkinson offered this presentation at a moment when few women demonstrated such a global focus and years before activist and academic feminist circles would claim transnational approaches as imperative.)

A complicated narrative came out of the Oklahoma meeting. When confronted with a powerful challenge to the purpose of International Women's Year, a group of Native women seceded in support of both the initial intent of the meeting and their own political goals—objectives that were in concert.[23] Not all Native women; however, acted in unison. While a handful supported the ERA and IWY's more progressive agenda, others had no interest in a feminist articulation of equality. Indeed, the two Native women advanced as delegates were decidedly anti-ERA.

Houston: The National Conference

After the statewide meetings held through the late summer of 1977, 2,005 delegates from across the country met in Houston for the national conference. From November 18–21, nearly 20,000 women, children, and men attended as participants and observers. Of these, 1,403 served as elected representatives, 186 as alternates, 47 as IWY commissioners appointed by the president, and 370 as state delegates-at-large. Some state conferences had so much success in attracting and nominating women of color, poor women, and women from rural areas that the National Commission appointed additional white and middle-class women as delegates-at-large in an effort to replicate state demographic numbers. Conversely, delegations hailing from states with more conservative and overtly racist factions, such as Alabama and Mississippi, asked the National Commission to appoint additional poor women and women of color as delegates-at-large to represent their states. In the end, North Carolina sent five indigenous women to Houston (including Ruth Dial Woods) and Texas sent two (including Owanah Anderson). Two Native anti-ERA supporters hailed from Oklahoma. No Native women served as national delegates from Louisiana or Florida. This absence of Native representation does not mean that Native concerns in their states did not reach the national conference, however. Delegates from Florida went with a charge to urge the national convention to consider carefully the representation—or lack thereof—of Native women. Many in attendance would have been aware of the Oklahoma fiasco; perhaps they would have also known about the role Native women played in resisting the takeover. Of most importance, all of these states, to greater and lesser degrees, advanced platforms that incorporated the concerns of indigenous women, who focused on tribal sovereignty, reproductive justice, child welfare, employment needs, health care, and cultural preservation.[24]

While at Houston, Native women delegates contributed in significant ways to the platform on reproductive freedom. The final reproductive rights plank stated: "Women who assert their right to control their own bodies oppose compulsory abortion, compulsory pregnancy, or compulsory sterilization." Regarding sterilization, delegates called for "strict compliance by all doctors and medical and family planning facilities with the Department of Health, Education, and Welfare's" 1974 regulations to ensure that all sterilizations were "truly voluntary, informed and competent." The resolution gave specific consideration to the experience of women who used federal facilities, such as Native women who used Indian Health Services (a subset of Health, Education, and Welfare). They also argued that cutbacks in federal funding for abortion resulted in increasing "the potential of coerced sterilization through 'bargaining:' that is, allowing a woman to have an abortion only if she also agrees to be sterilized." Native women and other feminists of color in Houston successfully extended the terms of reproductive rights beyond the concept of "choice" to include freedom from coerced sterilization. This was no small feat. Many of the women in attendance came to the conference regarding reproductive rights as synonymous only with birth control and abortion.[25]

In the minority women's plank, Native American women brought concerns about sovereignty to the table. The section on American Indian and Alaska Native women highlighted the "sovereignty of Indian peoples." It insisted that the "federal Government . . . guarantee . . . tribal sovereignty; honor existing treaties and congressional acts; protect hunting, fishing, and whaling rights; protect trust status; and permanently remove the threat of termination." Native women also demanded that Congress "provide adequate care through the Indian Health Service" and "forbid the systematic removal of children from their families and communities." Sovereignty, in short, existed at the core of each of these women's concerns, from fishing to parental rights. They advanced these causes by defining them as indigenous feminist concerns and incorporating them into those of the International Women's Year.[26]

Finally, Ohoyo, a Native American women's rights organization, emerged from the American Indian and Alaska Native caucus at Houston under the guidance of Owanah Anderson. The organization later incorporated in 1979 with the assistance of a Women's Education Equity Act Program grant. By 1980 Ohoyo claimed one thousand members, including women well-known in political and academic circles, such as Winona LaDuke, Paula Gunn Allen, and Rayna Green. Ohoyo members divided up into task forces to address particular issues of importance to them. Nearly two hundred of Ohoyo's members focused on Indian child adoption and seventy-four took up the issue of sterilization abuse. In addition to these concerns, members also addressed education, health care, and cultural preservation. While not all of Ohoyo's members attended the meeting in Houston, the conference itself served as the catalyst for the organization's formation.[27]

At the close of the conference, Billie Nave Masters, a Cherokee woman and then graduate student in social psychology at the University of California at Irvine, offered closing remarks in place of IWY Commissioner LaDonna Harris, who was ill. Masters structured her comments around issues of sovereignty, explaining that "one of the predominant forces that have caused Indian women and Native Alaskan women to become active in the movement is the fact that paternalism has been a destructive force that continues today for Native people." Masters argued that the federal government and U.S. citizens fundamentally believed that "Indians must be cared for" because they were incapable of making good decisions for themselves. This paternalism, which challenged the right of the tribes to self-determination, resembled the subjugation that all American women experienced in a paternalistic and sexist culture to varying degrees. In this tenuous and controversial way, Masters and other Native women placed themselves and their specific indigenous goals within a larger feminist framework for change.[28]

Conclusion

In *Indians in Unexpected Places*, Philip J. Deloria asks readers to reconsider where and when they situate Native Americans in modernity.[29] Stereotypes and unexamined assumptions combine to trap Native Americans in an ethnographic past and render invisible their very presence in the larger drama of U.S. history. While Native women rooted much of their political work in their tribes, a history of colonialism, and the imperative of sovereignty, they were not outside of the struggle for women's rights. Through their contributions to IWY, southern Native American women participated in a highly visible feminist project—one that they helped organize, operate, and bring forward into the following decade. Notably, President Jimmy Carter appointed Ruth Dial Woods to the continuing committee charged with maintaining the focus of International Women's Year; beyond meeting with the president, the continuing committee produced a newsletter and served as the official post-conference network.

Quantifying the effects of a specific action or moment in a longer movement for social change can be like "nailing Jello to the wall."[30] As such it is difficult to summarize immediate achievements for southern Native women as a result of their participation in IWY. That said, the entire IWY initiative, culminating in the conference at Houston and its subsequent report, provided an official way for southern Native American women to make the federal government aware of their pressing political concerns and needs outside of Red Power activism that was often seen as controversial and frequently poorly received. Second, IWY participants helped formulate the focal points of the broader women's movement going forward, including a strategy for comprehensive reproductive justice that addressed coercive sterilization and the right to parent. Finally, out of their IWY networking, Native women established Ohoyo to carry their political work into the next decade. While IWY rhetoric promised a more perfect union, Native southern women "engaged in the struggle for liberation" as they saw it and moved toward improved conditions in their nations, broader communities, and larger women's political causes.

Notes

1. IWY Oklahoma Meeting, Letter to Governor David Boren from Jill Holmes, June 20, 1977, Women's Rights Collection—International Women's Year, Sophia Smith Collection, Smith College, Northampton, Massachusetts (all subsequent cites from IWY are from the Women's Rights Collection—International Women's Year, Sophia Smith Collection, unless otherwise noted); IWY Oklahoma Meeting, Final Report of the Oklahoma IWY Coordinating Committee, 132.

2. For work on the Red Power Movement generally see: Troy Johnson, Joanne Nagel, and Duane Champagne, eds., *American Indian Activism: Alcatraz to the Longest Walk* (Urbana: University of Illinois Press, 1997); Troy Johnson, *The Occupation of Alcatraz Island* (Urbana: The University of Illinois, 1996); Joanne Nagel, *American Indian Ethnic Renewal: Red Power and the Resurgence of Identity and Culture* (New York: Oxford University Press, 1996); Alvin Josephy Jr., Joanne Nagel, and Troy Johnson, eds., *Red Power: The American Indians' Fight for Freedom* (Lincoln: University of Nebraska Press, 1999); Russell Means with Marvin J. Wolf, *Where White Men Fear to Tread: The Autobiography of Russell Means* (New York: St. Martin's Press, 1995); Dennis Banks with Richard Erdoes, *Ojibwa Warrior: Dennis Banks and the Rise of the American Indian Movement* (Tulsa: University of Oklahoma Press, 2004); and Stanley David Lyman et al., *Wounded Knee 1973: A Personal Account* (Lincoln: University of Nebraska Press, 1991). For women's experiences specifically see: Mary Crow Dog with Richard Erdoes, *Lakota Woman* (New York: Harper Perennial, 1991); Devon A. Mihesuah, "Anna Mae Pictou-Aquash: An American Indian Activist," in *Sifters: Native American Women's Lives,* ed. Theda Perdue (New York: Oxford University Press, 2001), 204–22; Elizabeth A. Castle, "Black and Native American Women's Activism in the Black Panther Party and the American Indian Movement" (PhD diss., Cambridge University, 2001); and Elizabeth A. Castle, "Keeping One Foot in the Community: Intergenerational Indigenous Women's Activism from the Local to Global (and Back Again)," in *American Indian Quarterly* 24, no. 2–3 (2003): 840–60.

3. *"To Form a More Perfect Union": Justice for American Women: A Report of the National Commission on the Observance of International Women's Year* (Washington DC: Government Printing Office, 1976).

4. For work on second wave women's activism see: Kathleen C. Berkeley, *The Women's Liberation Movement in America* (Westport CT: Greenwood Press, 1999); Alice Echols, *Daring to Be Bad: Radical Feminism in America, 1967–1975* (Minneapolis: University of Minnesota Press, 1989); Jo Freeman, *The Politics of Women's Liberation: A Case Study of an Emerging Social Movement and Its Relation to the Policy Process* (New York: McKay, 1975); Linda J. Nicholson, ed., *The Second Wave: A Reader in Feminist Theory* (New York: Routledge, 1997); Sarah Evans, *Personal Politics: The Roots of Women's Liberation in the Civil Rights Movement and New Left* (New York: Alfred A. Knopf, 1979); Susan M. Hartmann, *The Other Feminists: Activists in the Liberal Establishment* (New Haven CT: Yale University Press, 1998); Dorothy Sue Cobble, *The Other Women's Movement: Workplace Justice and Social Rights in Modern America* (Princeton NJ: Princeton University Press, 2004); and Benita Roth, *Separate Roads to Feminism: Black, Chicana, and White Feminist Movements in America's Second Wave* (Cambridge MA: Cambridge University Press, 2004).

5. Bea Medicine, *The Native American Woman: A Perspective* (Austin TX: National Educational Laboratory Publishers, 1978), 94.

6. Devon Mihesuah, *Indigenous American Women: Decolonization, Empowerment, Activism* (Lincoln: University of Nebraska Press, 2003), 8, 160, 162.

7. The planks on which participants voted included: the arts and humanities, battered women, business, child abuse, child care, credit, disabled women, education, elective and appointive offices, employment, the Equal Rights Amendment, health, homemakers, insurance, international affairs, media, minority women, offenders, older women, rape, reproductive rights, rural women, sexual preference, statistics, welfare and poverty, and the continuing committee of the conference.

8. *The Spirit of Houston: The First National Women's Conference: A Report to the President, the Congress, and the People of the United States* (Washington DC: National Commission on the Observance of International Women's Year, 1978), 9, 11, 17–77, 99.

9. IWY Texas Meeting, Planning the Texas Meeting, 9.

10. IWY Texas Meeting, Planning the Texas Meeting, 9.

11. Statistics on grants awarded: "5 to American Indians, 80 to Hispanics, 67 to Blacks, 54 to Caucasians, 4 to Others." Planning the Texas Meeting, 17. Planning the Texas Meeting, 11; IWY Texas Meeting, Resolutions, 89.

12. Interview L-0078, Southern Oral History Program Collection (#4007), Ruth Dial Woods, Interviewee, June 12, 1992, Interviewers: Anne Mitchell Coe and Laura Moore, http://docsouth.unc.edu/sohp/L-0078/menu.html, accessed October 12, 2016.

13. IWY North Carolina Meeting, Report from Mildred Jeffrey on North Carolina State Meeting for International Women's Year, Winston-Salem, North Carolina, June 17–19, 1977.

14. Ruth Woods interview, 11. Thomas Biolsi has suggested that for some indigenous groups abstention from voting was synonymous with a "no" vote. See *Organizing the Lakota: The Political Economy of the New Deal on the Pine Ridge and Rosebud Reservations* (Tucson: University of Arizona Press, 1988), 82.

15. Ruth Woods interview, 20.

16. IWY Louisiana Meeting, Louisiana Women's Conference, June 16–18, 1977, Pre-Conference Activities: A History of the Louisiana Women's Conference, Muriel Dees Arceneaux, Historian, 8, 55.

17. IWY Louisiana Meeting, Pre-Conference Activities, 98–99; IWY Louisiana Meeting, Part III: National Recommendations and Comments, 5; Employment, 94; IWY Texas Meeting, Summary of the Final Report to the National Commission on the Observance of International Women's Year by the Texas Coordinating Committee, September 1977, Office of the Governor, Attachment AA.

18. Ironically, despite this instance that indigenous women needed to speak for themselves, rather than having non-Native feminists presume to do so, this same resolution also urged "that the federal government, particularly in the fields of health care and education, consult with the Indian people as a whole before programs in these areas are implemented, and that Indians receive greater representation in all phases of national life." Perhaps this interpretation came from the handful of Native American participants present. IWY Florida Meeting, Minutes, Closing Plenary Session, Florida Meetings on the Observance of International Women's Year; IWY Florida Meeting, Office of the Governor, Attachment AA; IWY Florida Meeting, Attachments to Minutes of Closing Plenary Session, 7; https://www.flsenate .gov/search/results?q=lori+wilson+, accessed October 12, 2016.

19. IWY Oklahoma Meeting, Final Report of the Oklahoma IWY Coordinating Committee, July 18, 1977.

20. IWY Oklahoma Meeting.

21. IWY Oklahoma Meeting, Representative International Women's Year Caucus, 124; Action on Resolutions, 127–28.

22. IWY Oklahoma Meeting, Representative International Women's Year Caucus, 124; Action on Resolutions, 133, 137; IWY Oklahoma Meeting, Final Report of Coordinating Committee, Quotes from Participants, 1.

23. Native Americans on Coordinating Committee: Marie Cox, June Echohawk, Carmen Chasteen, Millie Giago, Deanna Jo Harragarra, Katherine Red Corn, Agnes Cowen, and Evalu Russell. IWY Oklahoma Meeting, State Coordinating Committee for the Oklahoma Women's Conference, 1977, Minutes of the First Meeting; Action on Resolutions, Agenda 149.

24. Caroline Bird, *The Spirit of Houston, What Women Want: From the Official Report to the President, the Congress, and the People of the United States* (New York: Simon and Schuster, 1979).

25. Bird, *The Spirit of Houston*, 71, 86, 83, 154.

26. Bird, *The Spirit of Houston*, 70.

27. Marge Emery, "Indian Women's Groups Span a Broad Spectrum," *Indian Truth* (1981): 8–9; Winona La Duke, *All Our Relations: Native Struggles for Land and Life* (Cambridge MA: South End Press, 1999); Paula Gunn Allen, *The Sacred Hoop: Recovering the Feminine in American Indian Traditions* (Boston MA: Beacon Press, 1986); Rayna Green, *Women in American Indian Society* (New York: Chelsea House Publishers, 1992); Owanah Anderson, *Ohoyo: One Thousand: A Resource Guide for*

Native American Women (Wichita Falls TX: Ohoyo Resource Center, 1982). (Numbers gleaned from index.)

28. Bird, *The Spirit of Houston*, 37–38.

29. Philip J. Deloria, *Indians in Unexpected Places* (Lawrence: University of Kansas Press, 2004).

30. Although a well-known idiom, I use it here in honor of Mike Green and the guidance he and Theda Perdue gave me when this research was at a much earlier stage.

Thirteen

Cherokee Ghostings and the Haunted South

JAMES TAYLOR CARSON

Tohi-gwa-tsu?

The translation of other languages is always tricky, but if one Cherokee speaker met another, they would not necessarily say, "Hi, how are you?" Instead they would ask each other if they were flowing well. In reply, they might say that they were flowing peacefully or even unhurriedly. They might also add that they felt upright and balanced. But if they replied in their equivalents of "so so" or "not so good," they would each know that something was wrong, not just with them but with the energy in which they both lived. Always an individual's actions implicate him or her in the flow of the world around them, and so life boils down to a constant struggle to remain balanced and to flow well.[1]

Why don't you take a look at the airport in Franklin?
—Theda Perdue

A little more than two hundred years before the Macon County Airport Authority ever imagined bulldozing the site of the old Cherokee town of Jore, the Quaker botanist William Bartram surveyed the scene and noted that the town he faced was "pleasantly situated in a little vale on the side of the mountain, a pretty rivulet or creek winds about through the vale, just under the village." While he could never know what a parking lot would be or even dread the thought of flying in a puddle jumper, he did have an eye for detail, and the most salient feature of Jore that he jotted in his journal was a well-tended grove. It was the only

one of its kind he had seen in his travels through the Cherokee towns, a home for what the town's inhabitants called the
"beloved trees" whose green leaves and tender shoots provided
the base for the celebrated, and emetic, black drink that people
across the region drank before undertaking serious discussions.
The grove marked Jore as an important town, a seat of discussion and deliberation, a space where people came to think and
to talk together, a place of respect, of order, and of eminence.[2]

It was vacant (except for a few Indians).
  —Perry Miller, *The New England Mind*

Scraping back the earth to bare the old town of Jore to make
room for the extra feet that would give the Franklin airport a
longer runway restaged the old script of the American frontier.
The municipal authority hoped to clear the land in order to
create new sources of revenue and job growth, and it turned to
bulldozers and backhoes to strip away the bushes, trees, and soil
that stood in the way. But what did the backhoe operator think
when the digger's teeth ripped away the right sides of two skulls
that had protruded from the earth? Did the archaeologists who
were on the scene to survey it panic about the event they later
glossed in their written report as an "intrusion?" What did the
man or the woman whose shovel exposed what the site report
documented as "the presence of teeth" feel? What goes through
your head when you disturb the dead? When you hear modern
metal break old bone? Did anyone wash themselves in running
water to rinse the contamination that had come by touching people who were supposed to be left alone?[3]

The bits of skull and teeth uncovered in the early days of the
Franklin airport extension project fall anonymously to us today
as "human remains." And while they were "human remains,"
they also were not. They were people who while in a state we
might agree to call dead were nonetheless also not. For Cherokees it has been said that there is no real death, no absolute
end. Because of grammar structures particular to the language,
Cherokees can describe actions that occurred in the past without locating them in the past. The language makes it possible
for things that, as some people might understand it, have hap-

pened, are happening, or will happen to all coexist within the same conceptual and lived space, as if in a room so to speak, and as people enter the room they partake in a sense of time that has neither a beginning nor an end but is just always. At the same time, everything a person can do can be witnessed by those who inhabit the room, by those who already have, and by those who hopefully will.[4]

Papers that consist of small sections joined by subtitles are the products of undisciplined minds.

—Mike Green

The Eastern Band of Cherokees was among the few of the South's first peoples to elude the inhumane expulsions we remember today as the Trails of Tears. The federal and state governments once rid the region of most of its fifty or so thousand original inhabitants, but if we recall the Cherokee notion of death and that room where everyone sits, we should not be surprised that what happened in the 1830s also happened yesterday and will happen tomorrow, too. From the Treaty of New Echota that underwrote the ethnic cleansing of the Cherokees' homeland to the Tellico Dam Project that flooded the Little Tennessee Valley to the defoliation of Nikwasi Mound to the extension of the Franklin airport runway to the reclamation of the Kituwah Mound, removal's everpresent shadow has shaped everything after and remains in place today to inform Cherokee responses to the unending and altogether unremarkable American myth that the "Indian" obstructed the "Progress" that Providence had ordained.

Cherokees still recall hiding in caves, gathering food from the land, evading soldiers, and waiting until it was safe to come out. Today around 13,000 Eastern Cherokees live in the United States, 9,000 of whom call the Qualla Boundary reservation in western North Carolina home. Their presence is in many ways a rebuke to removal and to the popular idea of the "vanishing Indian," a testimony to that gap that hangs perilously between what one historian has called "the willfully recalled and the deliberately forgotten past." And the most effective intermediary in exposing and perhaps even closing that gap has not been a Bureau of Indian Affairs agent nor even a Cherokee official but rather ghosts, the ones that emerge from the earth every time an archaeologist tests a shovel pit or a backhoe rips a trench, every time the old ground is disturbed to make way for the new. We all inhabit the same room together, and no one is ever really dead.[5]

> *Wherever I go, I got my mountains inside of me. They keep me steady. Headin' back to East Tennessee, I keep pushin' til I get 'em in sight again. When I see that first blue line rise up, I know I'm home.*
>
> —A trucker (qtd. in Marilou Awiakta *Selu*)

Life is just short.
And death comes quicker than it should, always.
I've learned that.
And then sometimes there are reprieves.
I've also learned that I wish I had it written down. Or at least remembered it.

I did, at one time. On a scrap of paper that I would share with each graduate student I taught, but then after my third office move I lost track of the sheet of paper and repeated searches of packed boxes, forgotten folders, and overstuffed drawers have proven fruitless.

What I lost was the record of Mike and Theda's doctoral genealogies. I'm scared to ask for it again, not because I am afraid of them, but because I lost something kind of sacred. Wherever it is I imagine it pulsating with a kind of low humming sound, maybe even glowing red. Like I imagined the scrap of paper I lost on which my great aunt, Nellie Miller Bennett, wrote the numbers of the regiments in which her uncles had served in the Army of Tennessee, including the name of the one who lost his leg at Chickamauga, a man who still stands in a photo behind a spindly chair at the bottom of which no left foot shows. But I can't remember his name now because I never asked her again. And now cannot ever. It's gone. She is dead.

And so too is that family tree of professors and supervisors except that I can recall a few names, some famous—Frederick Jackson Turner and Perry Miller—and some less so—Malcolm

Rohrbough, even though *Land Office Business* is a classic. The point of the tree was to show me where I had come from and, in a way, to explain to me who inhabited my work, my ideas, and my life. Writing history involves a kind of account settling, an attempt to say that what we remember or what we forget is not the whole story but that the whole story, even if it can never be ascertained, has more to say to us and about us than any partial recollection ever can, no matter our need for self-fulfillment. In this way, the history of the South is a history of hauntings played out over centuries. It is a tale that holds forth no resolution, no moral imperative other than the utter impossibility of the Golden Rule. Just being and belonging to a place that is as unsettled as the South, where the dead still speak to us about what we have done, exacts a toll on every effort to become who we think we are and what we think we do.[6]

The Puritan mind, as we know, found allegory congenial.

—Perry Miller, *The New England Mind*

For me the drive along Highway 74 just past Asheville through Waynesville and then by Cherokee to Chattanooga where my grandparents lived was always spooky. But I preferred it to taking I-40 up through Knoxville because that drive was boring, really boring, even though we got to glimpse Neyland Stadium. 74's winding lanes put me against so many deep drops that I dreaded it. Passing the turnoff to Robbinsville always made me wonder why Joyce Kilmer's parents named him Joyce and how Ronnie Millsap got around up there as a child. Each trip I'd check the kudzu that had turned a former roadside stop into a monstrous green hump but still had not reached the large rusting sheet metal kettle that stood above the decayed building, ready to serve giants from *The Jack Tales*, or so I imagined when I was smaller than I am now. And the AM radio gave out nothing but static from Waynesville through to this side of Cleveland. Only the kayakers that bobbed on the Nantahala provided an incongruous respite from what was otherwise, even to me as a child, a grim land even though I loved traveling through it because I felt like I had passed through something.

The names from all around where I grew up—Saluda, Keowee, Hiwassee, Stecoah, Etowah, Ooltewah, and Chickamauga—seemed even then to lie on the land more deeply than an Asheville, a Hendersonville, or a Fletcher ever could. Of the English names that comprised my childhood land, only Bearwaller Mountain resounded with the depth of time that I always craved. I had grown up knowing of pot hunters, arrowhead collectors, and bloody stories about the invasion of the Sequatchie Valley and took them as a child for what they were—remembrances of family relationships with the real and true people who had inhabited the place for millennia yet had largely disappeared from their land. It was the biggest ghost story of my life, the drive to my grandparents and the weekends that always followed, and it invoked every anxiety any Southerner could ever feel about having intruded, having expelled, and having taken. Never mind having also enslaved. Normal people get to feel proud of their roots. What do you do when you are a Southerner?

> The frontier is the outer edge of the wave—the meeting point between savage and civilization.
>
> —Frederick Jackson Turner, "The Significance of the Frontier in American History"

Small wonder a haunted region remembers some things and forgets others. But the way it is remembered and forgotten tells a lot about the living and the dead. For how long the stories have circulated who can say? William Gilmore Simms drew upon them to fashion the romantic South he imagined when he saw in his day headline stories of "Indian removal" and when he witnessed the sad march to Fort Sumter. In "Jocassé, A Cherokee Legend," Simms explained how the river got its name when an Occonnee maiden named Jocassé saw the scalp of Nagoochie, a warrior from the rival Estatoes, whom she loved. Full of despair she plunged herself into the living tide to be reunited forever after with her bloodied lover. Sadie Patton, who lived in Hendersonville during the Great Depression, was no Simms but recalled stories of other "Indians" who died because of love. One star-crossed maiden plunged off of "Jump-off Rock" when her lover failed to return from a battle against the Shawnees in the early 1700s while the beautiful Estatoe, who must have perished before Nagoochie was born, drowned herself in a river when her love for her father's mortal enemy could not be consummated. Pearl Webb of Pineola, North Carolina, recalled the same story about how the Estatoe River got its name. And an early explanation for the Brown Mountain lights holds true to this day. The lights that have danced and twinkled for centuries echo the lights of the torches born by the Cherokee women, come to seek the bodies of their husbands and sons who had perished in a battle with the Catawbas.[7]

It's all there, the story of the South, the conflict, the death, the nostalgia for people who in their day were mostly despised, and the mourning. But why love and suicide? And why do the land's invaders never appear? Such stories, of course, continue to underscore popular recollections of the region's past. "Braves" and "Maidens" are still remembered to have fallen in love and to have jumped off of mountains or into streams, old burial grounds still bother modern homeowners while stilled souls rise from time to time to avenge the pilfering of their graves or to search for long-lost family members. It is hard to dismiss such stories as frivolous, though, because they all touch so squarely on the South's disturbing origins. Indeed, the society in which we live today remains so wedded to the notion of the "Vanished Indian" that it never really bothers to ponder why "vanished?" Such ghost stories, tacky or harmless as they may be at first glance, invoke the past deaths on which our lives today are premised as seemingly benignant and arm's-length reminders of a history that is often remembered as romantic but that can be called nothing other than shameful, of the cleansing of the land, of the emptying of Keowee, Tocqua, and Chota, and of the deaths and dispossessions of untold thousands. Not one of whom, as far as I have ever found, was a love-struck maiden.[8]

By consigning the first people to such maudlin lives and deaths, the second people who told and retold the stories have represented the past in ways that enabled anxious settlers to claim ownership, not just of the land but of the knowledge that named it. Indeed, when such stories take their place within the larger premise of the story of the "vanished Indian," they effect in their own way a kind of removal, a dislocation of the first people from places that were once theirs and a substitution of noble suicide for less glamorous fates like smallpox, dysentery, famine, and murder. The deaths of Jocassé and Estatoe created the baseline from which Southerners could emerge as intact and "historied" people who could subsume the ugly story of how they got their land in tales that placed the peopling, the naming, and, presumably, the loss of the land in a deeper past that they had simply inherited rather than caused.[9]

If the ghosting of the South's second peoples that occurs in such stories as "Jocassé" and "Estatoe" works as a removal of another kind, it is also important to remember that the spirits that haunt the South's ghost stories are wholly different from those that come out of the ground when ancient burying grounds are disturbed, when colonization has to be enacted again so that today's "Manifest Destiny" can be renewed and reproduced across today's time and through today's space in the form of new shopping centers, residential subdivisions, hydroelectric projects, and runway expansions. No place is ever free from the past and so every day, whether we like to admit or not, we encounter ghosts. And in the South, the ghosts, more often than not, raise to the present the forgotten facts that have made the South such a haunted land, all of which unsettles everything, exposes our fragile foundations, and confronts the verities of modern life with its often unspeakable origins. The appearance of something from another time into ours puts us in a place not unlike that room shared by Cherokees where linear time ruptures, where the dispossession did not take, where the removals failed to cleanse, where the dead still live, where the "Indian" never vanishes, and where such simple-minded tropes like "Progress" and "Frontier" remain always in contest no matter the distance we trek between then and now. The postcolonial ghost story tells not the fanciful nostalgia of how a river got its name but instead heralds the return of a truth about how everything built atop it came to be.[10]

Conversion of the Indians is, inevitably, one of the seven purposes.
—Perry Miller, *The New England Mind*

In November 1979 the Tennessee Valley Authority flooded the

Little Tennessee River valley as part of the Tellico Dam hydro-electric project that, planners hoped, would pull the region into the "modern age." With cheap electricity, the TVA believed that light industry would flock to the region, outmigration for decent jobs would be staunched, and recreational properties for sale along the new lakes would pull in even more tourist and tax dollars. Among the variety of groups who allied to oppose the Tellico project were recreational fishermen who wanted the river to remain alive, environmentalists who seized upon the imperiled snail-darter as an emblem of the carnage they feared, and Cherokees who lamented the drowning of historic towns like Tocqua and Chota and Citico with their untold hundreds of cultural objects, sacred sites, and burials. People had been living in the valley for millennia, and in a flurry of archaeological activity in the years leading up to the flooding, the University of Tennessee and the TVA exhumed hundreds of people for study and then storage, in what I have no idea. Cardboard boxes? Canvas sacks? Of the roughly 1,200 people whose remains the social scientists unearthed, 185 were returned to the Cherokees for reburial in 1986 while the other 1,000 or so were put back in storage because they could not be definitively called "Cherokee." Some death sentence. If they are not buried and instead are only dug up, can they inhabit the room? The dead failed to block the Tellico project, but their activism, so to speak, enabled people to label the TVA and the UT archaeologists "grave robbers," as powerful a derogatory term as there is, and set the stage for future conflicts between Cherokee ghosts and capital developers.[11]

Here pause we by the ancient mound
For which no builder yet is found
And muse upon the vanish'd race
That left, without a name, a trace

—William Gilmore Simms, "The Mountain Tramp"

To be honest, there is a name and more than a trace no matter what Simms thought. A people called Tsa-la-gi settled in a place called Nikwasi where they founded one of the oldest Cherokee towns, a mother town. In the beginning, women lugged earth in baskets made of river cane to the place where the people had decided to build their council house. Men inserted a hollowed cedar trunk in the midst of the great pile of earth, like a straw in a shake, to make the fireplace for the house that would sit atop the mound. But no ordinary fire was kindled at Nikwasi. No, Nikwasi was home to the everlasting fire put on earth by the Thunderer to guard men, women, and children against the cold, and every year after the annual Green Corn Ceremony that marked the beginning of a new year, the people of Nikwasi would share their everlasting fire with nearby towns, children towns, and enact the kind of genealogical hierarchy that had ordered the towns' relations for centuries. According to the story, the fire still burns deep in Nikwasi Mound although a recent ground-penetrating radar scan failed to find it.[12]

Over time the inhabitants of Nikwasi changed but the mound remained and in the 1700s men from the towns that comprised the Creek confederacy attacked Nikwasi and overwhelmed its defenders. But then the mound opened and out poured thousands of "spirit people," the *Nunnehi*, the "people who live anywhere," who made themselves invisible and killed the Creek men, even those who hid behind rocks and trees because no obstacle could stop the arrows that sought their hearts. Only one man lived to flee back to his home with the message to never attack Nikwasi again. Years later new people arrived again and, again, drove out the older folk, and, in 1828, they renamed Nikwasi "Franklin." During the Civil War, however, when columns of blue horsemen threatened to burn the town, the *Nunnehi* exited the mound again to defend the village against hostile invaders, and no building burned in Franklin that day.[13]

It was Freeman Owle, a Cherokee man born just after World War II had ended, who told this story one evening to the Nantahala Hiking Club. And he told it not to skewer his audience, not to shame them, but to charge them with the responsibility they bore, as residents of Nikwasi, to tend the fire and to guard the home of the spirit people. "I'm respectful of Franklin, North Carolina," Owle told his audience, "you are one of the very few areas that has protected your mound, that is located within your village." The struggle to protect it began in the early decades of the twentieth century when the national campaign to create the Great Smoky Mountains National Park ennobled Appalachian landscapes and sacred Cherokee sites. As part of the mania for conservation and preservation that swept the region, Franklin's citizens saw the Nikwasi Mound as a kind of civic charter that established the antiquity of their town and, by extension, their own indigenous possession of the land. The mound was, the Macon County Historical Society declared, a "stately and silent reminder of a time, a culture, and a people of a bygone era."[14]

Indeed, around the same time Owle was born a developer had offered to purchase and then raze the mound, but its owner, W. Roy Carpenter, gave the town the chance to buy it for $1,500. The Nikwasi Indian Mound Association slowly raised funds, extended the purchase deadline, and raised more funds to complete the deal. Even the schoolchildren of Franklin pooled their pennies to help, and the town took it upon itself to preserve the home of the *Nunnehi* without alteration. But it did get altered. The land around it changed, an encircling fence was built, and one can only guess what the *Nunnehi* thought when in the late spring of 2012 a municipal crew sprayed herbicide on the mound to kill the grass that town aldermen thought was too costly to mow.[15] The town hoped instead that a low maintenance "eco-lawn" could be sown on the mound afterward to keep down costs. But as the original turf browned and the eco-turf failed to germinate, word of the balding mound reached the Eastern Band whose chief, Michell Hicks, wrote to the Franklin town board that Cherokees were "deeply offended by the use of herbicides on such a special place as Nikwasi." One alderman, Bob Scott, thought the town owed the band an apology, but the board as a whole refused in one of those stubborn unreflexive gestures that makes you wonder just how hard the heart can be.[16] Mayor Joe Collins, whose childhood Sundays were spent in the company of his aunts, uncles, and cousins who lived on Qualla Boundary, however, contacted Chief Hicks and expressed his regret for what had happened and invoked Franklin's past as Nikwasi in the hopes that "we will also share a common and amicable future." The spirit people had won their third victory.[17]

My parents always say, "If you meet a copperhead—snake or person—give 'em a wide birth. If you have to go in close, take a hoe!"
   —Marilou Awiakta, "Trail Warning"

Twelve landings a day were not enough for the managers of the Franklin airport because no small southern town on the make wants to be thought of as podunk. So in 1998 the airport's commissioners decided to expand the runway by 600 feet to meet the minimum 5,000 feet requirement, along with a larger safety area, for landing small jets. Development officials in Macon County had identified a need for jet traffic to support local business in addition to servicing wealthy vacation-home owners in the nearby community of Highlands. The short runway put Franklin at a competitive disadvantage relative to other towns of similar size.[18]

The debate that arose over the project echoed similar discussions in any town in America. One member of the Macon County Airport Authority remarked that the new runway "would project a much more progressive and prosperous image for the county."[19] In addition to boosting the town's tourism and economic development, it was also hoped that the project would make Franklin into an economic engine for the region and stop the out-migration that was taking so many young people away. Maybe the ghost of the TVA had haunted the town's civic administration because they also carefully skirted any real confrontation with the question of the dead.[20] Other members of the public, however, had doubts. Against arguments for development and progress, citizens of Franklin rued a repeat of the region's darkest history. "The Cherokee suffered during the "Trail of Tears," wrote one opponent of the project, "Will Macon Country make them to suffer again?"[21] James A. Bullman asked anyone with grandparents how they would feel upon learning that their graves would be bulldozed "so that some fat cat could land his larger plane?," while James W. Akins attributed it to the backroom influence of the "fat cats" of Highlands who wanted a place to land their fancy planes.[22] "Thank God for the fat cats," retorted the airport authority's chairman, "the fat cats up there spend a lot of money. They help keep our tax base low."[23] Cherokee graves, he did not have to say, do not.

The problem was that the project site, of which a little more than five acres would be touched directly by the construction work, lay atop the seventeenth-century Cherokee town of Jore which in turn lay atop multiple other layers of human life and death reaching back thousands of years. The rural site that had once been home to a dairy farm some five miles out of town had been, before that, a place where ten thousand years ago hunters abandoned or dropped a few spear points and where three thousand years ago someone learned how to make a clay pot, probably from someone else. Certain stone blades found on the site betrayed influences from the great Hopewell civilization of the Ohio River Valley that dominated life in eastern North America around, as one Asheville newspaper editor put it, "the time of Jesus." And around 500 AD the site became a permanent settlement where the people learned to cultivate maize, to construct large fortifications, and to build council houses atop earthen mounds. The vast bulk of artifacts unearthed from the site, however, reflected the lives led by the Cherokees who had planted and tended those trees that Bartram had so admired back on the eve of the American Revolution.[24]

> *No fraud upon the dead commit*
> —Philip Freneau, "Lines Occasioned by a Visit to an Old
> Indian Burying Ground"

The archaeological investigation that preceded the runway project surveyed the five acres that made up the project site, and what came to be known as the "impact site"—where the greatest concentration of artifacts and site features collided with the most intensive excavation and construction—was found to comprise about an acre. Initial hopes that the test digs would yield nothing of importance fell flat when the survey samples revealed that a major site sat beneath the coveted land. Subsequent investigations suggested that as many as four hundred burials dotted the area, meaning that, in the most basic way possible, the dead would have a say in what happened to them and to the airport.[25] Harold Corbin, chairman of the Macon County Board of Commissioners, however, doubted the dead, and uttered the kind of remark that, more than anything else, betrays the troubled soul of the colonial. In response to news about human remains, Corbin thought out loud, "I don't think they've ever identified them as human. . . . They could be cow, horse, or dog bones."[26] The survey, however, proved Corbin wrong, and all parties agreed that "the dignity of the buried remains [would] be respected." Achieving respect remained elusive though because of various competing pressures related to costing, scheduling, legal issues, and relations with what bureaucrats and modern managers like to call stakeholders.[27] To be sure, the Eastern Band played an important role in the subsequent negotiations and achieved some important objectives, but it was the dead who threatened most to kill the project because of their obdurate and unapologetic occupation of the land.

> The Indian was a common danger, demanding united action.
> —Frederick Jackson Turner, "The Significance of the Frontier in American History"

Neither the dead—but let's call them ghosts now because they have assumed an animated presence—nor the Eastern Band had legal rights to block the project because it was on neither federal nor Cherokee land. Nevertheless the airport authority spent years in talks with the ghosts and the Cherokees to ensure the project's completion with the smallest amount of disruption and dishonor. As always, money was a concern, too; this was, after all, the municipality that fretted about the costs of mowing the grass on Nikwasi Mound. The memorandum of agreement that came out of the protracted talks stipulated that the various pots of federal, state, and county monies that were to cover the expansion would provide $535,000 to fund the recovery of 25 percent of the artifacts located in the "impact site" that would be most disturbed by the earth movers, backhoes, and graders. Confusion ensued about the 25 percent figure, which accounted for just one-fourth of the two million dollars estimated as a minimum cost for a thorough and proper excavation of the site. Cherokees and members of the public thought that the 25 percent target applied to the entire site and felt insulted at such a meager recovery rate. Others called for 100 percent recovery of the artifacts to which the state archaeologist replied that such a target would be impossible to meet given that no one could ever know how much stuff actually lay beneath the ground.[28] As the Eastern Band's historic preservation officer, Russ Townsend, put it, "To do just 25 percent on such a resource I think is just a shame."[29] Dr. Michael Trinkley, the archaeologist commissioned to undertake the pre-construction site survey, was less circumspect. "It's an abomination," he stated in response to the 25 percent recovery plan, "its vulgar, it's obscene, and it is disrespectful."[30] Everyone knew the dead would either be disturbed or destroyed.[31] Indeed, Trinkley advocated for the project to be called off. Citing North Carolina's "Unmarked Human Burial and Human Skeletal Remains Protection Act," which sought to protect human burials and remains from "vandalism and inadvertent destruction," he labeled the extension project "unethical," while Townsend flatly refused to grant any permission to disturb, damage, move, or molest the graves because, really, they were not simply resting places for the dead but also where ancestors continued to live, breathe, watch, and do.[32]

> The obstacles to settlement were distance, physical barriers . . . and especially the Indians.
>
> —Malcom Rohrbough, *The Trans-Appalachian Frontier*

After the Eastern Band refused to sign the memorandum of agreement because of their opposition to the 25 percent plan, local and state authorities declined to push the project further; instead, heeding the ghosts' silent activism, they sought extra funding to undertake as complete an artifact recovery as possible from the entire site, not just the "impact site." The Federal Aviation Administration and the North Carolina Division of Aviation came up with an extra $700,000, which, while falling below the estimated total recovery cost of $2–$3 million, nonetheless broke the stalemate along with a revised grading plan that would ensure no grave would be troubled. While the band wanted 100 percent recovery, possible or impossible as that may have been, they most wanted to ensure that the dead could remain in the ground so that they could continue their rest in the mother whence they had come. In the end, thanks in large part to the ghosts' silent protests, the Cherokee belief that the dead should never be disturbed prevailed so that no man, woman, or child had to be removed from their final resting place in order to make way for Progress. But one wonders if the "fat cat" jets let them sleep in peace today because the dead are never ever really dead, just quiet, waiting for moments when they can give life to our places, join us in that room, and remind us that what we tend to forget always endures in the face of what we choose to remember.[33]

> *The very first rebuilding of the mound, it was the children who did it. Our ancestors are buried here. That's what they needed to see. When we begin to do these things again, who we are begins to mean something again.*
>
> —Tom Belt, "Research Report"

They remembered that the Kituwah Mound and its surrounding town was, like Nikwasi, a mother town that possessed an everlasting fire, but it was also more important than Nikwasi because it was the point of origin of the Ani-kitu-hwagi, the original people whom we know today as the Cherokees: it was the site of the original fire, and the place where the creator had handed down the law. At the time of the removals, about ten thousand years after the place was first inhabited, the state of North Carolina confiscated the site and auctioned it off. Over the decades it passed through various farmers' hands. The mound itself diminished almost annually under the cleaving power of the farmers' plows and the inexorable flows of erosion. By 1940 the site was home to some grazing cattle and a small airstrip that sustained an aerial sightseeing business. When the 309-acre parcel came up for sale in 1996, however, the Eastern Band jumped at the chance to reacquire their ancient home, and they applied the earnings from their casino toward the three and a half million dollar purchase price.[34]

The investment led many to ask what next? Some Cherokees touted the site's tourism potential, and some went so far as to suggest building a tourist train station, a resort, a golf course, or a NASCAR oval on the old town site. Too much money, pro-development Cherokees argued, had been spent for the land to lie fallow. Many of them recognized the imperative to balance development and conservation. Some, however, likened the site to "that graveyard we can't do anything with," to which others fired back that such proponents of development were "non-Indians." "It's sacred ground," one supporter of the site's preservation insisted, "It's not just future, it's history there." As such, shortly after the purchase Cherokees began returning to the site to perform small ceremonies and to pray on the hallowed ground. In 1998 Tom Belt organized children to visit the site and to place red clay at the top of the wounded mother to begin the process of renewing her promise and theirs, to repair the damage of the past and to restore the good and healthy flow. "You're talking about kids who can't speak Cherokee, who watch TV all the time," Belt noted, "All of a sudden they reach back in time and say that's part of who we are."[35] They enter the room.

It was Franklin all over again except this time Cherokees argued with Cherokees about the future they would share. The flow was bad. But Groundhog changed it all. Long ago Groundhog played tricks, like the time he sang his way out of the clutches of seven hungry wolves and lost only his tail in the bargain as he fled down his hole. The other animals had also punished him once, long ago, for an insulting remark he had made in council that had disrupted the flow. For his transgression his head was made to smell badly, but unfortunately the details of his transgression remain out of print because, the story collector asserted, "The story is a vulgar one, without wit enough to make it worth recording." Nonetheless, on March 14, 2000, Groundhog played another trick when he dug a hole in Ferguson's Field and bared a few broken human bones. Maybe he wanted to atone for his slander so long ago.[36]

Word of the bones spread and what everyone suspected came into clear view. A subsequent archaeological survey of the site that deployed more than a thousand small test holes revealed fifteen graves and, based on historic population patterns, the team estimated that there were hundreds if not thousands of burials on the site. Magnetic imaging further revealed numerous hearth sites that marked the centers of peoples' homes as well as one large hearth that marked the spot where the everlasting fire had burned and where the original law had been given to the people. Other burial sites, here and there, emerged from the murky electronic images. The people's presence changed everything, the site was alive, and the debates that had divided Cherokees closed up as more or less everyone agreed that the living had an obligation to protect Kituwah from anything that might disturb their people and their flow.[37]

Like the energy substation Duke Power proposed to build adjacent to the site in early 2010. In reply to the plan the tribal council passed a resolution declaring that "it is this tribe's solemn responsibility and moral duty to care for and protect all of Kituwah from further desecration and degradation by human agency in order to preserve the integrity of the most important site for the origination and continuation of Cherokee culture, heritage, history, and identity."[38] Duke Energy claimed to be surprised by the outcry that had followed their bulldozing of an area the size of two football fields on the adjacent mountainside where they planned to install the station to service, in part, Harrah's Cherokee Casino by way of 100-feet-tall utility towers carrying humming high-voltage lines. Backed by the council motion, the lawyer for the Cherokees, Hannah Smith, promised no compromise. "I think they're counting on us not to know the law," she said, "and I think they're counting on their Fortune 500 lawyers beating us."[39] More fat cats!

Duke Energy claimed it had the law on its side while Cherokees had nothing more than a charter embodied by the dead and the claim they held on the past, present, and future. And the support of the 290,000 Oklahoma Cherokees and 10,000 members of the United Kituwah Band of Cherokees. And the backing of Swain County officials where 40 percent of residents share that room with the Kituwah dead. The power of those ghosts that Groundhog had unearthed and the living whose spirits they animated to oppose the project kept Duke Energy at the bargaining table for months. In the end, Swain County officials identified promising alternate sites and the utility giant agreed to relocate the station out of Kituwah's lines of sight. The dead had ended talk of racetracks and golf courses and had pointed the community in a common direction, and once the flow had been established Duke Energy could neither withstand it nor turn it aside no matter the law. "It's almost Biblical in a lot of ways," said Tom Belt about the site and its power within the valleys of those ancient mountains, of that time when the children and the ghosts together helped the people see their way ahead.[40]

> Beyond the mountains the first American was still a dismaying problem.
>
> —W. J. Cash, *Mind of the South*

When he wrote *The Mind of the South*, W. J. Cash located the origins of the South's mind in the history of a frontier that rolled ever westward. Before settlers made their way across the land, it was, Cash wrote, a "wilderness," but not an empty one. "The noble savage" tracked what in his rude hands could only ever be a "wasteland" to await the arrival of "Civilization," and the wait was long, for it was not until, Cash asserted, "Andrew Jackson and his men of Tennessee could finally crush him" that the South's first peoples began to vanish from the scene.[41] The violence in Cash's story, however, is telling, for as he admitted with his allusion to Old Hickory's war against the Creeks, the real story of the South's foundation was not the frontier's unfolding nor God's sweet grace but rather the land's depopulation through the destruction of its original inhabitants.

> His greatest difficulty would not be the stones . . . and Indians, but the problem of his identity.
>
> —Perry Miller, *Errand into the Wilderness*

The mind of the South, and, for that matter, the history of the South, sits on piles of bones—a kind of Golgotha where the profusion of dry counties would make it hard to find wine to succor the lips of the martyr. Where Jem Finch could only have met Boo Radley because "General Jackson" had run "the Creeks up the creek."[42] Where Thomas Wolfe's Altamont was built atop a place much like Jore.[43] Where ancient mounds loomed in the shadows of Yoknapatawpha County's swamps and backwoods. Where students at the University of Alabama are honored atop a mound made not of clay and the everlasting fire but of the rubble of a dormitory burned to the ground by federal troops, and where "Osceola" prances on horseback to rally the Florida State faithful at halftime. Ghosts are everywhere and yet are rarely remembered for what they bespeak—an ancestry. Maybe not the benign and prideful ancestry we associate with family trees, but an ancestry nonetheless that refuses to keep silent in spite of the degree to which the South continues to deny its origins in invasion, ethnic cleansing, and forgetting.

When we confront such things as the Trail of Tears or the flooding of Tellico or the paving over of Jore and view them through the prism of the frontier, through the cost-benefit analysis of Progress, and through the divine mandate of "Manifest Destiny," we witness firsthand what literary scholar George B. Handley has likened to a "politics of oblivion" whereby what has been forgotten shapes the writing of history every bit as much as what has been remembered. And if we do not stop to think, we run the further risk of allowing "existing memories of conquest, enslavement, and colonization" to appear "as naturally born from history itself" in ways that absolve us of our complicity, if not with the deed then with the memory of the deed. By obliterating the humanity of the region's first peoples, their existence as people rather than as stone-like obstacles to Progress, we enact a kind of inhuman and atemporal logic, of locating the South's origins in a primordial natural world free of human agency, and of reproducing a history premised on elimination. Such are the hallmarks of how the Kituwah redevelopment and the Franklin runway project threatened to go, except that in such cases, as with Tellico, and as with Nikwasi, ghosts acted in their own defense and forced outcomes that would have been unthinkable a century before. If we allow ourselves the capacity to listen to the dead, to enjoin them in conversations about the pasts they lived and the present we share with them, then their hauntings will continue to condition what we choose to remember or to forget and our actions might be more thoughtful and maybe even our lives more complete.[44]

We don't think you should use the word "likely." What does it mean anyway?

—Mike Green and Theda Perdue

The people of Jore whom Bartram met likely would have held conceptions of death that varied considerably from what most of their descendants might think today although echoes of older practices can still be heard. No one lowers the dead in a fetal position into a pit along with shell ornaments, beads, mica plates, and bone rattles anymore nor do they any longer bury their relatives in the floors of their homes. But they do observe a week-long wake, wash themselves in running water after a funeral service or after coming into contact with anything of the dead, and hold fast to the basic idea that the dead never die. For such reasons we might consider that the past can, through the Cherokee language, be rendered as the present, still alive, still active, and still implicated in everyone's quest to flow well.[45]

Disturbing people who rest in the ground, however, breaks any good flow and leaves the world in a state of discord. Section 70-2 of the "Cherokee Code" states that Cherokee dead should never be disturbed. If they must, then the band prefers that reburial take place as close as possible to the site in question, and if that is not possible, then the dead are to be reinterred in a burial mound on the grounds of the Sequoyah Birthplace Museum in Vonore, Tennessee. It was there in 1986 that the people whom the TVA and the University of Tennessee had unearthed in advance of the Tellico Dam project were reinterred, and it is there today where, from time to time, unfortunate souls whose repose has been ended by archaeologists or excavators join the bones of their ancestors and descendants.[46]

But let us not lose ourselves in talk of skulls, teeth, bones, and the dead because if we are to listen to the ghosts then we must also account for a different way of conceiving everything sanitized by the phrase "human remains." It is easy today to dismiss ghosts as lame subjects for paranormal TV shows or as irrational holdovers from more credulous times, but they were there at Franklin and at Kituwah as beings in the present who sat with us in our lives and who knew no past, present, or future, but only now. And all they wanted was to be left alone, to lie untouched where they had lain for centuries, and everyone from the Federal Aviation Administration to the Franklin airport authority to the Band Council, in the end, heeded their counsel.

"They are still here," one Cherokee has said of the dead, "and if we disturb them we've upset the order and balance." Troubling the dead can also imperil the living, not just because of the loss of balance but because of the sacrilege associated with disturbing graves and the attendant disruptions to the flow in which we all live. When the dead are disturbed, when the ghosts are ignored, "Their existence—our existence—," one Cherokee concluded, "is wiped away." But that did not happen this time in Jore, in Nikwasi, and in Kituwah because people chose a different path, one that reconciled as best they could modernity and respect, that closed the gap between past and future, and that restored the flow thanks to the strong and silent activism of ghosts who wanted to remain in the room and to continue to exist in the balance and the flow that makes us all well.[47]

Tohi-gwu.

Acknowledgments

The author would like to thank Mike and Theda for everything they gave as well as Catherine, Tim, and Greg, and Cailin Murray who shared her fundamental idea about the power of ghostings as well as critical thoughts about an early draft.

Notes

The first and last epigraphs are from Heidi M. Altman and Thomas N. Belt, "Reading History: Cherokee History through a Cherokee Lens," *Native South* 1 (2008): 91.

1. Altman and Belt, "Reading History," 91–2.
2. William Bartram, *William Bartram and the Southeastern Indians*, ed. Gregory A. Waselkov and Kathryn E. Holland Braund (Lincoln: University of Nebraska Press,

1995), 82; Michael Trinkley, "Archaeological Testing of 31MA77, Proposed Macon County Airport Expansion, Franklin, North Carolina," *Chicora Research Contribution 312* (Columbia SC: Chicora Foundation Inc., December 15, 2000), 6; Christopher B. Rodning, "Center Places in the Cherokee Landscape: Archaeology of the Coweeta Creek Site in Southwestern North Carolina," www.tulane.edu/~crodning/cr_p_ms08122011.pdf, accessed December 5, 2012.

3. Trinkley, "Archaeological Testing," 37.

4. Altman and Belt, "Reading History," 93.

5. Robert A. Gilmer, "In the Shadow of Removal: Historical Memory, Indianness, and the Tellico Dam Project" (PhD diss., University of Minnesota, 2011), 5; Geary Hobson, Janet McAdams, and Kathryn Walkiewicz, eds., *The People Who Stayed: Southeastern Indian Writing after Removal* (Norman: University of Oklahoma Press, 2010), 77, 80; Michelle D. Hamilton, "Adverse Reactions: Practicing Bioarchaeology among the Cherokees," in *Under the Rattlesnake: Cherokee Health and Resiliency,* ed. Lisa Lefler (Tuscaloosa: University of Alabama Press, 2009), 32; W. Fitzhugh Brundage, "Introduction: No Deed but Memory," in *Where These Memories Grow: History, Memory, and Southern Identity,* ed. W. Fitzhugh Brundage (Chapel Hill: University of North Carolina Press, 2000), 6.

6. Renée L. Bergland, *The National Uncanny: Indian Ghosts and American Subjects* (Hanover NH: University Press of New England, 2000), 5; Arthur Redding, *Haints: American Ghosts, Millennial Passions, and Contemporary Gothic Fictions* (Tuscaloosa: University of Alabama Press, 2011), 8, 40.

7. John Caldwell Guilds and Charles Hudson, eds., *An Early and Strong Sympathy: The Indian Writings of William Gilmore Simms* (Columbia: University of South Carolina Press, 2003), 178–81, 196; Sadie S. Patton, *Ghost Stories and Legends of the Mountains* (Hendersonville NC: Blue Ridge Specialty Printers, 1935), 2, 38–39; Newman Ivey White, ed., *The Frank C. Brown Collection of North Carolina Folklore,* 5 vols. (Durham NC: Duke University Press, 1952), 1:632, 684; Michael Renegar, *Roadside Revenants and Other North Carolina Ghosts and Legends* (Fairview NC: Bright Mountain Books, 2005), 61–62; Terrance Zepke, *Best Ghost Tales of North Carolina,* 2nd ed. (Sarasota FL: Pineapple Press, 2006), 19–21.

8. Jean M. O'Brien, *Firsting and Lasting: Writing Indians out of Existence in New England* (Minneapolis: University of Minnesota Press, 2010), xiii; Frances Casstevens, *Ghosts and Their Haunts: The Legends and Lore of the Yadkin River Valley* (Boone NC: Parkway Publishers, 2005), 5, 94; Lee King, *The Beast of Rickards Road and the Ghost of Payne Road: True Ghost Stories from North Carolina* (Lincoln NE: iUniverse, 2007), 100–101, 135, 179; Steven Conn, *History's Shadow: Native Americans and Historical Consciousness in the Nineteenth Century* (Chicago IL: University of Chicago Press, 2004); Hobson, McAdams, and Walkiewicz, *People Who Stayed,* 7.

9. O'Brien, *Firsting and Lasting,* xiii, 4–5; Bergland, *National Uncanny,* 1–4, 40; Ken Gelder and Jane M. Jacobs, "The Postcolonial Ghost Story," in *Ghosts: Deconstruction, Psychoanalysis, History,* ed. Peter Buse and Andrew Stotts (London: Macmillan Press Ltd., 1999), 182; Colleen E. Boyd, "'You See Your Culture Coming Out

of the Ground Like a Power': Uncanny Narratives in Time and Space on the North-west Coast," *Ethnohistory* 56 (Fall 2009): 700.

10. Bergland, *National Uncanny*, 4–5; Boyd, "You See Your Culture," 700–701; Avery F. Gordon, *Ghostly Matters: Haunting and the Sociological Imagination*, 2nd ed. (Minneapolis: University of Minnesota Press, 1997), 3, 8, 207; Michael Mayerfeld Bell, "The Ghosts of Place," *Theory and Society* 26 (December 1997): 813; Redding, *Haints*, 37; Peter Buse and Andrew Stott, "Introduction: A Future for Haunting," in *Ghosts*, 14; Gelder and Jacobs, "Postcolonial Ghost Story," 188.

11. Gilmer, "Shadow of Removal," 1, 215–18, as quoted 215; Marilou Awiakta, *Selu: Seeking the Corn Mother's Wisdom* (Golden CO: Fulcrum Publishing), 43, 57; Jefferson Chapman, *Tellico Archaeology: 12,000 Years of Native American History* (Knoxville: Tennessee Valley Authority, 1985), iii, 61, 97; John R. Finger, *Cherokee Americans: The Eastern Band of the Cherokees in the Twentieth Century* (Lincoln: University of Nebraska Press, 1991), 155–56; William Bruce Wheeler and Michael J. McDonald, "The 'New Mission' and the Tellico Project, 1945–70," *TVA: Fifty Years of Grass-Roots Bureaucracy* (Urbana: University of Illinois Press, 1983), 168–70, 175–81, 183–88.

12. Rodning, "Center Places," 25; James Mooney, *James Mooney's History, Myths, and Sacred Formulas of the Cherokees* (Asheville NC: Bright Mountain Books, 1992), 240, 396; *Asheville Citizen-Times*, June 28, 2009.

13. Mooney, *Mooney's History*, 330–31, 337; Randy Russell and Janet Barnett, *Mountain Ghost Stories and Curious Tales of Western North Carolina* (Winston-Salem NC: John F. Blair, 1988), 58, 62; Hobson, McAdams, and Walkiewicz, *People Who Stayed*, 98–101; Trinkley, "Archaeological Testing," 27–28.

14. Nathaniel Francis Holly, "The Plasticity of Place: The Lives of Cherokee Sacred Places and the Struggles to Protect Them" (MA thesis, Western Carolina University, March 2012); O'Brien, *Firsting and Lasting*, xiii–xv; Hobson, McAdams, and Walkiewicz, *People Who Stayed*, 100; http://www.maconnchistorical.org/about-us/, accessed July 18, 2012.

15. Holly, "Plasticity of Place," 115–21; *Macon County News*, June 30, 2011; *Cherokee One Feather*, May 9, 2012; *Franklin Press*, May 11, 2012.

16. *Macon County News*, August 9, 2012; *Cherokee One Feather*, May 9, 2012; quoted, *Franklin Press*, June 13, 2012.

17. *Franklin Press*, June 13, 2012.

18. *Franklin Press*, March 3, 2009; *Franklin Press*, February 19, 2009; *Asheville Citizen-Times*, February 17, 2009; *Asheville Citizen-Times*, February 20, 2009.

19. *Franklin Press*, March 1, 2009.

20. *Asheville Citizen-Times*, June 14, 2001; *Asheville Citizen-Times*, February 17, 2009; *Macon County News*, June 9, 2011.

21. *Franklin Press*, March 11, 2009.

22. *Franklin Press*, February 18, 2009; *Franklin Press*, March 11, 2009.

23. *Franklin Press*, March 12, 2009.

24. *Franklin Press*, May 8, 2009; Trinkley, "Archaeological Testing," 10, 14, 43, 46–47, 51; quoted, *Asheville Citizen-Times*, February 20, 2009.

25. Trinkley, "Archaeological Testing," 1; *Franklin Press*, May 8, 2009; *Tuckasee-gee Reader*, February 17, 2009.

26. *Asheville Citizen-Times*, November 28, 2000.

27. *Franklin Press*, April 12, 2002.

28. *Tuckaseegee Reader*, February 17, 2009; *Franklin Press*, February 19, 2009; *Franklin Press*, March 3, 2009; *Franklin Press*, May 8, 2009.

29. *Franklin Press*, March 3, 2009.

30. *Asheville Citizen-Times*, February 17, 2009.

31. *Franklin Press*, March 3, 2009.

32. *Tuckaseegee Reader*, February 17, 2009; "Article 3. Unmarked Human Burial and Human Skeletal Remains Protection Act (1981)," 70–27.a.1, http://www.ncleg.net /EnactedLegislation/Statutes/PDF/ByArticle/Chapter_70/Article_3.pdf, accessed May 7, 2013. The North Carolina act preceded the federal Native American Graves Protection and Repatriation Act (NAGPRA) by nine years. NAGPRA, https://www .nps.gov/nagpra/MANDATES/INDEX.HTM, accessed May 7, 2013.

33. *Franklin Press*, April 3, 2009; *Franklin Press*, September 2, 2009; *Asheville Citizen-Times*, October 1, 1999; *Macon County News*, June 9, 2011; Andrea Cooper, "Embracing Archaeology," SAA *Archaeological Record* (May 2011): 13.

34. Holly, "Plasticity of Place," 143–47; "Research Report: Kituwah Mound," in *The Pluralism Project at Harvard University*, 2004, 1–2, 4; "Proposed Development of Kituwah 'Mother Town' of the Cherokee, Debated," *Cherokee Nations News*, April 20, 2000, www.thepeoplespaths.net/Cherokee/News2000/Apr2000/UBK000416Kituwah .html, accessed March 19, 2013; and Cooper, "Embracing Archaeology," 13.

35. As quoted, Holly, "Plasticity of Place," 148–57; *Wilmington Morning Star*, April 7, 2000; Thomas N. Belt as quoted, "Research Report: Kituwah Mound," 4.

36. As quoted, Mooney, *Mooney's History*, 279; Holly, "Plasticity of Place," 152–60.

37. Cooper, "Embracing Archaeology," 14; and "Research Report: Kituwah Mound," 5.

38. *Cherokee One Feather*, February 11, 2010.

39. "Duke Energy Project Threatens Sacred Kituwah Site," www.westerncarolinian .com/news/duke-energy-project-threatens-sacred-kituwah-site-1.1373195#.UUidiVdxp -O, accessed March 19, 2013.

40. As quoted, https://www.manataka.org/page2196.html; "Duke Energy to Move Electrical Tie Station to a New Site," www.duke-energy.com/news /releases/2010080202.asp, accessed March 19, 2013.

41. W. J. Cash, *Mind of the South* (New York: Vintage Books, 1941), 4, 9.

42. Harper Lee, *To Kill a Mockingbird* (New York: Warner Books, 1982), 8.

43. Thomas Wolfe, *Look Homeward, Angel* (New York: Charles Scribner's Sons, 1952), 7.

44. James Taylor Carson, "'The Obituary of Nations': Ethnic Cleansing, Memory, and the Origins of the Old South," *Southern Cultures* 14 (2008): 6–31; Handley, "A New World Poetics of Oblivion," in *Look Away: The U.S. South in New World Studies*, ed. Jon Smith and Deborah Cohn (Durham NC: Duke University Press, 2004), 27.

45. Cooper, "Embracing Archaeology," 13; Trinkley, "Archaeological Testing," 16–17; Hamilton, "Adverse Reactions," 35, 37.

46. *Cherokee One Feather,* December 2, 2011; Michelle D. Hamilton and Russell G. Townsend, "The Unintended Consequences of Prehistoric Skeletal Studies to Modern Cherokee Communities," in *Under the Rattlesnake: Cherokee Health and Resiliency,* ed. Lisa J. Lefler (Tuscaloosa: University of Alabama Press, 2009), 24, 28; Hamilton, "Adverse Reactions," 40; "National NAGPRA," *Federal Register* 76, no. 229 (November 29, 2011): 73568–660

47. Hamilton, "Adverse Reactions," 39.

Contributors

Mikaëla M. Adams, assistant professor, Arch Dalrymple III Department of History, University of Mississippi, Oxford

James Taylor Carson, head of the School of Humanities, Languages and Social Science at Griffith University, Brisbane, Australia

Tim Alan Garrison, professor and chair, Department of History, Portland State University, Portland, Oregon

Izumi Ishii, associate professor, Department of American Civilization, Tokai University, Kanagawa, Japan

Malinda Maynor Lowery, associate professor, Department of History and Director, Southern Oral History Program, University of North Carolina, Chapel Hill

Rowena McClinton, professor, Historical Studies Department, Southern Illinois University Edwardsville

David Nichols, professor, Department of History, Indiana State University, Terre Haute

Greg O'Brien, associate professor, Department of History, University of North Carolina, Greensboro

Meg Devlin O'Sullivan, assistant professor, Department of History and Women's, Gender, and Sexuality Studies Program, State University of New York, New Paltz

Julie L. Reed, associate professor, Department of History, University of Tennessee, Knoxville

Christina Snyder, Thomas Milton Miller and Kathryn Owens Miller Associate Professor of History, Indiana University, Bloomington

Rose Stremlau, assistant professor, Department of History, Davidson College

Index

Third Seminole War, 145
Thomas (Chickamauga), 90
Thomas, Robert (Cherokee), 76
Thompson, Mr. (British trader), 63
Tiger, Jimmy (Seminole), 150
Tiger, Martha (Seminole), 151
Tiger, Old (Seminole), 151
Tiger, Young (Seminole), 151
Tishomingo (Chickasaw), 108
Tishomingo, Chickasaw Nation, 205, 208
To Form a More Perfect Union: Justice for American Women (national commission on women's issues), 222
Tocqua (Cherokee town), 244, 246
Tonagi, 148
Townsend, Russ (Cherokee), 252
Trails of Tears, 240, 249, 257
Treaty of Hopewell (1786), 202
Treaty of Paris (1763), 50
Treaty of Paris (1783), 88
Treaty of Tellico Blockhouse, 89, 94
Trinkley, Michael, 252
the Trunk (Cherokee), 76–77
Tuckabatchee (Creek town), 63
Tucker, Lewis (Seminole), 150
Tulsa OK, 229
Tunstall, Martha G., 185
Turner, Frederick Jackson, 241
Tuscarora Indians, 96
Tuscarora War (1711–1715), 96
Tustenuggee (Seminole), 144
typhoid, 174

Ugulaycabe (Wolf's Friend, Chickasaw), 39
United Kituwah Band of Cherokees, 255
United Nations, 222
United States: Army, 35; civilization plan, 72, 166–67; Civil War, 130–33, 144, 175, 200, 205, 207–8; Commissioner of Indian Affairs, 182, 206; Commission to the Five Civilized Tribes, 189; Congress, 39–40, 107, 220–21; Constitution, 39, 113–14; Continental Congress, 86; diplomacy with Indians, 39; House of Representatives, 116; Indian policy, 138, 181, 188–89, 213; president, 221; secretary of interior, 212; Senate, 137; set-

tlement of California, 164–65; War Department, 39–40
University of Alabama, 257
University of California at Irvine, 232
University of Chicago, 9
University of Georgia, ix, 2
University of Iowa, ix, 3
University of Kentucky, x, xiv, 23
University of Nebraska Press: *Indians of the Southeast* series, x, 23
University of North Carolina at Chapel Hill, x, xii, xiv, 24
University of Tennessee, 10, 246, 258; archaeologists, 246
U.S. Telegraph (newspaper), 99–100
Utah, 170

Valley Towns region (Cherokee), 166
Van Buren, Martin, 99
Vann, Dawnee (Cherokee), 78. *See also* Dawnee of Oostanaula
Vann, James (Cherokee), 75, 81n15; house, 9
Verdigris River, 169
Vinita, Indian Territory, 206
Violence Against Women Act, 18
Virginia, 35, 85–86, 89, 116–17
Vonore TN, 258
Votaw, Carmen, 227

Walker, John, Jr. (Cherokee), 113
Walker, Tandy (Choctaw), 209–10
warfare: as marker of masculinity, 48, 50; to gain revenge, 48–49, 96–97; role of women in, 49
War of Jenkins's Ear, 35
Washington, George, 72
Watie, Charles (Cherokee), 169, 172, 175
Watie, Stand (Cherokee), 127, 130–32, 169, 174
Water, Thomas (Cherokee), 130
Watkins, Andrea Ramage, 32
Watts, John (New Tassel, Chickamauga), 90, 94
Waynesville, North Carolina, 227, 242
Webb, Pearl, 244
West: history of, 163
Western Carolina University, 3

Western History Association, xi, 10; "gang of four," 14; Lifetime Achievement Award, xi
West Florida, 39
West Point Military Academy, 84, 92
West Texas State University, 6–8
Whig Party, 117
White, Edward D., 117
White, Richard, 14, 19
Whiteside, William, 87
Whitley, William, 96
Wichita Falls TX, 223
Wilkes, Charles, 121
Willard, Frances, 182, 186; speaking tour, 182–83
Williams, Lewis, 117
Williamson, Andrew, 87
Willie, Frank, 149
Wilson, James Patriot, 95
Wilson, Lori, 227
Winston-Salem NC, 225
Wisconsin, 206

Womancatcher, Susannah (Cherokee), 166
Women's Christian Temperance Union (WCTU), 181–94; Band of Hope, 184; executive committee, 193; *Union Signal* newsletter of, 184, 189. *See also* Eastern Oklahoma Women's Christian Temperance Union; Indian Territory Women's Christian Temperance Union; Oklahoma Territory Women's Christian Temperance Union; Tahlequah Christian Temperance Union
Woods, Ruth Dial (Lumbee), 224–26, 230, 233
Worster, Donald, 14
Worcester v. Georgia (1832), 111
Wunder, John, 12, 31
Wynne, William, 95–96, 100

Yamasee Indians, 85
Yamasee War (1715–1717), 34, 85, 90
Yazoo (Choctaw town), 62

www.ingramcontent.com/pod-product-compliance
Lightning Source LLC
Chambersburg PA
CBHW020338270326
41926CB00007B/234